D1243184

REDEMPTION ALLEY

HOW I LIVED TO
BOWL ANOTHER FRAME

BOB PERRY

with Stefan Bechtel

RODALE. DISCARD

B
PERRY, B

Copyright © 2014, 2015 by Bob Perry and Stefan Bechtel

Rodale books may be purchased for business or promotional use or for special sales.
For information, please write to: Special Markets Department, Rodale, Inc.,
733 Third Avenue, New York, NY 10017

Printed in the United States of America

Rodale Inc. makes every effort to use acid-free ♾, recycled paper ♻.

Book design by Christina Gaugler

Library of Congress Cataloging-in-Publication Data is on file with the publisher.

ISBN: 978-1-62336-522-6 hardcover

Distributed to the trade by Macmillan

2   4   6   8   10   9   7   5   3   1   hardcover

RODALE.

We inspire and enable people to improve their lives and the world around them.
rodalebooks.com

$24.99
12/9/15
8B

114126035

I want to dedicate this book to all the people on the street
who didn't make it and to all the people in the rooms
who couldn't find their way home.

—BOB

AUTHOR'S NOTE:

Names have been changed to protect the innocent.
And to protect the rest of us from the guilty.

CONTENTS

CHAPTER 1

THE BEGINNING OF THE END

I WAS 20 YEARS OLD in the summer of 1972, and I looked like John Travolta's character in *Saturday Night Fever.* No, wait: It was the other way around. Travolta looked like *me,* 'cuz that movie didn't come out until a few years later and I'd been rocking out at the discos for ages by then—since even before "The Hustle" got big.

My best buddy, Cadillac Nicky, and I used to go down to this place in Paterson, New Jersey, called Mr. Stag's, and we'd buy more clothes in a month than some people bought in a year. There was this Jewish guy, Irv, who'd actually let us buy stuff on credit because we were such righteous customers. Other times, we'd go into the City to a place in the Village, on Sixth Street, where Doc Severinsen, the bandleader from *The Tonight Show,* used to buy his shit.

We were stylin', man!

I'd wear these real nice pants, with creases like knives. I'd wear these Italian knit shirts, like the gangsters wore. I had a couple of eight-, nine-hundred-dollar leather jackets that I'd wear, and another one, with a belt, that came down almost to my ankles, that must have cost 1,000 bucks. I had this one velour jacket with flowers all over it, that might seem kind of fruity today, but in those days everybody in the clubs loved it. I'd wear 2-, 3-inch platform shoes. I didn't go for the 5-inch ones, mainly because it was hard to dance in them.

Yeah. It was a time when white guys dressed up like black guys. I'd do my hair with one of them hot combs. Gold chains weren't popular in those days, but I used to wear a couple of gold "300" rings, that the Professional Bowlers Association gave out when you bowled a perfect game. And around 2:00 in the morning, when I went out to the after-hours clubs in Manhattan, or to this place called Mr. D's in Saddle Brook, with all the lights and people and music, I looked like a million fuckin' bucks.

Nicky had this totally pimped-out white 1968 Cadillac Eldorado. He would scrub and shine that thing until it looked like a white spaceship, like the goddamned thing just touched down from Mars. And when we showed up at Mr. D's on a Friday or Saturday night, he'd park that bitch right on the sidewalk in front of the club. These two brothers that owned the place let us do it, because we were the deal, man—we walked into the place and it was like one of them movies where, just for a second, everything stops.

Back in those days, though, all I really wanted was to float on top of the music and dance all night with all those hot women, all that heat, all that noise. I was a really good dancer—I kind of took lessons from this Hispanic girl, who would go out to the clubs with me and show me the moves. And since most guys didn't dance, I could dance with anybody's girlfriend and it was cool. It was like walking into a pinball arcade and playing every single machine for free.

The music in those days was Teddy Pendergrass, the Trammps, Marvin Gaye, Barry White, Double Exposure, the Jackson 5, the Bee Gees, Frankie Valli and the Four Seasons. (They got their name from a bowling alley in Jersey called the Four Seasons. Joe Pesci used to work there, before he got famous. That's where I met him.) All those songs with that pounding beat! "Stayin' Alive," "I Will Survive," "Ten Percent," "Shake Your Booty," "Black Skinned Blue Eyed Boys," "I'll Always Love My Momma." All that shit.

Everybody drank in the clubs, of course. And everybody did coke, too, but usually not too much because it was so expensive. But it wasn't like all that shit was no big problem. It was just, you know, party time. Coke was the club drug.

So where did a couple of 23-year-old kids have all that money to throw around? Well, first of all, me and Cadillac Nicky both worked full-time at my dad's appliance store in Paterson, PK Appliance, basically schlepping refrigerators and dishwashers all the fuck over New Jersey. That's the job we were trying to escape from when we'd get decked out to go to the clubs.

A much more entertaining source of income, of course, was Uncle Raymond, known by many as "the fat man," the smartest man I ever knew, who taught me and Cadillac Nicky and a few scary-looking older guys how to use our brains to consistently win money at the racetrack. When it was rainy, Uncle Raymond would wear a black fedora and a long, black trench coat and just park himself at the rail watching the ponies come pounding down the straightaway. That man had so much brainpower underneath that black hat that it was almost like a giant magnet in there, sucking up the right answers like iron filings in some science experiment. Unfortunately, Uncle Raymond's brains couldn't save him, or me, or anybody else, when the shit-storm finally came down.

And there were also times when I would make five or six thousand dollars in a night from "action bowling"—the after-hours betting game that drew all the gamblers and hoodlums and derelicts from all over the Tri-State Area. I might have been a hot-shit dancer in the disco clubs. I might have been a studly-ass dresser. But as a bowler, I was phenomenal. And I was the best action bowler walking.

Howard Barnett (childhood friend from Paterson, now a financial advisor in Virginia): I remember the first time I met Bob

Perry, at the Bowl-O-Mat in Paterson. Of course I'd heard of him by then—everybody had heard of Bob Perry. He was very nice to me, even though I was only 13 or 14. He went behind the counter of the snack bar and made me a sandwich, actually. He seemed to live at the bowling alley. But when I actually watched him bowl—that was something else. You don't have to be an expert in baseball to see that when Mickey Mantle swings, it's just different than everybody else. That's the way it was with Bob—it was just different than everybody else. It was amazing. It was a beautiful thing to watch.

"Fat Joey" Ardolino (bowler from New Jersey, now selling mattresses in Florida): One time I ran into Earl Anthony [one of the most famous bowlers on the West Coast] in Paramus Lanes. I was a teenager at that time. Anthony bowled anchor for D'amato Paperstock, and Bobby Perry introduced me to him. Bobby walked away and Earl said to me, "You know, he's the best bowler in the world," nodding his head, pointing to Bobby. Bobby was the best, unequivocally, without a doubt. Anyone who truly knows bowling knows that on a given night even a blind squirrel could find a nut. But a lion will always eat. Bobby Perry was a lion on the lanes. You didn't have to like Bobby, but when it came to bowling, you had to respect him. Anyone who didn't became the next victim.

Joe Tolvay (former bowling teammate): Bobby's future at the age of 16 was as bright as it could be in the sport of bowling. Everybody was jealous. When he picked up a bowling ball, he was "the man." His bowling ability got him a lot of free passes, whether it was league bowling or action bowling. People would sponsor him for anything. People used him to make money; they tried to take advantage of his abilities.

Here's what I'd do: During the day, for working at the appliance store, I'd wear my schmuck clothes that practically had "Bobby" printed over the shirt pocket. Then after work, I'd go out to dinner or whatever and then, at 11:00 or midnight, I'd change into my pimped-out disco clothes that I had nicely arranged on hangers in the back of my car, and me and Cadillac Nicky would make our big entrance at Mr. D's. After that, maybe around 1:00 or 2:00 in the morning, we'd change clothes again and go out to whatever bowling alley had some action. And I'd be a superstar again, but this time in a different way. Sometimes I wouldn't get home until 4:00 in the morning. Sometimes Cadillac Nicky wouldn't come home for 2 or 3 days. When did we sleep in those days? I dunno. I just know there was more than one time when me and Nicky were so tired that we dropped a goddamned Frigidaire.

Well, that's how it all started out, anyhow—with late nights, hot-combed hair, stacked-heel shoes, and a white Cadillac Eldorado. But before it was all over, people couldn't believe I was even still alive. I'm 63 now, and my health is pretty much shot from everything that happened—I got prostate cancer, diabetes, I got chemo burns in my throat and whatnot—and all those fabulous clothes are long gone. They're so long gone they're a joke. But here I am anyhow: A man who was destroyed, almost lost, found by an angel, and brought back to life.

I'm a friggin' miracle, really.

I grew up in a kind of ordinary house, with four sisters, on East Twenty-Sixth Street, in Paterson, New Jersey. It was in a neighborhood that was ethnically mixed-up—lots of Polacks, lots of Italians, lots of hard-drinking Irish. It was an okay neighborhood, I guess, but it was only, like, a block away from the projects, and my school was six blocks away from "Murderville," down on Governor Street, where there were bars on all the windows and the brothers hung out on the corners selling heroin. It was a big heroin area down there. Man, if you'd let one of them brothers stick his head in your car window, and you had a gold chain on, he'd grab that chain and yell, "five-oh!"

which meant the cops were coming, so you'd boogie out of that place so as not to get caught copping, and the brother would just run away with the gold.

In the old days, supposedly, up until the First World War or whatever, Paterson was known as the "Silk City of the World," because of all the textile mills that were there. But when I was growing up, all that was long gone. Most of them mills were boarded up, and that whole end of town was just a nasty, spooky ghetto.

Paterson wasn't a great place to be a small, shrimpy kid, but that's what I was. Big kids would corner me on the way to school and steal my lunch money. I always felt tense, like there was danger lurking around every corner. Plus, I was blind in one eye from a childhood accident. And there was another terrible thing that was happening to me then that I'll tell you about later, if I can. Nowadays people talk about dysfunctional families, but Paterson in those days was a dysfunctional town—it was a very mean, tough place for a skinny little kid like me.

Patsy Purzycki (older sister): I remember Bobby as being the kid that always got hurt. You know how there's always one kid like that? Bobby was an accident looking for a place to happen. A basketball hit him in the chin and he almost bit his tongue in half. He'd be walking down the stairs and he'd stumble and fall. Other kids saw him as clumsy and weak, I think. A target. That's why they were always picking on him.

There were more drunks living on my street than you can imagine— guys coming home shit-faced and yelling and screaming at their kids and their wives and whatnot. I think the only person on my street who didn't drink was my dad. And there was this other thing that would go on in my neighborhood, which was that some guy, like the Italian guy next door, would just kind of disappear. And I'd ask some older person where so-and-so went and they'd say, "He went to college." That was the terminology. It was only later that I realized, in my world, nobody went to college, especially thugs and tough guys. They weren't going to college. They were going to prison. Or worse. To the cemetery. So I guess you could say that, later in life, I had some real bad examples to look back on from when I was a kid.

Another big part of my life when I was a kid was the Catholic Church. My parents were very religious. If I didn't go to church every Sunday, that was sinful, and I'm telling you, that guilt followed me my whole life! I went to St. John's Catholic School in Paterson through grammar school. Those nuns were tough—they'd whack the back of your hand with a ruler if you weren't paying attention. Once a nun hit my left eye and it started bleeding. You did what they told you or you suffered the punishment: That was how I perceived the Catholic Church back then.

I also sang in the choir at church, because I loved to sing, and I was an altar boy. When I was 13 or 14 years old, my sister Pat would get up at 5:00 in the morning to take me to do 6:00 a.m. Mass. Then we'd get home and get on the bus and ride 50 minutes to St. John's Grammar School, all the way across town on the other side of Paterson. But I didn't have any experience of God or anything like that by being an altar boy, if that's what you're wondering. In fact, I figured if there was a God he was probably pretty mean, because of the Sisters of Charity and their rulers. One of the big reasons I was an altar boy, actually, was because I figured I could make a little extra money doing weddings and funerals.

But my father was a spiritual man, not just a religious one. He was a saint, really. He had this huge heart, a heart of gold. There were five kids in my family (four girls and me) and I guess you'd say we were just middle class, but almost every night there would be other people's kids sitting at our dinner table. There were something like 50 kids on our block, and some of those kids might be hungry, or the father was a drunk, or they'd be abused or just kind of forgotten. Taking care of those forgotten children—other people's children who were in need— that was my father's religion. That was one of the big things I learned from him. (Later on, at his funeral, you should have seen it! It was like the governor died, there were so many people.)

My family also had another big connection to the Catholic Church through my mother's cousin, who was actually a pretty big-shot Franciscan monk, called Father Benjamin. He lived at a place called Graymoor, a couple of hours from Paterson, north of the city. It was some sort of a spiritual retreat center, way up on a mountain, and when we were kids my parents would take us up there for picnics and whatnot. Father Benjy was this very jolly, round, bald-headed guy, around 5-foot-6, who wore a brown robe and sandals like all the rest of the monks up there. There were all these fields everywhere at Graymoor, and trails through the woods, and it was kind of peaceful, I guess, but I wasn't really that interested in all that nature stuff. I just wanted to be back home bowling.

In those days, in Paterson, there was really only one place except the church that felt clean and safe, a place full of light and people laughing. A place families could go. Really, it was a place sort of like the places in those impossible TV shows—*Lassie, Leave It to Beaver, The Adventures of Ozzie and Harriet, My Three Sons*—where people had little problems that always got solved in half an hour, and there were mothers and fathers and dogs and nice lawns and whatnot. Not like the rundown part of Paterson where I grew up, where things felt raggedy and edgy and I was never quite safe.

That place was the bowling alley. It was bright and cheerful and noisy, with the sound of jukebox music and tenpins clattering off the pin deck. I felt at home there. I felt safe. In Paterson, the place everybody went was a place called Bowl-O-Mat lanes. I started going there with my mom and dad and sometimes a couple of my sisters when I was just a punk kid, maybe 6 or 7. My dad was a good bowler who bowled in a league. Later on, just for use in bowling, he started going by the last name "Perry" instead of "Purzycki," which is my birth name, a Polack name. When I got a little older I changed my name to Perry, too.

My dad could tell at a pretty young age that I just had a gift for the game. I just understood naturally that you didn't want to hit the tenpins head-on; you wanted to hook the ball so it would come in, hard, in the "pocket" just behind the head pin. I had a knack for doing that, and I loved the sound of those pins clattering across the hard-maple lane when I threw a strike. My dad and mom screamed and yelled when that happened. I joined one of the New Jersey leagues, and by the time I was 12 years old, I was averaging over 200 a game.

Plus, you gotta understand: Bowling scores nowadays are way higher than they used to be in the old days, because of the introduction of synthetic lanes and high-performance balls (which we used to call "cheater balls" when they first came out). It's the same way new-fangled baseballs and bats have made it much easier to hit a home run than it was in Babe Ruth's day. So for a skinny little 12-year-old to be averaging over 200—that made people sit up and take notice.

Chuck Pezzano (prominent bowling writer and inductee into the Professional Bowlers Association Hall of Fame): Even when Bobby was 15 years old, you could see that he had a spectacular talent. It had to have been a natural ability, because he was too young to have much training at that age. He had a lot of guts, he wasn't afraid of anybody, and I thought right from the beginning that he could be great.

Mike Stella (bowler from North Arlington, NJ): I remember once Earl Anthony said to me, "There's only one bowler I fear on the PBA [Professional Bowlers Association] Tour and that's Bob

Perry." And Earl Anthony, of course, was one of the greatest bowlers ever.

This was a time when top professional bowlers could make real money. Not as much as professional golfers, but still, a lot. And, in those days, it seemed like bowling was a sport that was taken more seriously than it is now. Nowadays you only see bowling in cartoony movies like *The Big Lebowski*, but when I was growing up there were all these bowling shows on TV, like *Bowling for Dollars* and *Make That Spare*. And then, of course, there was all the TV coverage of the big professional tournaments, with big-money purses. That was before the Super Bowl High Roller tournament was started in Vegas, which became the biggest-money bowling competition in the country, with a total purse of over two million bucks and a first-place prize of $100,000. That didn't come around until 1981. Even so, I started to realize it might just be possible for me to have a golden career as a professional bowler—maybe even take my place among the Great Ones. People like Dick Weber, or later Earl Anthony and Mark Roth.

In 1964, when I was 12, my dad found out about this national youth bowling competition that was going to be held at the New York World's Fair in Flushing. This would be my first chance to get up on the national stage and show the world what I could do.

Two days before I was supposed to go to Flushing to this tournament, my dad gave me a croquet set for my birthday. He told me not to use it until after the tournament. I don't know, maybe he got a little worried about those long-handled wooden mallets around a 12-year-old kid. (So what did he give them to me for then?) Of course, me and this neighbor kid named Ricky unpacked the croquet set anyway and were playing with it in my backyard when Ricky somehow lost control of one of the mallets, which went flying through the air and smashed me in the left side of my face. It felt like a bomb going off in my head. It crushed my left eyeball and a bunch of the bones around it, too.

Patsy Purzycki: I was across the street at my girlfriend's house and I just remember hearing this screaming, and Bobby came out from behind the house holding his face and there was blood everywhere. Somebody called my dad at work at the appliance store and it seemed like he was there in 2 minutes. I remember Bobby lying there on the sidewalk, all covered in blood, holding my hand and saying, "Please don't leave me! Please don't leave me!" He seemed so alone.

People have said that I'm the queen of enablers—always the one to step in and help someone in need or even if they're not in need. And of all my three sisters and me, I was the one who was always the closest to Bobby. That day he got hit in the eye and came screaming down the street—I was 16 at the time, but that stayed with me the rest of my life. I think that was the beginning of many, many years of enabling that started out as kindness and got worse and worse as the years went by. If Bobby was hurt, if he needed money, if he needed a ride, if he needed an apartment, I made it happen, even when nobody else wanted him in the house.

You know, I eventually came to believe that Bobby and I were souls that have been intertwined for many lifetimes—sometimes as brother and sister, sometimes as mother and son, sometimes as spouses. It's like there is something we have to work out between us. And for me, it was enabling—reaching out to help him even when that was the worst thing I could do for him.

When I got back from the hospital, I had to lie on the bed in a dark room for weeks. Needless to say, competing at the New York World's Fair was out of the question. The doc thought maybe I'd be able to see a little out of that left eye, but when he took the patches off, it turned out that eye was almost completely blinded. To this day, I can only see a little bit of blurry light out of that eye.

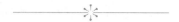

Patsy Purzycki: I believe to this day that Bobby suffered some major trauma damage that was never addressed when he got blinded. In those days, there was no counseling, no nothing—just a trip to the ER, then you're half-blind for the rest of your life. You've got to handle it on your own. The only thing I remember is that my father went to St. John's and told the priests and nuns not to hit Bobby with a ruler or a paddle, like they did. But that was about all the protection he got.

The great, golden bowling career I had imagined in my head, the chance to be somebody, to touch my dreams—all that seemed to fall away, like dust. I felt crushed, defeated. Just pounded down. But, I don't know what it was; somehow I just reached down inside myself and found a lion down there, ready to fight. I was pissed off at this fucking kid Ricky, of course. But mainly I was focused on getting up out of that bed and coming back to life. I didn't care if I only had one eye. I didn't care if nobody had ever heard of a one-eyed bowler. I wanted to get back to bowling and become the best athlete I could become—maybe even the best ever. So I started practicing like a maniac, bowling and bowling and bowling, trying to train myself to see down the lane with one eye and no depth perception at all. I trained myself to hit a mark on the lane over and over and over again, just exactly the same way, like a machine. Most people didn't even know I had only one good eye. One time I challenged another guy to bowl against me with both of us wearing patches over the left eye, and I crushed the poor dude. He didn't even know why.

Over the next few years, I started coming back, big time. I learned to use that same inner lion—that ferocious drive that had helped me overcome my blindness—to become a phenomenal bowler. I was still in my teens or early twenties when I won four regional titles. In one of them, I beat the legendary bowler Ralph Engan. I won the Regional Championship Classic tournament in Florida. I competed in the Firestone Tournament of Champions, a national championship.

I had a way of throwing the ball that just hooked harder than anybody else, and when that solid-rubber ball hit those rock-solid maple tenpins, they just exploded off the pin deck with an incredibly loud clatter. I loved that sound. It was so loud, so confident, so dominating, that it scared other bowlers; I could tell. One of the pin chasers where I used to bowl told me he could always tell when I was in the house because my strikes were louder and scarier than anybody else's. Bowling is a beautiful game, involving skill and strategy, and some of it has to do with psyching out the other guy. Intimidation. I was great at all that shit, and scattering them pins as if you were blowing up the dude was part of it.

Now, other bowlers not only admired me, they had started to fear me. Now, when I walked into the Bowl-O-Mat in Paterson or any of the other bowling alleys in Passaic or Nutley or Clifton or Hoboken or any of those other places, Lodi Lanes or Wallington Lanes, with my hot-combed hair and my fancy pants, everybody looked at me. Everybody knew who I was. I was like a movie star. Because when I got up to bowl and addressed that line, I was fearless. I was practically unbeatable. When people went up against me, they couldn't win. I'd beat their brains out. I'd wipe the floor with them. I was the best. And I was still just a kid. Who knew how far I could go? I had no idea how blind I really was, or how far down the wrong road I was getting ready to go.

CHAPTER 2

UNCLE RAYMOND

I DUNNO. It's possible this is a story about a guy that got everything too easy. A guy that was cursed by God or the Devil saying, "Go on, help yourself. Have another! Everything is free." All I knew was that I just kept winning. The trophy shelf at my parents' house started getting more and more crowded. In 1973 and then again in 1974 (when I was in my early twenties), I won the Met Writers Regional Bowler of the Year, given out by the Metropolitan Bowling Writers of America, which meant that I was the best bowler on the East Coast.

In those early days, I was totally focused on the sport of bowling. I was like a top athlete in training—no drinking or drugs or staying out late or horsing around. I was bowling, almost every day. Monday nights, I'd bowl for the action. Tuesday nights, I'd bowl in the Bronx. Wednesday, I'd bowl in the doubles leagues against the best bowlers in the East. Thursday nights, I'd be back in New York or Long Island. Friday was Lyons Lanes and Saturday was the big money, in the tournaments. I was not only learning how to play the lanes, I was also learning how to psych out my opponents—how to dominate them, mislead them, how to play them like a fiddle. I had a real good teacher, Al Fuscarino, and he taught me a lot about the game, how to play the outside or the inside, how to work the angles. He also helped me develop a swing that nobody else had—this tremendously high back swing, which creates a great knee bend and a powerful hook that just demolishes the pins.

By the time I was 17, Al told me I was destined to be the best.

In those days, in the bowling alleys, everybody bragged about how good they were. But everybody was not as good as they said they were. Except me.

I started winning all kinds of legitimate trophies and tournaments— the official stuff. At the same time, though, there was this whole other world that was going down—late at night, off the books, when the bowling alley was closed to the public. Like I said, it was known as "action bowling." It was where the hotshot young bowlers, like the gunslingers in the Wild West, got to compete for money. The bowling alley would fill up with shadowy older men, gamblers and gangsters, who would bet big money on the superstars like me.

It didn't take me long to figure out that you could make a whole lot more money as a late-night action bowler than you could as a doofus in the local league playing pot games. Even my dream of winning national tournaments again started to pale in comparison to the money I was already making. Who needs clean money for hard work when you can get dirty money a whole lot easier? And I was quickly developing a reputation as one of the best money bowlers anywhere.

Plus, action bowling was a whole lot more fun. I was great at winning money because I loved the game: It was exciting and complex; it involved not just skill but cunning, intimidation, bluffing, strategy, and human psychology. I instinctively knew how to scare the shit out of my opponents, rattle their cages, mess with their minds.

Stepping out onto the approach at the top of the lane, it's almost like you're walking onto a stage. For a few seconds, you're the center of attention. And if you were someone like me—the guy who was probably going to win a lot of money—you never knew who was watching. Especially when I started one of those runs where I'd be throwing strike after strike after strike.

One night, before the action started, a guy walked up to me out of the shadows while I was sitting in the settee area, getting ready to bowl. He was this huge man, not very tall, but he probably weighed 240 pounds. He was "fat" like an oak tree was fat. He had dirty blond hair and was wearing glasses. And he was wearing a fedora, like Frank Sinatra used to wear. He was always wearing a hat whenever I saw him after that—that hat and glasses, so he looked like an old hoodlum. He was 17 years older than me, not old enough to be my dad, but old enough to be my older brother or uncle.

"How ya doin'?" the guy says.

"Okay."

"Wanna bowl? Five or 10 bucks a game?"

I just laughed.

"Fuggedaboutit," I say. "No way, man. I'll CRUSH you."

I was an arrogant sonofabitch in them days.

"No, seriously—I'll bowl you," the guy says.

"Look, mister, you can't win. You cannot win. Piss off, man."

"Well, let's bowl anyway. I can afford to lose a few bucks."

So after a while, just to humor the old guy, I threw a few games with him. And I destroyed him, just like I said I would.

But this guy—who turned out to be Uncle Raymond—he was pretty smart. Actually, very smart. He'd been watching me and all the other action bowlers from the shadows for a long time before he came up to talk to me. He knew all about me. He'd been making money off me for months. He also knew a lot about horses, too, and according to him, at least, he'd been making a lot of money at the track. He told me he was in the trucking business, bringing shrimp and seafood up from the Gulf and moving scrap metal and other stuff from one foundry to another all across the East Coast, from Pennsylvania down to the Deep South.

We kind of hit it off, I guess, and after that Raymond started coming around the bowling alley quite a lot. He'd sit there at the bar drinking Manhattans made with Seagram's VO—that shit is like rat poison, and it makes people mean—watching me bowl. Sometimes he'd come with this real old guy, a plumber named Nicky, who would fall asleep at the bar half the time.

One day Raymond asked me to give him a ride someplace. So I took the wheel of Raymond's car and drove him and Nicky the

Plumber over to someplace near North Arlington, where he lived, I guess to meet some guys. He told me to wait in the car while him and Nicky the Plumber went upstairs, so I did, and after I got done driving, he handed me a little wad of cash. Whenever I got through driving him, he'd always pay me.

So that's the way it started to go. I started driving Raymond and his friends around in his car—these guys were always drinking, and I guess they needed a "designated driver," even though nobody used that term in them days. They were always going to see people. I'd drive them someplace and these guys—big guys, nicely dressed, always smoking—they'd get out of the car and go into a house or an apartment. I'd always wait in the car. I think they liked me because I was always reliable and they knew I wouldn't blab about where I'd taken them. I would just shut up and drive, and at the end of the night, Raymond would give me cash. Then I'd go to the after-hours clubs in New York and party.

I don't know when it was, exactly, but at some point I started calling Raymond "Uncle Raymond," and he'd tell people I was his nephew, Bobby. There was one other kid, Bobby Schumacher, that Raymond also called nephew, so sometimes us two Bobbys would wind up driving Uncle Raymond around from place to place, like we really were his nephews for real.

And, okay, look: I ain't stupid. I grew up in a bad part of Jersey. There were a lot of towns that were known to be places that were "mobbed up." There were a lot of diners known for having a lot of Mob sit-downs. But the thing is, you just didn't talk about it. You didn't go sticking your nose into it. Except for people like Bobby Schumacher, who wanted to be in the Mob in the worst way and eventually wound up serving some serious time for it.

Uncle Raymond? I didn't know what he did in his private time. I didn't know what he really did for a living. I actually didn't believe he was in the Mob, even though he definitely knew people who were. I came to think he was probably "in the rackets," as they say in Jersey, meaning he might have had a legitimate business but part of the time stepped over onto the shady side of the street. Maybe most of the time. Anyway, I just knew he was very nice to me, like a real uncle, that he was the smartest man I ever knew, and that over time I came to admire him more than any other person I ever met.

Patsy Purzycki: Uncle Raymond was a heavy man who drove a Lincoln Continental and smoked constantly. He was always at the bowling alley. More and more, Uncle Raymond became a fixture in Bobby's life. It worried a lot of us. Supposedly Raymond was in the Mafia—that's what people said. And considering where he was from, North Arlington, I wouldn't doubt it for a minute. But all I really knew was that when you were around him, you felt his power. You felt protected. You felt safe. I also know that he slowly gained total control over Bobby—and that Bobby was already on his way over to the dark side when he first met Raymond. My father saw all this. He saw Raymond almost becoming Bobby's father. And even though Raymond was a Polack, like our dad, I believe to this day that our dad would rather have seen Bobby dead than go all the way over into Raymond's world. But it was happening no matter what my dad or anybody else did.

Frankly, I believe that Raymond is the one who ruined Bobby's life. The day Bobby changed forever was the day he got involved with these people.

Joe Tolvay: Bobby talked about Uncle Raymond a lot—"I gotta go do such-and-such for Uncle Raymond" or "Uncle Raymond will take care of this or that for me"—but I never actually met him. I sometimes wondered if he was fictional. I just know that Uncle Raymond was Bobby's savior. He gave him a lot of power.

About this same time, the best thing that ever happened to me, happened. Her name was Debbie LaRusso.

I'd met Debbie at the Paramus Lanes, in Paramus, New Jersey, a couple of years earlier, and God, she was beautiful! She looked like Barbara Streisand. She was everything a man could want. Blonde, about 5-foot-5, with a fantastic body—a wonderful body. She had one of those bodies that was so curvaceous you could see her naked through her clothes—her breasts, her hips, her thighs, her ass.

You kept trying not to look at her, but you couldn't. She was a good bowler herself, and as we got to know each other, I'd come to watch her bowl, and she'd come watch me bowl in tournaments. I know she loved it that I was a big star in the bowling world. Plus, we couldn't keep our hands off each other.

I guess it was a little unusual for that time, but we were so crazy about each other that we moved in together, first in Garfield, New Jersey, and then into a one-bedroom apartment with a garage on East Sixteenth Street in Paterson, because it was cheaper. It was a nice little apartment, and pretty cheap (our rent was $237 a month). We had a dog named Jackson that somebody gave us—he was half beagle and half German shepherd—and we were both very attached to that dog. We lived there in that little apartment, just the three of us—me, Debbie, and Jackson—like a little family.

Debbie had a real good job with this insurance agency, so she made a good income. Unfortunately, her mother hated me and the people I had started to hang out with. She was really angry and worried whenever she saw me leaving the bowling alley with Uncle Raymond and these other older guys wearing long coats and hats. She kept warning Debbie against getting involved with me and those scary-looking men.

One day I got Debbie a little ring and asked her to marry me. But when her mom found out, she exploded. She told Debbie, "If you marry Bobby, I'll disown you." I couldn't let that happen, of course. So we just lived together without getting married. Debbie would have married me if she could, and I would have married her, too. But we couldn't. My sisters—especially Patsy and Jeannie—they just loved Debbie. She was like part of the family.

But it wasn't just that Debbie's mother didn't like me. Looking back on them days now, 40 years later, I can see that my whole life was starting to run off the rails, but I had no fucking idea what was starting to happen to me. I had no idea where I was getting ready to go.

Partly, it was all that easy money—being able to go down to the bowling alley pretty much day or night and walk away with a fistful of cash. Alcohol was all over the place, but so was coke. And now I could afford enough of it to get myself into trouble. So I started drinking and doing blow all the time, whenever and wherever I could get it. And I couldn't get enough of that stuff. My nose had started to close up; I think I had a deviated septum already, but I just kept going. Without really knowing it, my life was gradually getting taken over by booze and dope and all the lying it takes to keep that going.

In July of 1981, just after my dad died, I went out to Vegas for the first annual Super Bowl High Roller tournament (known as just the "High Roller" at the time). It was the kind of huge national tournament I'd dreamed of ever since I was a little punk kid, and this was the big kahuna, the biggest of the big. It cost you $1,100 to enter, but if you won your first two matches, you broke even. So I went out to Vegas, all full of my own shit and swagger, but also heartbroken because my dad had just died. I won my first five matches, though, and then I got knocked out. I had a few grand in my pocket, so I started drinking, snorting blow, and then I got totally out of control, just drunk and obnoxious as hell. A bunch of bowlers were throwing dice, and I got mad and threw the dice everywhere. I was impossible, but I didn't know it. I did not realize how far down I'd already fallen.

After that, Debbie and I started arguing, mainly about my staying out half the night and drinking. I'd go out to have a couple of drinks, then wind up at the after-hours clubs and not get home until 5:00 in the morning or something. I'd be lying all the time. I'd tell her, oh, I had to help Uncle Raymond with something, or I had to go into the City to make some money, or I had to go meet somebody about a job, or this or that. But it was all a pack of lies, and I think she knew it. My whole life was turning into a pack of lies.

In them days, the PBA (Professional Bowlers Association) would give you a gold ring if you threw a 300 game, a perfect game. By that time, I was getting so good that I had at least 15 or 20 of these rings (although I'd already sold some of them for dope). Well, one night Debbie takes a hammer and just starts smashing the shit out of them. That made me mad, of course, and we had another big fight over that. All her friends were telling her to get away from me, to get away from the gamblers and hoodlums I'd started hanging out with. I didn't want her to leave, but I couldn't stop drinking and doing drugs, pretty much around the clock, really, and lying to cover it all up. It was tearing me apart. I was on the wrong side of the street, I can tell you that.

Patsy Purzycki: My bedroom was right next to Bobby's at home, and one time I went into my jewelry box and found $40,000, cash. You gotta understand: We were a nice middle-class family, and we didn't have money like that. It was like drug money. It was scary. And then the very next day, it would be gone and Bobby would be broke again. I didn't know what was going on, but I started to get very frightened for him. I didn't know what was going to happen next, but I just knew it was going to be bad.

CHAPTER 3

RUBY RED

BACK IN THOSE DAYS there was a guy named Arthur Prysock, a black jazz singer who had this big, soulful baritone voice. He had some big disco hits, but the main thing people remember him for is a beer commercial he did in the '70s where he sang, "Tonight, tonight, let it be Löwenbräu." Helluva thing to be remembered for, huh? Well, Arthur Prysock and his wife were big supporters of bowling for kids in Harlem. Lots of these youth bowling events they did were in a place called Lenox Lanes, on Lenox Avenue in Harlem. Every once in a while I'd go down to Lenox Lanes with other local bowling professionals to do some kids' event.

One night, after I finished bowling for Arthur, I had a few vodkas and smoked some pot, and I was just hanging out at one of the tables in the bar at Lenox Lanes, watching the action, and this guy came up to me.

He knew who I was—everybody knew who I was.

And I knew who he was—everybody knew who he was.

He was known as "Ruby Red," and he was a pretty unforgettable guy. A black guy, 6 feet tall, who was an outrageous dresser even though he was kind of a quiet guy. He'd wear a full-length red fur coat and a red fur hat, with red pants. Sometimes the fur was white or gray or green or black, but there was always fur all over the place. He'd wear these real expensive shoes—everything he wore was expensive. He was loaded with gold—chains, rings, all kinds of bling. He always drew a crowd wherever he went, and I knew that he was feared. I knew he had to be a tough guy to be feared like that.

Everybody said that Ruby Red and his brothers were loaded with money. Supposedly they were some of the biggest heroin dealers on the East Coast, working out of Harlem.

I had heard that Ruby Red was at the action in New Jersey on Friday nights because that was the predominant place where people went to bet for a lot of money. After midnight, on Friday nights, in Jersey, is where it was all happening.

"Hey, Money Bowler—what you doing here?" Ruby Red says to me. "Money Bowler": That's what he called me. (Later he sometimes just called me "Money.")

"I was here for Arthur's thing," I say. "The youth bowling thing."

"Are you bowling?" he says, meaning, was I bowling for the action.

"No."

"Why not?"

"There's no money here, man."

"Well, I heard if we beat you, we can make a lotta money."

"That's true, but you gotta have a lotta money to win a lotta money. You don't get nothin' for nothin'."

Like I said, I was an arrogant sonofabitch in those days.

"How much is a lot?" Ruby Red says, and then he reaches in his pocket and pulls out this big fat wad of hundreds, folded over and wrapped with an elastic band, and throws it on the table. There was probably, I don't know, maybe $5,000 in there.

"Is this enough money?" he says.

"No, that's not enough," I say.

I mean, just arrogant as hell.

He throws down another wad on the table.

"Is this enough?"

"No, sorry," I say.

He throws down another wad.

"Is this enough?"

"No."

Then Ruby Red calls over another black guy, maybe one of his brothers, and the two of them start throwing wads of money down on the table, until the entire table—it was one of them bar tables, not too big—was completely covered with money.

The truth is, I was kind of just kidding. I had never seen so much goddamned cash in one place in my life. I mean, it might have been $50,000, cash, or more, on that table.

"Okay," I say. "Sure—I'll bowl your guy. Where do you want to do it? We can't bowl here, that's for sure."

I knew that if this match really happened, it would attract all the degenerate gamblers and mobsters and hoodlums in New Jersey to the action. And the white mobsters weren't going to come to Harlem. They just wouldn't do it.

Plus, you had a situation where, if they did come, you'd have guys with tens of thousands of dollars in cash leaving the bowling alley late at night, and if somebody tried to rob them, it could turn into a real ugly situation. The guns would come out, and there'd be black gangsters shooting at white gangsters and the whole nine yards.

"Let's just bowl in Jersey," Ruby Red says.

"Okay," I say. "You pick the house."

So Ruby Red and a couple of his guys wrote some names on pieces of paper and put them in a hat. Then Ruby Red picked one: Olympic Bowl, in Belleville. I found out later that all the pieces of paper had Olympic Bowl written on them—he was already trying to rig the match. Olympic Bowl was next to Newark and Nutley, and it sounded okay to me, even though I'd actually never bowled there before. At that point, 23 years old and totally full of myself—invincible, unbeatable, a lion on the lanes—I figured I could crush Ruby Red's guy anytime and anyplace. It didn't really matter who the guy was, or where we bowled. The guy was dead. I was already counting my money.

"Okay," Ruby Red says, "You pick the time."

"Next Sunday night, 10 o'clock."

"Okay, see you then. Just be sure your guys bring a lot of money."

By this time, it was obvious to me and everybody else in my life that I "belonged" to Uncle Raymond. I was part of his crew, part of his outfit. Uncle Raymond was like one of them great big fish in the ocean that's got a whole lot of littler fish swimming alongside him.

A "crew" was sort of like a Mafia-type setup, even though Uncle Raymond wasn't in the Mob. If I went somewhere and told people off, those people couldn't do anything to me until they went to Uncle Raymond and got his permission. If somebody slapped me, they'd have to answer to Uncle Raymond. When I went out on one of these swag jobs in the middle of the night, I knew that Uncle Raymond would protect me if we got into trouble. That's the way it worked.

One of the crew was me, of course. Nicky the Plumber was always around, too. I figured out later that Nicky the Plumber was an old, old friend and also kind of a first lieutenant to another of Uncle Raymond's friends, Bobby Cabert. Cabert really was in the Mafia. Cabert and I just kind of hit it off from the beginning—maybe because I was always making him money, maybe because I just liked his style. He looked and acted and sounded like a gangster. But whatever Cabert's personal life was, who else he hung out with, it was none of my fuckin' business. Years later, when Cabert died in federal prison, the *New York Times* pointed out that Joe Pesci's character in the movie *Goodfellas* was based on him. That's the guy who is kind of a psychotic killer, who shoots this kid who is waiting on their table in the foot, and then kills him. Which doesn't surprise me, because Pesci knew Cabert. And Cabert sort of was like that gangster in the movie—kind of dangerous and unstable.

Then there was this new guy who'd started hanging around a lot. Some people called him "Johnny Boy," but Uncle Raymond just called him "the other guy" or "your friend." Like he'd say, "What happened to the other guy?" Or, "Are you gonna give your friend a ride, or what?" It was like Uncle Raymond was afraid the feds were listening in, even if we were just standing there at the bowling alley or sitting in a bar.

People said "the other guy" was a hoodlum, a gangster, from Ozone Park in Queens. He'd spent 2 or 3 years in federal prison. He was only about 10 years older than me, but he had this silvery hair all done up nice, and most of the time he had a nice tan. The old ladies said he looked like a movie star. He had a pretty deep scar on his right upper lip that made him look like he was sneering a lot of the time. He also walked a little funny. I found out later that it was because when he was 14 years old, he was trying to boost a portable cement mixer from a construction site and the thing tipped over and crushed his foot. I picked up a few other tidbits about the guy, just from people talking, even though this was the kind of guy you had to be extra careful knowing anything about. Like that he came from a family of 13 and grew up real poor. That when he was my age he used to run with a bunch of thugs and knuckle-breakers called the Fulton-Rockaway Boys. And that he loved to bet—on the horses, cards, dice, and sports events like action bowling.

There was another thing I learned pretty quick about Johnny Boy: If you were a winner, if you made him money, he loved you. And I was a superstar out there—the best action bowler there was. Another good part of it was that Johnny Boy told me, if I ever got into trouble, just to call him. He was a thug, I guess, an enforcer. But he was also a guy who genuinely liked people in general, and me in particular.

I'd picked Sunday night for the match with Ruby Red because Sunday night, after all the league play was over and all the mothers and fathers and kids were gone, when the bowling alley was closed to the public, was a perfect time for action bowling. That's when everybody who was there was a gambler or a gangster, or both. On Sunday nights there was nothing else to bet on—the racetracks were closed, football was over for the weekend. All that was left was bowling, and there were bowling alleys all over the place. That's why bowling turned into such a huge betting sport, an action sport, a money sport. There was a whole lot more money won—and lost—in these late-night action games than any of the professional bowlers were making on the pro tour.

I knew that. And so did Ruby Red.

"Who's your guy?" I ask Ruby Red, wanting to find out who I'd be bowling against, although it really didn't matter all that much.

"Guy Fisher," he says. Guy Fisher, a black guy, was a good bowler but absolutely no contest against me. It was a total mismatch. I was going to humiliate and destroy this guy.

I got back to the apartment late that night. Debbie was already asleep, so there was no big argument, but first thing the next morning the phone rang. It was Uncle Raymond.

"Why were you in Harlem last night?" he says, kind of accusing me.

"How did you know I was there?"

"Somebody told me."

"Who told you?"

"None of your business."

I had no idea how he did it, but Uncle Raymond always seemed to know where I was at. He had people watching me. He could protect me and love me and sometimes I could do no wrong. At the beginning, I wasn't afraid of him at all—why should I be? But later, when I did bad things and started to get him mad at me—really, I broke his heart—then he started to get scary.

"Look," I say, "I was up there for one of Arthur Prysock's things for the kids. I met up with that black guy Ruby Red, the guy with the fur coats. He wants to bowl for a lot of money."

"How much money?"

"The most cash money I ever seen in my life."

"How much is that?"

"I don't know—50, 60, 75 thousand maybe. But if word gets out, I think people will show up with hundreds of thousands."

"Yeah, that nigger has got a lot of money," Uncle Raymond says.

(I don't mean any disrespect—that's what he said.) "Where does he want to bowl?"

"Olympic Bowl, over in Belleville."

"When?"

"Next Sunday night, 10 o'clock."

"Why so late?"

"Because it's the best time. This guy and his brothers and them guys—they're loaded. They've got piles of cash. He says we gotta show up with a lotta money, so you gotta call your friend to make the match." Meaning: I was asking Uncle Raymond to call Johnny Boy and all his mobster friends to come to the match and bring plenty of cash to bet.

"Okay," Uncle Raymond says, "so I gotta go away for a few days but I'll be back by the end of the week. What you doing this week?"

"I probably gotta work for my dad at the appliance store, and I'll go practice at the Bowl-O-Mat."

"Well, don't you be stayin' out all night drinkin' like you do. You make sure to watch your ass and don't screw around. Practice. And don't drink so goddamned much."

"Okay," I say.

But, in reality, I kind of didn't give a shit. I guess I didn't actually believe that this match would really happen. Guys were always trying to set up action games for big money, and it usually didn't happen. Shit like that just never happened. But I just knew, if it did happen, I would beat the living shit out of whoever stood up to me.

I was at Lyons Lanes on Monday or Tuesday night and I happened to run into Ruby Red, all decked out in his fur coat and fur hat and whatever.

"We still on for the match at Olympic Bowl on Sunday night?" I asked him.

"Yeah, and you better bring a lot of money," he said.

By then, everybody seemed to have heard about the match. People were getting their cash together, getting excited.

Commotion was in the air because all kinds of people were coming.

And because there'd be so much betting going on, anybody could get in on the action, even with a hundred bucks. There'd be the big main bet, and all kinds of side bets also. Lots and lots of action, just like the gamblers loved.

Even so—don't ask me why—I still didn't really take Ruby Red seriously.

So on Monday night I bowled in the big league in Paramus, with some of the best bowlers in the country. I told a lot of people about the match and that there was going to be a lot of money there. They said they'd already heard about it. The next night, I went out for a couple of drinks and then to the disco, and I wound up staying out half the night. Then I went out and drank all night Wednesday. As usual, Debbie got really pissed at me when I got home so late. Afterward, she just got up and went to work without speaking to me. But that was not so unusual. I was used to it by now. Thursday was always a good disco night, so I went out that night, too. On the way back home I just wanted to stop somewhere and have a drink, and the next thing I knew I was drinking all night long. Again.

The truth was that I didn't really practice at all. I didn't really care. I didn't really give a rat's ass, for some reason. The truth—the truth that I had never really looked square in the eye—was that I was lazy, I was egotistical, I was unbelievably arrogant, I was completely blind, and most of all, I had turned into a round-the-clock alcoholic and a dope addict.

I was, actually, getting into very serious trouble in my life.

My boat had already gone over Niagara Falls, and I was going down.

But, at the time, I just thought I was the greatest boater in the world.

CHAPTER 4

PISSING OFF JOHNNY BOY

SATURDAY MORNING ROLLED AROUND, and Uncle Raymond called.

"Where you been?" he says.

"Do you mean have I been practicing, minding my own business? Yeah, sure. I been doing that."

"That's not what I heard."

"Well, maybe you didn't hear right."

"Where are you now?"

"I'm home, at my apartment. With Debbie."

"Come over to my house."

"I can't. I might have to work for my dad today, in the store."

"I just got home, and nobody knew where you been. Where you been all week?"

"I was working."

"Did you practice?"

"Yeah, sure."

"I want you to come over to my house."

"Why?"

"'Cuz I got some things for you to do."

Then he switches to his growly voice, very threatening:

"Perry! Come over here!"

I didn't really want to. Sometimes he was a real headache to be around because he was always bitching at me, and I couldn't drink when I was over there. He was always keeping an eye on me, and he'd make me do these bullshit jobs around his house. But I went over there anyway. It was the middle of the day, and he could tell that I had already been drinking. He didn't say anything about this, though. He made me mow the grass, clean up the garage, that kind of shit.

"You gotta bowl tomorrow," he tells me in that way he had that was really threatening at the same time it sounded friendly. "Either you show up here first thing tomorrow morning—and no fuckin' drinking!—or you just stay over here tonight."

I didn't stay over at Uncle Raymond's that night. But Sunday morning he called me at 8:30.

"Come over here," he says.

"I can't—I gotta go bowl at Palladium Lanes."

Palladium Lanes was in Orange, New Jersey. I used to go over there to bowl on Sunday mornings a lot. Uncle Raymond didn't give me no grief about it, because at least I'd be practicing, but by one o'clock I'd had a few drinks at the bowling alley, and I was starting to get a little toasted. Afterward, I went over to Uncle Raymond's house, and all we did was drive around and run errands, and then we picked up the "other guy" in Queens, around Ozone Park. Then, sometime after 9:00 that night, we drove over to Olympic Bowl in Belleville, which was about 5 miles outside the City, maybe 45 minutes from Queens.

And when we walked into that bowling alley, I'd never seen anything like it. The place was packed. There must have been 200 people there that night—every lowlife gambler in New Jersey was there—black, white, Hispanic, hoodlums, mobsters, heroin dealers—anybody who had money to bet was there, and they were ready for the action. Nobody knew where anybody else got their money from, and nobody was gonna ask. All I knew was that Ruby Red's guys seemed to be loaded with it.

I wasn't scared. I felt good. I felt like a winner, like I always felt. I was the guy who couldn't lose, and I was ready to go up against this joker. I even had a guy carrying my bowling balls. I walked in with my hot-combed hair and my fancy leather jacket, surrounded by the *Who's Who*—Uncle Raymond; Johnny Boy; my friend Bobby Cabert, the gangster; Nicky the Plumber, the gangster's apprentice; and some other big, scary-looking guys. This was not a bunch of "fugazis"—phony gangsters, a bunch of fake Italians. This was for real.

Because—oh, yeah, maybe I forgot to tell you—the guy people called "Johnny Boy" or "the other guy" was actually the silver-haired mobster John Gotti, who eventually became the head of the Gambino crime family and wound up dying in the federal prison hospital in Springfield, Missouri, after being given a life sentence for all kinds of crimes. I know he put out the hit on former Gambino boss Paul Castellano and all that. But all I got to say is, he was never anything but nice to me. (Well, except for this one particular night we're talking about here.) I just knew him as a guy who loved to gamble, a guy who loved action bowling, a guy who loved people. And he loved me, especially, at least he loved me when I won.

It's funny, though: I never actually called him by his name.

I didn't actually call him anything.

"How ya doin'?" he'd say to me.

"Okay."

"That's good. Did you come to bowl?"

"Yeah."

"Let me know who you're gonna bowl."

"Okay."

And that was it. That was how we'd say "hello."

Other times, I'd just identify the guy by the places I'd seen him. Like when somebody asked who the guy was, I'd say I'd seen him at Hollywood Lanes, downstairs, on Queens Boulevard. Or I'd seen him at Garden City, Long Island. And later, I'd say I seen him at the action in Deer Park, but by then I was on the long, slippery slide, and I don't remember too much.

On this particular night, I was John Gotti's golden boy. I was going to make this tough guy and his pals a shitload of money.

Like I said, I had never bowled at Olympic Bowl before, but I knew it was a Brunswick house (run by a big chain of bowling centers), and I knew I did good in Brunswick houses, plus it was in New Jersey, my home turf, so how hard could it be? That just shows you how arrogant I was: Here was this huge money match, and I hadn't even taken the trouble to bowl there.

Olympic Bowl was a 36-lane house, 18 lanes on a side. So since Ruby Red had picked the house, I got to pick the lanes. I picked the end pair of lanes, 17 and 18, right on the outside, because I had been told by older bowlers that those are the toughest lanes in the house, no matter where you go. Nobody ever bowls good on end pairs. I wanted to make it as tough as possible on the other guy, because I knew I would do great no matter which lane we used.

You gotta understand: At that level of play, every little thing makes a difference, including the way the lanes are oiled. When the lane is dry, the ball behaves differently than if it's oiled. People who own bowling alleys, and people who like to bet in them, have also figured out that there are ways to rig the game by oiling, or not oiling, the lanes, depending on who is bowling. A lot of bowlers are terrific in the lane conditions they're used to, but they can't adapt to different lane conditions. Being able to adapt is what makes the difference between somebody who is good and somebody who is great. I was convinced I could bowl great on any lane, in any condition, anywhere, against anybody. So who needed to practice?

Once we got there, I got out of my fancy clothes, just put on dungarees and a T-shirt, and then I went up to the bar. All I needed was a vodka-and-orange-juice to grease my wheels. But the fucking bar was closed. I asked the bartender for a drink anyhow, but he said it was against the law to serve me.

I walked back to the lane, just a little bit panicked, picked up a ball and addressed the line to throw a few practice balls, just to get the feel of the lanes. And the first ball I threw hooked sharply to the left and thunked into the gutter. I threw a gutterball! Holy shit. I couldn't believe it. I hadn't thrown a gutterball since I was a little punk kid. I threw again, and again, and again, but I couldn't get lined up. My timing was way off. I was amazed. I was just off. I already felt tired, and the match hadn't even begun. The truth was that I was hungover, but I wasn't prepared to admit that. I just thought I couldn't seem to throw the ball hard enough to hit the pocket.

I glanced over at the other bowler, Guy Fisher, and I noticed he wasn't doing much better. But he was still doing a lot better than me.

"You ready?" he said, after a few more practice throws.

"Yeah, sure," I said, even though I knew I wasn't. I could tell everybody was getting impatient. Some people had gotten there at, like, 6:00 p.m., and they'd been waiting all that time.

I figured the first game would start off with a bet of two, three thousand, but the first bet was $6,800. That was the main bet, but with all those gamblers, and all that cash, there were lots of other smaller bets going down. Gamblers will bet on anything. I looked around this crowd and there were a whole bunch of guys who were big and strong that I had never seen before, who had lots of money and who had been told I was the best money bowler that ever lived. And they'd just seen me throw a gutterball. I had no idea what they were thinking now.

Well, the first game I got killed. I couldn't believe it. Guy Fisher threw a 210, which normally I could have easily beaten, but I only bowled 160. It was nothing but splits, and the lanes were hooking real bad. I had only seen the ball make that kind of extreme hook once before in my life. I was a great curve bowler sometimes, but tonight I seemed to be fighting everything—fighting to get in line, fighting the lanes, fighting the hook, and fighting those two guys behind me who had all this money on the line and were putting all this pressure on me.

After the first game, Gotti walked up to me.

"What's the matter?" he says. He was looking at me funny, like he was surprised and a little suspicious. And you don't want to make John Gotti suspicious.

"The lanes are hooking real bad," I say. "I can't throw the ball hard enough to hit the pocket. I'm just not lined in yet—don't worry. I'll get it."

Actually, though, I was worried. Still, Guy Fisher was throwing the best he could and was only hitting 210. I just needed to get back to my usual game, and I could demolish this guy.

The next game, the main bet went from $6,800 to $13,000. Ruby Red's brothers parlayed their bets—whatever they won in the first match, they bet again. They had confidence in their guy, and the second game went in his favor, too. In fact, it was no contest whatsoever. I was totally off. Terrible. The other guy was getting looser, and I was getting worse.

After the second game, it was Uncle Raymond's turn to come up and grill me.

"Is this on the up-and-up?" he asks. I heard that same pissed-off suspicion in his voice.

He was suspicious that somebody was paying me to take a fall, to deliberately lose, because I could probably actually make a lot more money that way than by winning.

"Of course this is on the up-and-up," I say, starting to get angry myself. "Why would you ask me that?"

"Because you look terrible!"

"The goddamned lanes are hooking."

"Then throw the fucking thing harder!"

But the lanes were so dry that every time I threw the ball it would curve to the left. I couldn't get my timing together. It was like a pitcher in baseball, hitting the dirt instead of the strike zone. Actually, I knew what I needed to make me right: A goddamned drink. A goddamned vodka-and-orange-juice.

In the third frame of the third game, it was Gotti's turn to come up and rattle my cage.

"How come we ain't making any money?" he says. "Are you tankin'?"

You could tell he was getting really, really mad. He was not one of these guys who yelled when he got mad; he was quieter. But you got the point. This was a guy who'd gotten where he got by intimidating people, and he was pretty goddamned intimidating right now.

"You tell me the truth: Are you fuckin' tankin'?"

"No, of course not!"

"Well, that's what it fuckin' looks like!"

"I got some problems."

"Well, get rid of your problems, and start bowling! We're losing a lot of money here!"

The third bet was for $26,668. I remember this number, because it was the most money I ever bowled for in a single game. People were getting all excited by now; you could hear arguments over money in the back, all these complicated bets going down.

"What the fuck's going on?" Gotti kind of half-yells at me. "I want to know!"

"I need a goddamned drink. I've spent this whole week trying not to drink, and I need a goddamned drink!"

"What kind of a drink?"

"A mixed drink—I need some fuckin' vodka and orange juice."

"Well, why didn't you say so?"

"I asked the guy up at the bar earlier and he said the bar's closed. It's against the law."

"Well it's open now."

Gotti shoved his way up to the bar and confronted the bartender, who was standing there watching the action like everybody else.

"My guy needs a drink."

"Bar's closed."

"My guy needs a drink, you hear me? Open the bar and gimme a bottle of vodka!"

"The bar's—" then I guess the guy got a real clear shot of John Gotti, the pissed-off mobster, and figured he'd better open the bar.

Fuck the law. Gotti came over to where I was with a bottle of vodka, some orange juice, and a glass. I filled the glass about three-quarters full of vodka and orange juice, knocked it back, and poured another. Right away I stopped being tired, stopped being exhausted. I got an oomph, started getting lined in. I relaxed, my concentration came in, and I stopped worrying about everything and everybody. This is what was supposed to happen in the first game, not the third, and it would have if I'd had a drink before the match started.

By the fourth frame of that third game, before I had a drink, I was down by 42 fuckin' pins. But then I started to throw. I took another drink and threw two strikes. Then he threw two strikes.

Then, as I walked past the guy up to the line, I kind of growled at him, "Throw bad, you fuckin' rat!"

The vodka was kicking in and my old, arrogant, sonofabitch, fuck-you self was coming back. My asshole self.

Then I threw two strikes. He threw two strikes. By the last frame, the guy was standing at 254. He was doing pretty good. Real good, actually. All I needed was two strikes in the 10th to win.

"Lock the doors!" I yelled out. "This guy is dead!"

Then I threw the ball. I thought I threw it perfect. But it went sailing down the lane, off-center, and only knocked down nine pins. Guy Fisher won, 254 to 247—three in a row.

By now the place was going nuts. Ruby Red and his guys were winning all kinds of money, and other guys were losing all kinds of money, and the guy who supposedly cannot lose, was losing.

But then I looked over at Guy Fisher and he was sitting down, taking off his bowling shoes. He'd won the first three games, but I was coming back, big time, and he could see it. The kid knew he could not win against me.

I walked over to him.

"What are you doing?" I say.

"I'm quitting," he says.

"Why are you quitting?"

"Because you're drinking. I've seen you before, and when you're drinking, you can't be beat. There's no way I can beat you."

Ruby Red and his guys might have given Guy Fisher 10,000 bucks for bowling three games, so that was a good night for him. But this is also what is known as "bad action"—when somebody is winning and they quit while they're ahead. The guys who are losing don't get a chance to win their money back, and they tend to be seriously jerked around about this.

"You can't do that," I say.

"Who's gonna stop me?"

"They are."

"Who are they?"

"Them guys," I say, hooking my finger over at Uncle Raymond and Bobby Cabert and "the other guy."

Then Ruby Red walks over.

"What's going on?" he says.

"Your man's quitting," I say.

"So? He's allowed to quit," Ruby Red says.

"No, he's not."

"Who's gonna stop me?" Guy Fisher says.

"Nobody stops Ruby Red," Ruby Red says. "He does what he wants."

So then Uncle Raymond and "the other guy" walk over. "What's the matter?" they say.

"Well, we got two problems," I say. "Number one is, this guy is quitting" (and here I'm pointing at Guy Fisher, who has stopped taking off his shoes). "And number two, this other guy says that's okay" (and here I'm pointing at Ruby Red).

So then Gotti jumps in. He gets right up in Ruby Red's face.

"You told us to bring a lot of money, and we brought a lot of money," Gotti yells at him, probably busting the guy's eardrum. "There could be three, four hundred large out in this crowd. So here's what's gonna happen. Lock the doors, nobody's going home! We're staying here until I win all your money, or you win all our money, or somebody gets killed! I will kill you or shoot you where you stand."

This was no longer the John Gotti I knew, the guy who loved people, the guy who loved me and loved to bet on bowling. This was the John Gotti who scared the shit out of people.

Ruby Red just stood there for a second, with his full-length fur coat and his fancy shoes and all his bling.

"Let's bowl," he says.

I guess he figured "the other guy" was serious.

Well, by then I was getting seriously toasted on vodka and I bowled fantastic. I just crushed the poor bastard, nine out of the next 10 games. I fuckin' cleaned his clock. It wound up one of the ways Gotti said it would: With Ruby Red and his guys losing all their money.

So Gotti went up to Ruby Red and handed him a big wad of cash—maybe 10 or 20 thousand.

"Here," he says, "here's some pocket change to get you home."

"I don't need your money."

"Go on, take it anyway—no hard feelings. I don't want any repercussions over this. Maybe we can do business together in the future sometime."

This was the way things were done in those days. It was a standard gambler's thing. You never let a guy go home broke. For one thing, you wanted to be able to gamble against the guy some other time in the future. And also, it was just a matter of etiquette, kind of "honor among thieves." So Ruby Red took the money.

I put my bowling balls in my bag and me and Uncle Raymond and "the other guy" walked out to my car in the parking lot. We got in the car in our usual way—Raymond in the front passenger seat, me in the driver's seat, and Gotti in the back seat, directly behind me.

"So we did good, huh?" I say. I'm happy. I'm rubbing my hands together. I knew I did great those last 10 games.

"How did you like how I bowled?" I say.

"You were terrific for those last 10 games," Uncle Raymond says.

"So you think we did good, huh?" I say.

"Yeah, I think I did good. We won a lot of money. How much do I get?" I ask as I start turning the key in the ignition.

That's when Gotti reaches around from behind me, grabs my whole head in his hands like a melon, and slams it into the driver's side window so hard it cracks the glass. Then he slams it into the glass again and again, as hard as he can, and the glass starts to shatter in my face. The side of my face splits open and blood gushes everywhere.

"You think you did good, huh? You think you did good? Don't you ever, EVER do that to me again!" Uncle Raymond yells at me, right up in my face.

Then he grabs my head and takes his turn, slamming it into the glass a few more times until the glass is busted all over the place and there's blood splattered all over my clothes, all over the seat.

"You put us in a real bad spot—we put big money on the line and you showed up with your head up your ass! You could have lost us a lot of money!"

I have to say, thinking back on it now, I was not totally surprised when this happened. I really did put them in a big-time bad situation because, first, they thought I was tanking and, second, for the first time in my life, I really wasn't ready to bowl. I showed up hungover and out of practice and way off, mentally. I'd had no desire to practice or anything.

On the other hand, they weren't looking to kill me or anything; they didn't throw me out of the car onto the ground. They didn't want the cops coming around. This was just a family argument. They just wanted to smack me around, teach me a lesson.

Still, I was busted up so bad—bleeding all over the place—that Uncle Raymond had to take the wheel. He and Gotti both felt bad about what they'd done, I think. Uncle Raymond drove over to his doctor's house, someplace in North Arlington—by now it was, like, one o'clock in the morning—and he got the doc up out of bed to stitch me up. It took 40 stitches to put me back together, the doc said. I got $4,000 and 40 stitches out of that night.

When I finally got home, I told Debbie I fell down the stairs.

I don't know if she bought it, but at least she didn't throw me out of the house.

The way our relationship was going, I considered that a good night.

CHAPTER 5

THE EMPTY ROOM

LOOK, YOU GOTTA UNDERSTAND: Debbie LaRusso was the love of my life. She was fantastic—beautiful, caring, sexy, funny, somebody who cared about the stuff I cared about, somebody who fit into my family as if she was born into it. She was so kind to my mom and dad and my sisters. She was the woman most guys are never lucky enough to meet in their lives.

Yet I was lucky enough to meet her, fall in love with her, and most amazing of all, she fell in love with me, too. If there ever was a person for me forever, it was her.

If everything had worked out like I thought it was gonna, we would have gotten married and spent the rest of our lives together. We'd have had grandkids by now. I'd be Grandpa Bobby.

Who wouldn't love a woman like that? But it didn't go down that way.

Not at all.

And it was all because of me—because, by the time I was 25, I was turning into a lying scumbag and an addict. And I lost the love of my life.

How do you live with regret like that?

All these years later, I still don't know exactly how.

The night of the Ruby Red match, Debbie wasn't there. She didn't want any part of that shit. Plus, it was kind of a total guy thing—I don't think there was a single woman in the crowd that night.

But she also wasn't there because I was leading two lives now. One was the life where I loved Debbie, and kind of divided my time between our apartment and my parents' house in Paterson. That was a life full of love and hot meals and going to the bowling alley with this great, funny, beautiful lady. And the other life was the late-night life, full of jacked-up, coked-up energy, booze, action bowling, the excitement of big bets hanging on a single moment, getting drawn deeper and deeper into a world full of people like John Gotti and Bobby Cabert and other shadowy, dangerous characters. I started to act and think and lie like these guys did.

I don't remember how I first met them, but I started hanging out with some guys in the Bergen County Mob—real lowlifes they called Crooked-Eye Phil and Little Al and Malinky. And one day I gave these Bergen County mobsters a major league gambler, this guy Chuck, who was involved with the "Coupon King," the guy that invented grocery store coupons or whatever. This guy Chuck had too much money for his own good—he'd bet four or five thousand a match, $50,000 in a night, like it was nothing.

When you bet $5,000 on a game, of course, you had to lay down an additional $500 as the vig, the juice, the percentage. That money went to the Mob or whoever "owned" the game. So if you got a guy betting $50,000 a night, the vig alone is big enough to get the Mob interested.

So this guy Chuck goes out and bets a lot of money and wins a lot of money, until one day he doesn't. He gets crushed. And he winds up owing the Bergen County Mob, like, $20,000 to $30,000 in vig. And right after that, Chuck pulls a Houdini act and disappears. He don't come around no more.

This is a really, really bad idea.

But since the Bergen County boys can't find Chuck, they send Little Al over to see me. Little Al is little, but he's tough.

"You need to pay up," he says.

"I'm not paying nothing. I don't owe you a thing. You need to go find Chuck yourself."

"Where is he? Where's the guy live?"

"I don't know where he lives. That's your problem."

Then Little Al starts getting real nasty with me, all up in my face with that weird spooky glint in his eye.

"If we can't collect the vig, I'm coming after you, you little prick. I'm holding you responsible."

Meanwhile, while I was slipping into these sorts of situations with all kinds of degenerate characters, I was also slipping deeper and deeper into the grips of that beautiful white powder called cocaine. What had started out as a little club drug now and then had turned into a driving obsession, almost like a reason for living. I couldn't stop. What started out as recreational use turned to extensive use and then to totally abusive use. Every dollar I made action bowling went straight up my nose, or down my throat.

And gradually, something else had started to happen: Drugging may start out as this big social party scene, this club scene, but after a while it starts to turn into something completely unsocial. You start to get more and more focused on your own little self, and your next high: How am I gonna get the money to get high? How am I gonna score? How am I gonna get loaded? How am I gonna get the money to do it again? I wasn't Debbie's boyfriend no more. I was the boyfriend of booze and little razor-sharp lines of white powder.

Patsy Purzycki: Things got a lot worse than Bobby has ever admitted—a lot of it he doesn't even remember, I'm sure, because of the blackouts. More and more, people didn't want him coming around. His nose was always bleeding, and people were afraid of getting AIDS from him. Also, you couldn't trust him with anything. You didn't know what he was gonna take, to buy drugs or booze (even though, in all those years, strangely enough, I never once saw him take a drink). But then he started getting violent when I confronted him. That's when things really started getting scary.

Debbie wasn't stupid. More and more, she was getting suspicious and mistrusting of me. And I gotta say, she had good reason. I'd tell her I was going to be home at 8:00 or 10:00 that night or whatever and then I wouldn't show up until midnight or 2:00 or even after sunrise the next day. And, look, I wasn't any sort of womanizer. I wasn't carrying on with some other lady at the clubs. I was carrying on with alcohol and cocaine.

By December 1978, when I was 26 years old, I'd been deeply involved with Debbie for a couple of years. And, like I told you earlier, we would have been married if Debbie's mom hadn't threatened to disown her if she had done that. So most of the time we were "living in sin."

Then, on December 18, 1978, on a Monday just before Christmas, something happened that I will never forget, something that showed what sort of magical stuff Debbie was made of.

The whole thing kind of began a couple of days earlier, on Friday. That day, my sister Patsy calls me up and asks me if I want to go to a party in Totowa, New Jersey. I tell her I am bowling but will come pick her up after that. So I go pick her up and we go to this hoity-toity house, and when we get there and knock on the door, this tiny little peephole opens up, like where the boogeyman would look out, and then somebody opens the door and lets us in. This is the sort of place I don't belong. And when we go inside, it's this big spaghetti-bender party. I say "spaghetti-bender" to mean Italian, not mobbed-up.

And I'm sort of wandering around the party awkwardly, kind of stumbling into the potted plants or whatever, 'cuz these ain't my people and I don't belong here, and neither does Patsy. And then I look into the next room and I see this huge guy starting to fuck with my sister, and I can tell she's a little drunk and that she doesn't like it. So I go charging in there. I go right up to the guy, who is, like, 6 or 7 inches taller than me. I've always been a bantamweight, but bantamweights are scrappy.

"Hey, man, stop fucking with my sister," I say to the guy. "Get out of her face!"

The guy turns toward me, and he's like one of them battle robots in the video games. I suddenly realize—too late—how big he is.

"Fuck you, man," the guy says, and then he rears back and cold-cocks me in the head—wham!—and I go flying through the air, all the way into the next room. That dude must have been ex-military or something. There's blood spurting everywhere, blood on the expensive oriental carpets and the furniture and whatever. Patsy doesn't normally get too worked up about shit, but she goes over and grabs some $4,000 vase or whatever and cracks it over the dude's head. Then we both leave the party real quick (probably just as the cops arrive).

Patsy drives me over to Wayne General Hospital, in Wayne, New Jersey, to get my face stitched back together, and I don't get home to my parents' house until, like, 4:00 in the morning. My face has been seriously rearranged, and it's all bandaged up. I look like Jack Nicholson in that movie *Chinatown*. So that's how the weekend starts.

Then on Sunday, Patsy asks me to help her deliver some Christmas gifts to clients of the cosmetics company, Chelsea Cosmetics, that she's working for. Ironically, the gifts are all bottles of booze—Jack Daniel's, Bolla and Valpolicella wine, and whatever. So I agree to help her, even though my face is still in awful shape. The next day, Monday, we go down to midtown Manhattan to deliver these Christmas gifts to her clients at Macy's and Gimbels and whatever.

And after a little while Patsy is just—I dunno, she's going too slow. So I grab 10 bottles of wine and two bottles of Jack Daniel's and go upstairs at Gimbels and I say to some guy, "Hi, my name's Bob Perry, and this is a Christmas gift from Chelsea Cosmetics."

The guy gets all flustered and he says, "Oh, we can't accept gifts unless they're mailed."

And I fight the urge to do some surgery on the guy's face with a bottle of Jack Daniel's, and I get out of there just in time.

So I go downstairs to the street, and I'm standing there on the corner of Avenue of the Americas and Broadway with a crowd of people waiting for the light to turn, and I look over and here's this absolutely spectacular brunette standing there. I mean, there are plenty of fabulous women in New York, but this woman is out of this world. She distracts me completely. Then the light turns. I step into the street. I hear her say to me, "Look out!" And the next thing I know, it's like a freight train slams into my body doing about 60, and I'm being dragged down Avenue of the Americas smashed into the bumper of a taxicab like a bug. I'm feeling a mixture of shock, surprise, and unbelievable pain.

Finally the cab stops—it went almost from Thirty-Fourth Street to Thirty-Third—and I vaguely remember all kinds of people crowding around, including the beautiful brunette. (I didn't do this just to get your attention, darlin'!) I think the fuckin' cab driver would have driven away if it hadn't been for all those people.

I remember drifting in and out of consciousness. I remember being unable to feel anything from the waist down. I remember terrible pain in my face, which the antenna of the cab had ripped open—for the second time that weekend! And I remember a New York City policeman looking down at me. He throws a coat or something on top of me.

"This motherfucker is dead," he says.

I remember thinking, "I'm dead. I can't believe I'm dead."

Somehow or other, Patsy sees all the commotion and realizes it's me sprawled in the street, and she comes rushing over to the place where I'm lying on the pavement. She's hysterical.

"Bobby! Bobby! Bobby!" I hear her yelling.

I hear the cop saying, "Don't move," which is hysterical, because, like, how am I supposed to move? I've been whacked in the head by a wrecking ball, and I'm completely paralyzed from the waist down.

Then I hear Patsy's voice, far away.

"Bobby, Bobby, Bobby!"

Then, at some point, I manage to throw the cop's coat back and yell out, "I ain't fuckin' dead!"

The inner lion that had come back over and over again in my life had just showed up.

"I ain't fuckin' dead yet, you asshole!"

So an ambulance comes and drags my sorry ass off to Bellevue Hospital (the place they send the nutjobs, which happened to be the only hospital available). When I get there, they load me on a gurney and this guy pulls off my dungarees and I just scream, the pain is so incredible (both my legs were busted up and broken). There are, like, 10 gurneys with bloody-looking guys lying there in the waiting area. These guys are handcuffed to the gurneys. One of them tells me they are all there 'cuz of a riot at the jail on Rikers Island. The guy tells me I look worse than any of them busted-up convicts. Boy, this has been a helluva weekend so far.

Patsy can't stop crying. She calls my dad's appliance shop and my dad is busy, so he sends over this huge guy who works in the shop. The guy is, like, 6-foot-6, and they call him "Thumbs." Thumbs can carry a Frigidaire on his back up two flights of stairs, but that doesn't do me much good now.

But what does do me a lot of good is when Patsy calls Debbie and she shows up in my hospital room, immediately, like an angel. And Debbie comes to see me every single day for the next 167 days, while I was in and out of the hospital. The girl never missed a single day. I mean, wow. What a woman. Do I deserve that?

Absolutely not, but this is a story about a guy that always got more than he deserved.

Almost as soon as I got in the hospital, the doctors started giving me Percodan, a powerful, addictive narcotic, to help relieve my pain. I guess they didn't know I was a junkie in training. And, of course, being a junkie in training, I never told them.

The cab had busted open the bone in my left leg. It ripped off the ligaments in my right leg. It ripped the shit out of my face. And all kinds of other stuff. But here's the worst part of it: I held the world responsible for what happened to me. As I would learn much later, in sobriety, it's your own attitudes and resentments that do the most damage, and it's only when you fix all them bad attitudes that you start to heal.

But I wasn't ready for that then. Instead I figured, since the world done me wrong, that it was fair when the doc gave me 60 Percodans for a month to eat them all in a week and ask for more. I didn't care if I was getting addicted to Percodan. It felt good, and God had done me wrong. I deserved it.

Uncle Raymond had a different explanation for what happened. He called me at the hospital the day after I got in there.

"So who hit you?" he says.

"Hit me? Nobody hit me. A cab ran over me."

"Yeah, right," he says. "You know everybody's saying the Bergen County Mob done it."

"The Bergen County Mob? Crooked-Eye Phil and Little Al and them guys? Raymond, you gotta be crazy. I got run over by a taxicab in midtown Manhattan in the middle of the day, with about a thousand other people standing there watching."

"Well, think about it. You had a dispute with them bastards over that little creep Chuck's debts. Basically, you told them you didn't owe nothing. They said you did. And that was, what, a couple of weeks before this cab thing happened?"

I had to admit, Uncle Raymond had a point. But I still thought what he was saying was ridiculous. I didn't believe that's what happened. What I believed, deep down, was even more ridiculous—that

God hated me and was punishing me. And it wasn't until I got over that idea—years later—that I finally started becoming a whole person.

But for now, I had to take care of some business. Because Little Al and them guys would not back off. They couldn't find Chuck, so they were going to try to extort 30 grand out of me. It didn't matter if I was a fuckin' cripple. It didn't matter that I didn't have the money. Finally I agreed to have a sit-down with these guys, in a restaurant owned by the Bergen County Mob, on Route 6. I told these guys I was going to bring some friends, my Uncle Raymond and a friend of his named Bobby.

So I show up at this restaurant, a little early, on crutches, with both my legs in casts. It wasn't like this makes these guys any more sympathetic, though. Little Al gets in my face again, mocking me.

"So where's the fabulous uncle of yours? Did he forget about you?"

And just about then Uncle Raymond and Bobby Cabert walk through the door. (And those two guys—I'm telling you—you could just look at them and know there was trouble coming.)

Uncle Raymond comes through the door like a bull elephant, ready to knock something down. Bobby Cabert is dressed meticulously, like he always was, wearing $200 pants, a beautiful sports jacket, a nice hat, with them aviator-type glasses he always wore. Nothing is out of place.

I never saw Cabert do nothing crazy, like Joe Pesci's character in *Goodfellas*. When Cabert did his business, nobody was around. But when he walked through that door, dressed to the nines, somehow you just got the idea that you'd probably better tiptoe out of there.

"How ya doin'?" Little Al says, which is what everybody always says in New Jersey.

"Whaddya mean, how am I doin'?" Raymond says, belligerent. "How do you think I'm doin'? Whaddya think I'm doin' here?"

Little Al looks over at Bobby Cabert, and he must have recognized who he was. Everybody knew who he was.

"Listen," Al says, "We didn't really realize—"

"Yes you did," Raymond says. "What the fuck are you trying to do to my nephew? He don't owe you shit."

And then Bobby Cabert gets in the guy's face, and then Uncle Raymond does, too, like a tag team.

A few minutes later, when they left the restaurant, that 30-grand debt had just gone away, like a soap bubble that just popped.

A few days after that, Uncle Raymond tracked down Chuck the gambler, and they had a nice little chat. Maybe they had tea. And after that, Chuck paid up.

That's how things worked, if you were connected to guys like Uncle Raymond and Bobby Cabert.

Meanwhile, incredibly enough, I had this angel, Debbie LaRusso, who had come to my room every day with unconditional love and sometimes flowers, back when I was in the hospital. At first I had worried that I would never walk again, much less bowl. But once the docs started to fix my legs, operating on both the left and right legs, I had been transferred into a wheelchair and then onto crutches. After I got released from the hospital, I went to stay at my parents' house for awhile (because I didn't have to climb so many stairs), and Debbie would come to visit me there every day after work. Think about that.

The cab driver's insurance company paid for all of them months in the hospital. I hired some shyster lawyer down on 125 Broadway and he got me, like, $20,000, even though I should've gotten $2 million.

Now that I had been released from the hospital to my parents' house, I was a "new man." On a personal level, I felt more in love with Debbie than ever. Professionally, I felt I would soon be as good a bowler as anyone on the planet—about ready to become nationally known, just as good as anybody.

Physically, though, I was still on the mend, hobbling around on these crutches that the doctors led me to believe might be a permanent deal. They didn't say so, but it was obvious they thought I might be a crutch-monkey for good.

A while after this—maybe a year or so—I was in the bowling alley with my crutches. There was a guy named Ralph Abbott, whose older brothers I knew from school, bowling this other guy named Larry. Larry owned a bunch of sporting goods stores. And Ralph Abbott, even though he was only 17, was really a fantastic bowler. But he was also a fuckin' loudmouth, and he was trash-talking Larry, big time. It started to really piss me off. Who did this kid think he was, disrespecting this older man? But the kid wouldn't quit. Then he turned to me. He was aware that I was watching, and also that I used to be one of the most formidable bowlers on the planet.

"If you didn't have crutches, I'd bowl you now!" he said, in a very mocking, sneering way. And the next thing I know, I was trying to throw my crutches away and put this little creep in his place. I didn't succeed—that happened a few months later—but the inner lion had come out again. When I was driven to it, I had this savage desire to succeed, to overcome adversities, to climb back into the winner's circle. When the lion came out, there was almost no stopping him.

When I got out of the hospital, I gradually shed not only the wheelchair, the crutches, and the casts but also the whole idea of myself as a crippled guy. Now I was back on my feet, good as new. Unfortunately, that also meant that I slipped back into my old habits of staying out half the night, drinking, and snorting blow. There was only one change: Now I had a new addiction, to Percodan.

For me, drugs and alcohol were like peanut butter and jelly—one went with the other. When I drank, I wanted to do drugs, and when I did drugs, I drank. I couldn't stop.

Was this any way to treat a good woman? No, especially not one who nursed me back to health for 167 consecutive days. But this was not a matter of manners. This was addiction—in fact, multiple addictions. More and more, I was becoming a slave to them. Even when I got back into my groove and started bowling real good, I'd sometimes win a $10,000 purse—and within a couple of days, I'd be broke again and trying to come up with some big lie to tell Debbie about why I got home so late.

Sometimes we'd go into the City and I'd drop her off somewhere and tell her I'd be back in an hour and then I'd be gone all night. Things were getting worse and worse. We just couldn't get along. I have to say, looking back, that I can hardly blame her.

Debbie was a real good bowler, and she liked the whole bowling world, and she really loved Bob Perry the bowler. She knew that I was a guy who could go all the way, become nationally known, win all the top tournaments, win a lot of money. But she could also see that, from time to time, I would make mistakes under pressure. It was like I was cracking, but slowly. She was watching me deteriorate. She was watching the drugs and booze obliterate me.

Then, finally, things hit absolute bottom. One night Debbie told me she was gonna make dinner, a meatloaf, and to be home by six o'clock. But it was closer to 11 o'clock when I walked in the door. I was hammered, and trying to cover it up. That was my life: I was one thing but trying to pretend I was another. I was bleeding from the nose but pretending I wasn't. Debbie was sitting there with black smoke coming out of her ears. She was fuckin' furious. Poor Debbie! Living with an alcoholic was making her old, and you could see it in her face.

"What are you so mad about?" I say, kind of innocently and surprised.

"Where have you been?"

"I had to take Raymond into the City."

"Bullshit."

"I'm not lyin', Debbie! Raymond had some business in Queens, in Ozone Park. The whole thing ran real late. Then we went to the track, because he had to meet a guy over there. I tried to call you."

I knew she wasn't going to buy my story, but I stuck to it.

"I don't believe a word you say, Bobby. Every time you open your mouth, you're lying."

"Look, I told Raymond I would take him around tonight. Whatever it was he was doin', it ran late. I can't help it! Whaddya want me to tell Raymond? To drop his business and come back here so I'll be on time for dinner?"

"Bobby, I made you dinner and asked you to be here at six o'clock. I wanted to sit down together, like a regular couple. Why can you never, ever do what you say you're going to do?"

"I told you! Raymond's business ran late! Why don't you ever believe me?"

Everything kind of ratcheted up from there. When you're defending a lie, like I was, your voice tends to get louder and louder as if, if you yelled loud enough, your story would be true. Poor Debbie. All she wanted was to have a nice meal with me at six o'clock, and here I was this raving, drunk lunatic in the kitchen screaming at her.

The meatloaf sat in the oven, getting colder and colder. Well, one word led to another and then the "F-U's" started. I was trying to defend an indefensible position and there was no place to go except to a higher volume. Our little apartment was not that far from other little apartments, and I'm sure our neighbors could have heard what was going on. It's possible somebody called the cops—I don't remember. I just remember that this fight with Debbie kept getting worse and worse, in this tiny kitchen. Finally she pushed me, hard. I pushed her back, hard. And then she slapped me in the face so hard it felt like she broke my nose. When somebody hits or slaps you in the face, it makes you go kind of crazy. Then, next thing I remember, she picked up a knife. It wasn't a butter knife, neither—it was one of them big, sharp kitchen knives that you'd cut a turkey with.

"I'll fucking kill you!" she yelled.

And then, I dunno, I guess we both realized how bad this argument had gotten, how scary it was. It was actually the worst argument either one of us ever had. By far. We were about 2 seconds away from doing something we'd regret for the rest of our lives.

I remember, years later, when I was in prison, I was talking to my mom at the time the O.J. Simpson verdict came out.

"You think he killed those two people?" she asked. "I know you know. 'Cuz you were there. Debbie told me about what happened that night. She told me how close it got."

But instead, kinda suddenly, Debbie and me both sat down, slumping into chairs at the kitchen table. We were both scared. We were both sad and confused. Then we both started crying.

"Look, Debbie," I said to her, pleading, with tears coming down my cheeks. "I can't live like this! We can't live like this!"

Then the remorse came up, like a big boiling flood. This was not a "dispute"—I was 100 percent wrong. I was not right in any sense. I had thrown a bad blow to the woman I loved. My actions were terrible. This was one of the most major league awakenings I had ever had.

"Oh, God, I'm so sorry. I'm not going to be like that anymore. I promise."

But my promises didn't mean shit. And the next day, when Debbie told my sisters and her friends what had happened, every one of them told her to leave me immediately. They told her to move out of the house. And my two closest sisters, Patsy and Jeannie, both stopped talking to me.

A couple of days later, I found that meatloaf, stone cold and untouched, in the oven.

Heartbreak. That's what you feel when the love of your life is leaving you, and it's all because of you.

Over the next few days and weeks, I was practically begging, trying to get Debbie to forget everything that went down. But no matter what I did, the addiction won. If I drank I drugged and if I drugged I drank, and I couldn't stop. When I laid down next to my loved one at night, I was so happy to be there. But I stank of booze. She wasn't happy that I was there. She didn't tell me she was leaving, but I knew something was going to happen.

Meanwhile, I had an angry fight with Patsy over my drinking, and I punched a hole in her wall. My sisters had seen this anger in me, and by now they considered Debbie a part of this family. More and more, they considered me the outsider, the dangerous one, the guy that had to be thrown out to protect everyone else. The wolf.

"You get rid of him—you gotta get rid of Bobby," they kept telling Debbie.

And I kept begging her not to listen to them.

It was not too long after that terrible fight that I had to leave to fly out to Reno to the national championships. I didn't win the tournament, but I did pretty good. And then there was this huge snowstorm—24 inches fell—and I got stuck in the Denver airport for almost a whole day. On the way home, I called Debbie from Chicago.

"I'm probably not going to be home when you get there—my mom and I are going to a show in New York," she told me. "Get somebody else to pick you up at the airport."

Things were not going well at that point. I tried to apologize to her for everything. She told me she was okay and everything was good and all that stuff.

So I call my friend Pepsi to come pick me up at the airport. He drives me back to the apartment in Paterson, and I get out of the car and I can see Jackson, our dog, at the window of the apartment up on the third floor. This is kind of unusual. But I am eager to see Debbie.

You've got to understand that by now not only was my relationship with Debbie on edge, my whole life was teetering on the brink. In the classic alcoholic, dope-addict way, I was just completely in denial about what was going on in my life, or in the lives of people around me. I mean, I had no car, I had no money—I just spent everything I had on booze and drugs and partying—and everybody was mad at me. Even my own mother, who lived on East Twenty-Sixth Street, wouldn't talk to me anymore. Too much lying, too much stealing, too many alcoholic blackouts. Once I had called her on the phone.

"Who is this?" she says.

"Bob Perry, your son," I say.

"Don't ever call this number again."

Click.

That was my life.

So I go bounding up the stairs to our apartment to see Debbie, carrying my little travel suitcase, and I unlock the door and bust into the living room and . . . it's completely empty. Jackson comes up to greet me, but there is nothing in the apartment except a mattress on the floor, a shower curtain, and a pile of my clothes. There's no food in the refrigerator, not even a toothbrush in the bathroom. All the utensils are plastic.

Debbie—beautiful Debbie!—has left me.

She's gone.

This sweet woman with the gorgeous body, who loves me to death—she's gone. She has given up on me.

There were no cell phones in those days, of course, so I go over to the neighbor's apartment to use the phone, but they don't answer the door. I go downstairs to use the phone at the pizza joint next door to call Debbie at her mom's house. She doesn't answer. I call everybody, but nobody answers. It turns out, everybody knew she was leaving me, except me. Finally, I call my sister Jeannie, and she picks up, but she doesn't want to talk to me either. She says I should call my other sister Patsy, who always gives it to me straight.

"Debbie left you—she moved out," Patsy says. "She's had it with your shit. Everybody else has, too."

Waves of loneliness wash over me. I am devastated.

Even now, over 30 years later, I can remember that empty apartment, and I feel that same devastation. Even now, I can't get that feeling out of my body.

Even so—believe it or not—it still wasn't enough to wake me up.

Even getting dumped by Debbie, the love of my life, was not enough!

I was heading down, and I had a long, long way to go before I hit bottom.

CHAPTER 6

THE FULL FUCKIN' SKID

IT'S BEEN MORE THAN 30 YEARS since Debbie left me, but right now I can still feel what I felt the day I returned home to find her gone. The shock. The emptiness. The hollowness. The fear. When Debbie went out of my life, it suddenly made me realize how hollow I already was inside. I had a hole inside myself so deep and so wide that there was nothing that could ever fill it.

Except for her.

But she was gone.

Now there didn't seem to be any reason for living. It was just me, Jackson, an old mattress, some plastic forks and spoons, and a pile of hot-shit disco clothes from Mr. Stag's in a big empty room. I was lost. I never realized how much I depended on Debbie. I started talking to people in the bowling world, and I found out that there was a lot of sympathy for her, that people were helping her way more than they were helping me. Maybe I thought I was hot shit, the greatest, but other people seemed to have a different opinion. That made me feel even more alone.

About a week after she left me, I wheeled around a corner at the supermarket with a shopping cart full of beer and practically ran into her.

"Oh, hi," I said, very casually.

"Hi."

"You doin' okay?"

"Yeah."

"Where you living?"

"I'm back at my mom's."

"How's that goin'?"

"It's okay."

"Well," I said like a real tough-guy, "you do what you gotta do."

We chitchatted a little and then, realizing my heart was breaking and that all that wise-guy stuff was just bullshit, I started begging. I practically got down on my knees.

"Look, Debbie," I said. "I'm so sorry for what happened. It's all my fault. I've got no defense for what I've done. But I promise you, if we ever got back together, I wouldn't do dope again, ever. I wouldn't stay out late no more. I'd earn money and not spend it. I'd bring it home. And you know what an incredible money bowler I am—the best. We could still have such a beautiful life together, Debbie."

She just stood there in the cereal aisle with all the Cheerios and Wheaties, with a look on her face that said, "I ain't buyin' this shit."

But for my part, I think I actually believed it when I said it. I didn't even realize I was lying like a rug.

A few months later, I had to take Jackson to the pound and give him away. I couldn't take care of myself, much less a dog. Debbie's mom didn't want to take the dog, either. So I asked Debbie to come with me to the pound and give him away. We both cried, but giving Jackson up was the responsible thing to do. The home Debbie and I had made together was gone.

I kept on living in that empty apartment for a couple of months, with no furniture except that old mattress, no TV to watch, no food except maybe vodka and chips. When I wanted to call somebody, I'd walk three blocks up the street and call my old partner in crime, Tommy Lorenzo. He'd help me out with a few bucks, and we'd go score some dope together and party. For a little while, everything seemed good again.

One day I went over to bowl on a team in Paramus, but it turned out they were all friends with Debbie and her mom and they threw me off the team. They were all couples bowling together in a league; they'd heard about me from Debbie, and that was enough for them.

Once or twice I called Debbie at her job at the insurance place. She didn't have anything much to say, except that she didn't want to see me. She said she was done. She was fine living back with her mother.

So then I decided to give up the apartment. I couldn't pay the electric bill. I could still make a lot of money bowling—I even won a couple of big tournaments for five or 10 thousand—but drugs and alcohol sucked up all of my earnings. I could barely afford food. Meanwhile, nobody was talking to me—not Patsy or Jeannie or anybody else. Even Uncle Raymond didn't seem to come around no more. He was such a powerful presence in my life that his absence weighed on me, like a boulder on my back. I knew that he loved me, and I knew that his not being there meant he did not approve of my life.

The only person who would help me out was Tommy Lorenzo. Sometimes we bowled and I'd give him a lesson. Sometimes we'd get in on the action bowling on a Friday night. But whatever we did, we'd always wind up in the City, seriously loaded on something or other. More and more, I'd wake up out of a blackout afterward, someplace I didn't recognize.

I was finally able to talk to my sister Jeannie, and she let me stay at her house for a few weeks. But then she started getting nasty with me, so I moved in with Patsy, which didn't work out either. So I moved into my mom's one-bedroom apartment in Haledon, New Jersey. She apologized for being so nasty to me on the phone, and I apologized to her for everything I had done. My mother still loved me then, and I loved her, too, despite all the shit that had gone down. But by now nobody else in my family would talk to me, so mom's apartment was the closest thing to "home" I was going to get. One day she bet $100 and won $5,000, and she recarpeted the whole apartment.

My own life used to be like that: magic, golden, easy. But now, somehow, I had turned into a 30-year-old man waking up hungover in his mom's apartment, and all the big dreams of my life—a wife and family, fame, riches and national championships—seemed like stupid, busted toys.

Even so, I wasn't ready to give up. And the main thing I wanted—the thing I always wanted—was Debbie LaRusso. Now I decided to do everything in my power to see if I could get her back.

Maybe you can't believe this now, but when I was 30 and all pimped out in my disco clothes and blow-dried hair, I looked like the tits. In the bowling world, I was still famous all over the East Coast. But the main thing I had going for me was my mouth. I could talk my way into or out of almost anything. So I decided to try to talk Debbie into taking me back.

I'd get her on the phone, or sometimes even in person at the bowling alley, and I'd joke and beg and plead with her, promise her I'd do things, or not do things. I promised her I'd never do dope or stay out all night again. I wouldn't get fucked up. I'd straighten out and get better. I'd even go to rehab. I'd work hard to make money and not spend it all. I told her I had saved up $10,000. I'd get us a nice apartment. Maybe I'd even learn to cook.

I don't know why, but Debbie finally bought it. And about 6 months after we broke up, we moved into another apartment, this time in East Rutherford, New Jersey. It was nice. And for a while I was really, really good. We had 6 or 7 months of happiness together in that apartment. I didn't stay out late. I made sure I wasn't too fucked up before I got home. I was polite and sweet to her.

But the seeds of trouble were already there. That 10 grand I told her I had saved up? I made it selling coke. (I didn't say nothing about how I got it, but I think she suspected.) And I said I would stop doing drugs, that I would change, but the amount of effort I put into changing was zero. It was only a matter of time before my old, bad self, the junkie self, my hungry, empty self, would come back again.

And it did. One night I came home about 4:00 in the morning shit-faced drunk and coked-up to the max. Debbie came stumbling into the kitchen and we had another big fight. I admitted to her, finally, that it was time for me to get some help. I realized that unless I got some help getting rid of this monkey on my back, I would lose Debbie for good. Finally Debbie had had enough of my shit. Actually, she was a saint for lasting as long as she did.

I remembered this old geezer named Billy that I'd known for quite a lot of years from seeing him around bowling alleys. He told me he'd once been this terrible drunk, but now he was in this program of recovery. He never beat my brains in with it, but he told me this program would always be there if I ever felt like I needed it. Billy had been sober a long time, maybe 15 years or something. I never lost Bill's phone number—I'd kept that ratty scrap of paper in my wallet even when there wasn't anything else in there. I'd run into Billy from time to time.

"You still in that program?" I'd ask.

"Yeah."

"Can I call you if I need to?"

"Yeah."

I thought maybe I'd call Billy, but the next morning Debbie made me call St. Joseph's Hospital in Paterson, and they recommended this free detox program called Straight & Narrow. Debbie drove me over that same day and I stayed there 6 days. I was a complete mess. My life was falling apart and I didn't want to lose her. It wasn't just that I couldn't breathe anymore because my nose was so fantastically stuffed up from cocaine. It was that the whole inside of my head was like a block of wood. But, more than that, deep down, even though I still looked fairly good and could talk a good game, I was a completely lost soul. There was just a lonely path down a lonely road where a person should have been.

There was this thing inside of me that I could not get rid of, and I would not understand it until years later. All I knew was that if I took a drink, I felt better, so I kept on drinking and doing blow until the next thing I knew I was gone, in a blackout. I didn't know anything about blackouts, had never heard of them. I just knew that more and more nights I'd get home and not know what happened the next day.

It was like my whole life was getting sucked down into a black hole, like one of them stars that sucks up all the light.

When I got out of Straight & Narrow, I felt pretty good. There was still shit draining out of my face, but I could breathe a little bit better and I felt kind of hopeful. But that wasn't good enough for Debbie. She insisted that I go to this 21-day program she found out about called St. Christopher's Inn, which was part of this very woo-woo rehab place called Graymoor Spiritual Retreat Center that was run by a bunch of Franciscan monks. It was someplace upstate, far away from the City. I didn't tell Debbie this, but I remembered Graymoor from when I was a kid and we used to go up there to visit my mom's cousin, Father Benjy.

Debbie wasn't fooling around. I was only in the apartment for 1 night after Straight & Narrow before she drove me up to Graymoor. She seemed kind of happy, like maybe things would change. Like maybe there was a chance for us. I just felt sick and scared and desperate. I really didn't want to do this shit.

But when I got up to Graymoor, it was like walking into a different world. All the monks were wearing brown bathrobes and sandals, like from the Bible days. Everything was real quiet. And the monks greeted me with open arms because Father Benjy had lived up there and was buried there. He was some kind of a big muckety-muck in the Franciscan world, so I figured these old gray-headed geezers would give me a break up there. It was going to be great. I had an inside track at this joint.

They gave me a bed and showed me the dining hall and the room where AA meetings were held. Part of the day you had to pray and part of the day you had to work.

So they gave me a little job in the intake area, checking in new people who would come through the door.

The first few days, I was trying to pay attention and be good, but after a little while the place started to really grind on my ass. The people who came in the door? They were pathetic derelicts and junkies and losers. They looked and smelled terrible. Almost all of them were homeless. What was I doing here? I mean, I wasn't like these people at all. I was one of the greatest bowlers on the East Coast, maybe the whole country. Hell, maybe the world. I was one of the greatest action bowlers walking. I could make thousands of dollars in a night, easy. I had a great apartment in East Rutherford. And I had the greatest girlfriend in the world. I had never even been arrested (yet). I was just doing this because I didn't want to lose Debbie, that's all. I went to a couple of AA meetings, but they were total bullshit. I mean these guys—what a bunch of pathetic nutjobs. Spilling their guts, and probably lying through their teeth, too. They talked about "The Steps," but I didn't know anything about that and didn't want to, either. I was sitting there in these rooms, listening to all this. I had not had a drink or a line of blow in 12 or 13 days, and these people were driving me batshit.

There was this one old guy at Graymoor, maybe 40 or 50 years old, who they kept on as a maintenance man because he was too messed up in the head to be able to function outside. He was what they call a "wet brain" drunk, a toothless old guy who basically cooked his noodle from so many years of drinking. He was going to be at Graymoor for the rest of his life. But even though he moved real slow and had trouble understanding everything, he was loved by everybody around the place.

They called him Old Man John or some such thing.

For some reason, Old Man John had it in for me. He kept coming around, bothering me, being nasty to me, getting up in my face.

So one day I start being nasty back to him.

"I ain't like you, bro," I say to him. "I ain't like you!"

Then I start yelling at him, belittling him—I guess just because I was going out of my mind up there. And besides, he wouldn't get out of my face.

One of the monks, a guy named Brother Pious, overhears what's going on and comes in from the next room to bust my chops.

"Listen, Perry, unless you change your life, you're going to wind up like this man if not worse before you know it," he says. "If you don't change, you'll wind up in jail or dead or both. And soon."

It was complete garbage, of course. Horseshit. Brother Pious just didn't like me. Well, I didn't like him neither, the grizzle-headed old fuck.

The next day I am playing basketball with this kid from Brooklyn and he is being a little prick, pushing and shoving, trying to trip me up. I pick up the basketball and hit him with it. So Brother Pious calls me on the carpet again.

"There is no room for violence here," he says.

"You should see what this kid's been doing to me!" I say. "He's being a total jerk. He's acting out!"

"This boy has serious problems that you know nothing about," Brother Pious went on, his voice getting darker and angrier. "Go out and die on the street! You have no humility! You have no respect for anything or anybody! There's no room for you here. I should give your bed to somebody who could actually use it."

"I'm not like him or any of these fucking people in here!"

"You're worse than these people in here. Unless you change, there is no hope for you."

"Man, I don't belong here."

"No, you don't," Brother Pious says. And he hands me a bus ticket back to Manhattan.

When I got to the City, I called Debbie and told her I'd done real good at Graymoor—so good, in fact, that they let me out early. When she came to pick me up, she could see that I looked and sounded a lot better, since I'd been clean and sober a couple of weeks, eating good food and actually sleeping at night. She was happy for me, and happy for us. I called Uncle Raymond and he was real happy for the both of us, too.

It seemed like everything was turning around for me.

Then, 2 weeks later, I discovered crack.

The second I tried it, I knew I was gone. Because crack was better than life. There was this kid named Dennis who lived around the corner from us in East Rutherford, and he was the one who introduced me to the drug that changed my life forever. (This was around 1984, when crack was a brand-new thing.) I went over there one day and he showed me how you load these little white rocks of crack cocaine into a straight glass stem with a little bit of Brillo stuffed into the end of it for a screen. Then you torch the crack with a butane cigarette lighter and—wham!—in a second that shit hits your brain like a freight train and you're gone. It's like sucking down 30 bottles of beer in 1 second, like the most perfect, most blissed-out you've ever felt in your life. And then, after about 4 seconds, it starts to fade and all you want is to do it again. You'd sell your pet puppy, sell your girlfriend, sell your mother to get more. And people do.

I was already a full-blown drunk, but crack escalated my drinking through the roof. It also escalated my lying, especially to Debbie, to cover it all up, and my hustling and stealing, because I had to pay for the shit somehow.

Because nobody could tell if you were smoking crack—it didn't have a smell, it didn't make your eyes red—I started thinking I could just do crack all the time and get away with it. The obsession started taking over my life. Then the paranoia and the weirdness started setting in. I became convinced that people were after me, following me, watching me, everywhere I went. More and more, I was turning into a creature of the shadows.

Joe Tolvay: Bobby used to always think he was better than everybody else in the bowling world, and the thing is, he was. But then he got in with the wrong crowd, and after a while nobody trusted him anymore. He turned into a con man, a like-able con man. People thought he was just scamming them all the time, and I'm pretty sure he was. One time he came in with this Aiwa stereo system—must have cost a couple thousand dollars—that he was selling for $200. I gave him the money, took the stereo, and the next morning when I came in, it was gone. That's when I knew he was in big trouble.

At the same time, I started to hate the high I once loved. I hated the smell of the stuff, and especially the smell of all that butane you had to inhale to get high. It was disgusting. (Some people smoked crack by setting fire to cotton balls dipped in 151-proof rum—that's why they sometimes call crack "151"—but I couldn't afford that.) Every time I went out on the street I would say, this is the last time, but I didn't do anything to change, so nothing changed.

More and more, I kept ending up in New York City at 3:00 in the morning, in places I would never have dreamed of going when I was just smoking pot or drinking vodka.

I'd find myself in some crack den in an abandoned building, looking over my shoulder, convinced somebody was coming for me. I used to be such a snappy dresser, but now I'd wear the same shit for days or weeks or months, first because I didn't care, and second because I couldn't afford new clothes—I was spending it all on booze and crack. I'd win a few thousand in a bowling tournament or in the action, but I could never manage to pay the rent. Debbie had to do it. I was completely dependent on her financially.

Meanwhile, my body was deteriorating. I rarely took showers anymore. I couldn't sleep. Sometimes I'd wake up at 2:00 or 3:00 in the morning, slip out of bed from beside Debbie, and drive into the City, into the middle of the apocalypse in the South Bronx, to cop drugs. I hated myself while I was doing this, but I did it anyway. I could easily have gotten shot or robbed or mugged in there. But I couldn't live with it and I couldn't live without it, so there was no real way to live at all.

It was inevitable, I guess. But finally, for some dumb reason, or maybe no reason at all, I smoked crack in front of Debbie at home. That was it. She told me to leave, like I knew she would, and I left without any fighting. I guess all the fight had gone out of me and I was just surrendering to a life of darkness and blackouts and death. I packed a bag full of clothes and I left on my reign of self-pity.

Patsy Purzycki: I don't remember exactly when this happened. All those terrible days are just a blur. But one day I found out that there was this statue of the blessed Virgin Mother called Our Lady of Fatima, that used to travel the world, and it was in our parish for a few days. She was known to perform miracles. So I went to the church to see this beautiful statue. They were selling books about her in the vestibule, and I took one home and read it in 2 days. It told all about the miracles that were attached to the statue—like that she wasn't allowed in Russia, but somehow the soldiers overlooked her and she was able to be seen by those poor people over there. And I started to think, "Maybe it's true—maybe there really are miracles."

I called my sister Jeannie, and she told me that the statue was going to be in our parish only one more night. I told her, "I'm coming to pick you up, and we're going to see the statue one more time." So we went to the church, and as we got into the procession of people walking by the statue, I said to the Blessed Virgin, "I can't do this anymore. I give up. Bobby is out of control. I am turning him over to you." I couldn't stop crying.

Of course, Bobby wasn't mine to turn over, but that's the way an enabler thinks—as if his whole life was my responsibility, as if I could save him myself. Now, I had to do this in order to stop trying to save him from himself. I knew this could mean that

Bobby would die—in fact, I thought he probably would. But I was the one who was dying from the fear and worry and anxiety. Bobby was killing me, and I had to let go.

Once again, I started trying to patch together a series of couches to sleep on, since I no longer had a bed of my own. My sister Jeannie let me sleep on her couch for a few weeks, but I'd be coming home drunk at 7:00 or 8:00 in the morning, and she hated the whole thing, so she threw me out. After that, Tommy Lorenzo would get me one-room fleabag flats that you could rent by the week, but I never stayed longer than a month, usually because I hadn't paid the rent. So then I'd move on to some other place to stay, just for a little while, until things went bad again.

Meanwhile, I always wound up hanging out at bowling alleys, either bowling for the action late at night, or just hanging out there because that's where I always felt comfortable, where I felt welcomed. Besides, I was Bob Perry the great bowler—everybody knew me and the bartenders would supply me with enough free booze to survive.

Believe it or not, at some point in the mid-80s, I got together with an old bowling pal, Mike Foti, and we set what was then the world record for doubles bowling. (That means two guys bowling three games each.) I threw 267, 279, and 299 (845) and Mike bowled 248, 267, and 279 (794).

And I actually managed to get myself out to Las Vegas to the High Roller a couple of times during those terrible years I was living on the edge. I think it was 1985 or 1986 or something—it's all kind of foggy. Somehow or another I would hustle up the money to fly out there, I'd sleep on a guy's couch, sweet-talk somebody into sponsoring me (paying the $1,100 entry fee), and then I'd step up to the line like nothing was the matter.

People that knew me said later, though, that they could see I was starting to come seriously unglued. I'd be wearing nasty pants and dirty shirts, with dirty, greasy hair. Me, the hotshot with the hot-combed hair and the Mr. Stag's disco threads!

I'd win my first couple of matches, and then the other guy would throw a lifetime best, or I'd have a rotten string of bad luck and I'd be knocked out. Or, at least, that's what I told myself. I didn't tell myself: You're flabby, out of shape, undisciplined, drunk, and homeless, and it's a miracle you've even won a single match. I mean, I knew I could win if I could get straight, but I just couldn't get straight. Drinking always took me out of it.

So then I would react to defeat by drowning my sorrows in vodka and one long, skinny line of coke that would have gone on forever if I could have afforded it. It was a good thing I bought a round-trip ticket, because otherwise I'd have been too broke to get back home. Yeah, "home"—a fleabag rented room, or somebody's couch like a 19-year-old kid, or, before long, Forty-Second Street.

I couldn't see myself at all: This sad, raggedy man in his midthir-ties, who was once a sweet-faced kid who dreamed of touching his inner greatness and winning a national championship but was now just a fading has-been.

I had become hopelessly, helplessly addicted to crack, and I would sneak away at every opportunity to make love to that little glass pipe. Finally, I went all the way. Over a period of 2 days, I smoked something like 500 vials of crack. (A "vial" is a little plastic, stoppered tube about 2 inches long, containing a couple of rocks of crack, which in those days sold for around $5. Yeah, that's a $2,500 high.) I'm not sure I even knew this at the time, but it's obvious to me now that I was trying to kill myself. I wound up in Wayne General Hospital, where I was in a coma for 10 to 12 hours. Then I was transferred to St. Clare's Hospital in Boonton, New Jersey, where I went through 7 days of detox.

Amazingly enough, my sister Patsy was right there through this whole thing. How did I ever get so blessed with long-suffering women? And how did I ever turn into such a fuck-up? Brother Pious was right: I was on the road to sad, pathetic ruin.

Patsy Purzycki: I don't know if Bobby even remembers this, because of all the blackouts. I mean, you can't imagine how bad things got. But one time, just before he became homeless and it had gotten really bad, nobody wanted to have anything to do with him. You couldn't trust him in your house. He would steal to stay alive, and you never knew what he might take. Medicine, checks out of a checkbook, spare change, anything. But being the queen of enablers, I told him he could stay at my house one last time, with one rule: No drugs in my house. (One last time! Can you believe that? His insanity was making me insane, too.)

So then a couple of days later, I came home one night and looked in the room where he was staying, and I found all these tiny little glass bottles or tubes scattered around on the dresser, and other stuff like matches and tinfoil. I never saw crack before, but I knew what it was. I freaked out. When he came home, I went crazy, and then he went nuts, too. We got into a terrible physical fight—terrible—and were almost trying to kill each other. He was scary violent, and it took everything I had in me to throw him out on the street. For someone who had been enabling him his whole life, and who loved the Bobby I remembered so much—not the crazed addict Bobby who was trying to strangle me—it was a miracle that I was able to do that. But it was the best thing I could do for him, even though it broke my heart and I could not stop crying afterward. I cried for days. There was nowhere left for me to turn except to do the hardest thing in the world for me to do. And it took a miracle to do it.

Once I got out of the hospital, I jumped into Alcoholics Anonymous the same way I did everything else: Way over the top. For 35 days,

I went to three meetings a day. I was staying at Patsy's house and on my best behavior. Then somebody asked me to bowl in a big tournament, and I agreed. My old friend Tommy Lorenzo was betting money on the match, and he gave me a ride to the bowling alley one night. He asked me if I wanted a line of coke, and without hesitating one single second, I said yes. And before you know it, there I was again: Getting loaded on coke and crack, swimming in a sea of vodka and orange juice, staying out half the night. Not too much later, Patsy threw me out. And I was on the street again, sinking back into a permanent blackout so I wouldn't have to face what my life had become.

Mike Stella: It was absolutely incredible, probably the most amazing thing I have ever seen in bowling. It's about 2:30 in the morning. My son Larry and I are at Wallington Lanes, in Wallington, New Jersey. Bob Perry walks in off the street. He looks like shit. Dirty clothes, dirty hair, just wearing gym shoes or whatever. He looks like he's a little drunk or stoned or something. He doesn't even speak to Larry and me. He goes over and pulls a ball off the rack, just the house ball. (The serious bowlers, of course, will come in with their own shoes and eight or 10 or 16 balls, for all kinds of lane conditions.)

So Perry goes up to a lane on the bottom floor, and he throws a perfect game: 300. Twelve strikes in a row. Boom. Then he goes upstairs to the lanes on the second level and throws another 300. Boom! And then he goes up to the third tier and throws another perfect 300 game. Boom! I mean, that's three perfect games in a row—a "900 series."

Then he yells, "I'm the greatest fuckin' bowler in the world!" throws his hands up in the air and walks out.

I think I practically fainted. I mean, you got any idea how hard it is to throw a 900 series? It's practically impossible! In the whole history of bowling, with 70 million Americans bowling every year, somebody has bowled a 900 series only something like 23 times. And Bobby did it in crummy street shoes, with the house ball, drunk.

Larry Stella (Mike's son): Yeah, I saw that, too. I couldn't believe my eyes. Bob didn't say anything while he was doing it, either. He just did it. Then he yelled, and he just left. I still can't believe it.

Here's the kicker to that story: I got no memory of this happening at all. My whole life had become a blackout. Even throwing a 900 series in street shoes.

CHAPTER 7

THE RAT AT THE BOTTOM OF THE WELL

I HAD NO FUCKIN' IDEA how I got here. How the fuck *did* I get here?

I had no idea where I even was.

All I could see around me was a depressing sleazeball apartment, with two or three people passed out here and there. On the table there was a rubble of drug paraphernalia—crack pipes, matches, tinfoil, empty vials, butane lighters. I looked out the window. This place must have been up on the 35th or 40th floor. It looked like the South Bronx down there—in other words, like hell.

And I was waking up out of a blackout. Again. I looked at my hands. They were covered with black grime and blood. I wiped my nose and the back of my hand came away with a long skid mark of fresh blood—my guts were seeping out through my nose. A flash of fear came over me: Did I have cancer in my nose or sinuses, after all these years of drug abuse?

I staggered over to the telephone and called my friend Tony, at Tri-State Telephone, in Manhattan. For some reason I could still remember his number.

"Where are you?" he says.

"The South Bronx, I think."

"What are you doing there?"

"I don't know, man. I don't know. Can you come get me?"

"Look, Bobby, I'm at work in the City. Why don't you get a cab?"

"I ain't got no money."

"Just jump in a cab and get over the GW Bridge, and I'll come pay the fare when you get over here."

I walked out of the apartment and at the elevator there were some really ratty-looking people standing around, but as soon as they looked at me, they moved away. They didn't get on with me. I rode the rattletrap elevator down to the "lobby," which looked like a shooting gallery or a bad alley, and walked outside. It was the Bruckner Expressway in the South Bronx, a real bad place to be, even in daylight.

I felt exhausted and sick. I needed something to drink, bad. Oh, my God. I knew I was hemorrhaging in my face—the inside of my nose and sinuses were all gone from doing crack and coke. My septum was totally shot. How long could I keep abusing myself like this and still live? Or had I already died?

I had gotten so worried about this nose thing that once (when I still had money) I went to an ENT doc and he said, "I'm not going to repair this because I can't."

"I'm not in here for that," I said. "I want you to check for cancer in my throat."

But he just said, again, "I can't touch that nose, there's too much damage."

Joe Tolvay: The things Patsy went through for Bobby! I remember that she promised God that if Bobby could get straight, she would dedicate her life to helping other people. And I believed her. But with Bobby, things just seemed to get worse and worse.

All I knew was that everything was so raw in there; every time I smoked crack all those fumes and chemicals and butane just burned the shit out of the inside of my face. But I just kept smoking it anyway.

It was insanity, and I knew it. But I couldn't stop.

I walked out into the street and tried to catch a cab, but once a cabbie got a look at me, in that neighborhood, he'd stomp on the gas. I looked like a homicidal maniac fleeing a murder scene. Finally, a cab driver, who I guess wasn't paying attention, pulled over and I climbed in the back.

The driver takes one look at my bloody, grimy face in the rearview mirror and starts to scream.

"Don't hurt me! Don't hurt me!"

"I'm not gonna hurt you, man! I just need a ride to the other side of the George Washington Bridge!"

When we get there, I climb out.

"How much?" I say.

"No, no, no! I'm going now!" and he goes flying off like a bat out of hell.

A few minutes later Tony pulls up in his big car.

"What the fuck happened to you?" he says.

"I have no idea."

Tony took me back to his office to get cleaned up, gave me 20 or 30 bucks, and dropped me at Tommy Lorenzo's house. But I was pretty sure that when Tommy came home, he wasn't going to be happy to see me. And if Tommy wasn't happy to see me, nobody was going to be happy to see me.

I knew Patsy had had it with me by now, and who could blame her? By now I was a guy living in hell, and everywhere I went, I brought hell with me. I wasn't just destroying my own life; I was destroying the lives of everybody around me.

I'd come to whatever crummy room I happened to be staying in at 5:00 or 6:00 in the morning, sleep a little, then get up and go hustle and bullshit to get a little cash for a drink or a vial. I didn't want to be in the day. It was all about existing, about making it through the next 12 hours. People? They were just ways of getting booze or dope. Meanwhile, I'd be coughing up blood from my nose, and now all my top teeth seemed to be rotting out. They'd started to get all discolored and loose. My body was falling to pieces.

Every day I'd say, "This is the last day; I'm not going to live like this no more," and then that day I would live like that. Again. By the end of almost every day I'd wind up in New York City, in the certain places where people do drugs, sometimes in abandoned buildings where the junkies shoot speed and heroin. Then, when Port Authority closed at 1:30 in the morning and all the people I used to hustle were gone, I'd get a subway token and ride the train to Brooklyn and the Bronx. I'd ride it until 6:00 in the morning, kind of dozing, trying to forget my life. I hadn't looked at myself in the mirror in months, maybe years, but I knew I looked pretty bad because nobody would sit next to me. I guess they thought they might catch something.

I'd get off the train and go help a guy unload a truck for a couple of bucks, or push his hot dog cart 10 blocks, always trying to figure out where everybody was, where I could hustle a couple of bucks off somebody to score a bottle of vodka or a couple of them sweet little rocks that were stealing my life away. Because realistically, I wanted what booze and dope did to me more than I wanted life. And it didn't matter how guilty I felt about it. I just kept doing it.

It was absolute hell, living like that.

It was hard to imagine that things could get worse.

But they were about to.

Because, even though it might have been shabby and depressing, at least I had a roof over my head. For a while I was living in a room at the YMCA for $55 a week, but I had to leave because I never made rent. (What I mean is, I made rent but didn't spend it on rent.) Then I was sleeping on a series of couches—I was "couch surfing" before they called it that. Finally, I wound up sleeping in my friend Dennis's laundry room. But, hell, it was a room. I was too wasted to notice it was a wet, nasty basement.

For a while I had a job delivering beer (of all things) for Nash Distributors. I'd return the truck on Thursday night, get my $600 pay, go into Manhattan, and wake up out of a blackout somewhere a few days later, dead broke. What kind of a life was that?

The jump from that kind of life to being completely homeless was not much of a jump at all. I'd been getting closer and closer to the edge for years. In fact, in a way, "homelessness" was a state of mind, and I'd been homeless for a long time before I was actually living on the street. I had no ability at all to create a warm nest that would be safe for a woman or a child, like a man is supposed to. All I knew how to create were nightmarish holes where I could hide away with my crack pipe and my bottle for a few hours, until I got kicked out. Again.

I started trying harder and harder to convince Jeannie or Patsy to let me stay at one of their houses for a while, that I'd be good this time, that I wouldn't drink or smoke crack no more, that I was making all this money from action bowling and could even pay them something. We had angry fights, almost to the point of somebody getting killed. But basically what it all came down to was, I was wrong, I was lying, I had no intention of quitting, but I was telling them I would. As they say in the rooms of AA, "Denial is not a river in Egypt," but I was denying, denying, denying.

Patsy Purzycki: Things got so bad with Bobby that I was in a state of constant panic about what would happen next. My sisters? They didn't want anything to do with him anymore. Didn't even want to hear about him. And I couldn't blame them. For a while Bobby was working down in the produce markets delivering grapes and whatnot, and I guess he must have been stealing, because one day I answered the doorbell and there were two big, dumb, mobbed-up-looking guys standing there.

"Where's your brudder?" one of them said.

"I don't know."

"Where's our money? If he don't give us our money, we're gonna cut his hands off."

I slammed the door in their faces, but I stayed scared because these people really do those things.

Another time Bobby came home and he could barely walk—his knees were three times their normal size, and all black and blue. He said a bowling ball came up out of the return and hit him in the knee. I'm sure what really happened is that somebody beat the hell out of his knees with a baseball bat. And once he came home with his right thumb wrapped up in an enormous wad of bloody bandages—he claimed it was an accident, but I have no doubt somebody stuck his thumb in a car door and slammed it as retribution for something he did. When you go over to the dark side like Bobby did and you let God out of your life, nothing destroys you quicker than booze, dope, and gambling. And Bobby was addicted to all three—and paying for it all (when he couldn't win enough at bowling) by stealing.

Then, one day—I don't know which day it was, they were all the same—I had finally worn out my welcome with every single person in my life, even my beloved saintly sister Patsy, even Tommy Lorenzo and Tony, and all my teammates and friends in the bowling world. Everybody. Nobody wanted to see my ugly face no more. Nobody trusted me. Nobody wanted to hear my line of bullshit no more, about how I had a big tournament coming up and I was gonna win so much money it should probably be illegal and I was gonna pay everybody back and all that. They'd heard it all before, and they just didn't want to see me or hear from me anymore.

So I took the train back to New York City, where I knew my way around, where I knew how to hustle, where I could get crack and coke and booze and where I thought I could survive. I knew the places where people sold drugs, like near the entrance to the Queens-Midtown Tunnel on Thirty-Sixth Street.

I had my favorite bars: One on Forty-Fourth Street, another all-night place on Forty-Second Street and Ninth Avenue, a couple of bars on Tenth Avenue, and some really dingy places by Port Authority. Midtown Manhattan has been really cleaned up since those days, but back then that whole area was filled with sleazy strip clubs and bars and peep shows and other stuff any decent person wouldn't want to know about. That's where I lived, if you could call it that.

Sometimes I'd stop at an all-night liquor store and get a bottle of vodka for a couple of bucks, get a paper cup with ice and orange juice, and pour in the booze. It would be like a little campfire that would keep me warm on the street corner all night. Then all I had to do was find some dark place to curl up and sleep, hoping the animals wouldn't kill me, and get free of my life for a few hours.

Where did I get the couple of bucks for the bottle? Well, I never panhandled—I lived off the kindness and loneliness of strangers. I'd sit down at a favorite bar somewhere, get to talking to some lonely businessman from Cincinnati, and figure out how to get the next drink. Maybe the guy was a little put off by my appearance, but he was drunk and he was one of the last guys at the bar. The guy would tell me his sorrows, and I'd drink and listen all night long. He would introduce me to some other guy—"Hey, meet my friend Bobby"—and we'd all tell our sad stories and drink while somebody else paid. That was my specialty: Getting other people to pick up the bar bill. Sometimes the guy would have some coke and we'd take turns doing lines in the bathroom, or he'd ask me to go score for him and I'd come back with some blow. It was all about existing. It was all about making it through the night. A lot of times, we'd sit there and drink and talk until the joint closed.

I'd be the guy's best friend for a couple of hours, until he got tired or had to leave, and then I would walk out of the bar and suddenly I would have to face my life. There would be nowhere to go. I'd hit this big wall of emptiness, like a faceful of icy air.

If it was wintertime, I'd linger in the bar as long as possible. Then the place would close and I'd have to step out there onto the street freezing to death. I never carried nothing, not like these homeless people you see nowadays with their shopping carts and whatnot. No bag, no backpack, no nothing. Most of the time I wore a ratty, old winter coat my mom had given me, with lots of pockets. And it's amazing how many people forget their gloves in a bar.

Maybe I didn't carry all that other shit because I wasn't really homeless. I was Bob Perry, the great bowler, just a little short tonight. Little did I know that being "a little short tonight" with no place to go would last for 7 years, from 1986 to 1992. The truth is that during those years I was a homeless crack addict on the streets of Manhattan, and whatever great thing I might have done in the past, or hoped to do in the future, did not matter at all.

Winter turned to spring turned to summer turned to autumn—the years rolled on and I just got sicker, more pathetic, more desperate, my body more filled with death and disease. I started to look like a vampire, with discolored skin and scabs all over. I never washed. And, one by one all my top teeth got infected and pus-filled and loose, and I just yanked them all out. When I closed my lips, my mouth must have sunken in like a rotten pie, but I never looked in the mirror to see it.

I was just one cold winter night away from being an unidentified corpse in the morgue.

Without money, New York City is a very cold place, especially in the winter. If you go into a restaurant to use the toilet, they'll kick you out unless you buy something. So I figured out two places I could sleep (without ever admitting to myself that I was homeless). One was a kind of coal cellar under the sidewalk on Forty-Second Street—really, just a hole in the ground, where I'd curl up in the dirt like a rat. The other was inside one of them cubicles at a peep-show house, also on Forty-Second Street.

These peep-show houses were open all day and all night, and most of them were run by Indian guys, but the one I went to was run by two white guys named Freddie and Frankie. At 2:00 a.m. these places would be filled with businessmen, sick and demented fucks watching porno, absolutely crazy sick human beings. I'd pay Freddie and Frankie a couple of bucks and they'd let me into this tiny room, almost a cabinet, where people watched porno, and I'd sit in a chair and put my feet up and try to sleep for a few hours. I was the richest homeless guy Freddie and Frankie knew, showing up almost every night at 2:00 or 3:00 in the morning. They'd let me in, and then a few hours later they'd kick me out, back onto the street, lots of times before it was even light yet. That was my home address: I was paying rent to sleep for a couple of hours a night in a filthy peep-show house.

At the very beginning, before they knew me very well, Freddie and Frankie sent their bouncer after me when I walked in with a crack pipe loaded with a couple of vials of rock. That dude busted my face, and I had to go to the ER and get stitches. But I left the hospital AMA (against medical advice), and I went back to the same place. I think the bouncer felt bad after he beat the shit out of me. After that we were friends, and he'd let me in. Him and Freddie and Frankie started calling me "Poppy" because I looked like I was a hundred years old, even though I wasn't even 40 yet. That's what passed for my "home" and my "family" at that time.

All the peep-show houses had bouncers, and they had guys that washed the floors all night long. Otherwise they'd get too sticky, I guess. Not many people robbed them though, so even though it wasn't too comfortable or sanitary, it was fairly safe.

The worst time on the streets of New York is about 4:00 in the morning, a couple of hours before daylight, when most businesses are closed and the animals are on the prowl. And I mean animals. It's hard and heartless and dangerous out there. You've got to watch yourself, otherwise you could wind up knifed in an alley for no reason, or OD'd on some bad dope you just bought. And I knew from St. Christopher's Inn that you can die from withdrawal, and I worried about that, too. That's why I tried to stay hydrated at all times. (That's a joke, kind of.)

Sometimes I would take the train out to New Jersey and go to Lodi Lanes, in Lodi, where everybody knew me and I could get all the booze I needed to survive. I'd go there and for a while I'd hardly feel homeless at all. There was a sweet lady who worked the front desk and the snack bar and she'd sneak me food. Sometimes I'd help clean the lanes, and she'd even let me sleep there, laying down on a hard bench with no pillow back in the corner. Well, at least it was warm and safe.

By now, though, I was starting to look permanently filthy, and it was hard to hide that I was living on the street.

I'd wear some old pants for months at a time. When it got cold, I'd spend 20 bucks on a thermal shirt, socks, and sweatshirt and wear them all winter. I'm sure I smelled like a sewer. Inside, I knew my life was wasting away. I wanted to die every day. I was dying constantly, throwing up all the time, sticking my finger down my throat to get the pus out. It was terrible.

Why didn't I try harder to get sober? Why didn't I beg and plead to be let into some rehab somewhere, to try to put my life back together? Why didn't I go back up to St. Christopher's and fall on my hands and knees in front of Brother Pious? Why, why, why?

There is no "why." Addiction has no "why." My life was insanity. I was living a life of endless death, but I couldn't stop, and I guess I didn't want to. So I'd shuffle over to the dingy bar around the corner from Port Authority wearing my nasty winter jacket even in summer— and go inside, looking to find a lonely guy to get me loaded for one more night.

I'd sometimes go to that disgusting men's room at Port Authority to clean up a little, but only my hands, because they were usually almost black with grime. I never washed my whole body, in years, because if you took off your clothes, the animals would steal them. Like, what are they going to do with a homeless guy's nasty, old winter jacket? Put it in a homeless museum?

I have to say, I was not totally without friends in those terrible years. There was a guy named Bob Collins, and his sister, who I got to know well. They were a nice middle-class family living in New Jersey, and they knew I was having some really hard times. I had helped both of them with their bowling when they were younger. Their father, who was disabled, was a very nice man who loved to play cards. He used to go play cards in Lodi. He knew all the wise-guys and bookmakers, but he was a sweet, kind man.

Anyway, Bob Collins and his sister and father were always nice to me, and they'd invite me to their house for Thanksgiving. Can you imagine? I don't know how they stood the smell. But they acted like I was just another friend from the old days, somebody who had helped them when he was able to help. And I can't tell you how much I appreciated that.

Even so, it was totally obvious to me and probably everyone else that I was on the fast train to oblivion. There was no way I could live like this for very long.

With all my top teeth rotted out, I could only eat soft foods, like hot dogs and pizza and scrambled eggs. There were all kinds of sores up inside my mouth and sinuses, and on my face. My bones ached. There was poison through my whole body. I still cough up blood to this day, more than 20 years later.

So one winter day in Manhattan, around Forty-Second Street, I ran into this guy named Homeless Louie. I'd seen him around, picking through garbage cans and whatnot. He looked like hell, like me.

"Why don't you come downstairs and see my room?" he says.

"Okay," I say, kind of curious to see what he's talking about.

So he leads me into Port Authority, down some stairs, and down some more stairs, and finally he jumps over the rail and lands in the gravel beside the tracks. I follow him into this dark, greasy chamber with big pipes overhead, and then he leads me into this smaller chamber, almost pitch black, where he's got pieces of cardboard spread on the floor.

"See? It's my room," Homeless Louie says. "It's pretty warm, pretty safe, and it's free."

He lights a little candle stub and holds it up. Now I can see a couple of little cardboard Chinese food boxes. They're swarming with cockroaches.

"Hungry?"

"I don't think so."

"Want to see my pet?"

"Okay."

And Homeless Louie lifts the candle a little bit higher and points over into the corner. And over there in the dimness, scrambling around like a dirty dog, is an enormous sewer rat.

The thing must have weighed 25 or 30 pounds, like a little pig fattened up by human garbage. It was one of the most disgusting things I had ever seen.

"Lemme outta here!" I yell.

And I bolted out of that place as fast as I could run. My life had been coming unraveled for a long, long time, but somehow this was the absolute bottom. I couldn't go no lower. I had no more will to live any more days of death. I was ready to end it.

I ran up onto the upper deck, up the big stairway, and out onto the street. It was freezing cold and snowing a little. There was a garbage truck trundling down the street, and I ran in front of it, hoping the death would be quick.

But the driver veered sharply away from me and collided with a power pole. He threw open the door and I heard him screaming after me.

"You dumb fuck! Whassamatter with you!?"

I went stumbling off down the street.

Bob Perry, the great.

I couldn't even succeed in killing myself.

CHAPTER 8

THE ADDICT AND THE ANGEL

I DON'T KNOW HOW MANY DAYS or weeks it was after I tried to throw myself in front of that garbage truck outside Port Authority that I came out of a blackout and found myself sitting in some sort of a bowling center with a friend of mine, Jackson Gist. Jackson was this huge black guy, maybe 6-foot-3. I'd met him at the bowling alley when he was bowling around 144 average. By the time I was done helping him, he was an over-200 bowler, and he won a lot of money. I really helped him, and he kind of owed me for it.

But now it was, like, 8:00 or 9:00 in the morning, a gray winter morning, a Sunday, and the bowling alley was closed and empty.

Jackson is in my face, yelling at me.

"Look at you!" he's yelling. "Look at you! You coulda been the greatest bowler in the world and you're just a bum! You're just a drunk and a dope addict! You smell like a dumpster, man. You make me sick! You're pissing your talent away, and there's nothing worse than wasted talent. What's the matter with you? What's the matter with you, man?"

Look: I was just coming out of a blackout, and I had no idea where I even was. In those days, I never "fell asleep," like normal people do. I passed out. If you fell asleep on the streets of New York, that's when you'd get robbed or beat up or killed. And I never "woke up," either. I just came out of a blackout. This was normal to me.

"Shut up," I tell Jackson. "Go behind the bar and get me a fuckin' drink."

Jackson, apparently, had a job cleaning the lanes on the night shift; this place, it turned out, was Eclipse Lanes, a bowling center in Hasbrouck Heights, New Jersey, about 6 miles outside the city. As my head started to clear and I looked around, I recognized the place. I'd bowled here lots of times before, probably made a lot of money here, too. Probably threw some 300 games, maybe even won some championships here. Whatever.

I was also familiar with Eclipse Lanes because that's where I used to go to meet Tommy Lorenzo when he needed drugs or I needed some money. Tommy was in the family business and had an office about 10 minutes from Eclipse Lanes. Whenever I called him, he'd be there right away. Tommy was the king of enablers, and when we got together, we'd just feed each other's addictions—he'd give me money to pay for a few nights in a hotel or a bottle of vodka, and I'd go cop dope for him. Then we'd get wasted together. This is what we thought of as a good time.

Eclipse Lanes was also a good place for us to meet because it was right by one of them greasy burger joints. All they served was soft stuff, stuff a toothless guy could eat. I was like an 80-year-old man, even though I was only 39. The joint was cheap, too: You could get four of them little tiny hamburgers, fries, and a Coke for, like, three bucks. I used to call them "murderburgers," because they'd give you diarrhea for days. But that was the sort of stuff I lived on, whenever it occurred to me to eat something at all. You could say that the way I fed my body was the same way I fed my soul: Just cramming some cheap, nasty shit in there without really thinking about it.

Right now, though, I just needed some vodka, that sweet poison that was killing me. I needed to go back to sleep and black it all out again. Jackson went behind the counter of the closed bar and fished me out a bottle of vodka.

"You gimme that bottle or I'm gonna take it from you," I say, real threatening.

And I would have, too, except Jackson just handed it over to me. I guess he saw that look in my eye and gave up.

"Listen, Bobby," Jackson says, "you gotta get outta here because if Joe comes in, I'll get fired."

Joe was the owner, and he was a real nasty guy who hated me. Even though I'd once had a part-time job at the bowling alley, Joe had already told Jackson more than once that he'd fire him if he ever came into the alley and saw me inside. Sometimes, if Joe showed up when I was there, I'd go hide in the ladies' room. I was a drunk and a drug addict and he was probably afraid I'd rob the place, which was a reasonable fear. But I never stole anything from there. I was always just going there to meet Jackson or Tommy Lorenzo.

Now Jackson was telling me to get lost or he'd get fired. So, once again, I was getting pushed out onto the street because I was an unsavory character—unwanted, useless, dirty, unsafe.

Before I left the bowling alley, I fished around in my grubby pocket and pulled out one whole quarter. God knows how it got there. Then I pulled out something else: A folded-up piece of paper with Billy's name and number on it. That guy who told me to call him if I needed to. The guy in that program.

The pay phone in the alley cost 50 cents, so I borrowed another quarter from Jackson and called Bill. Here I was, this big champion bowler, and I was so broke I had to borrow a quarter to make a phone call. Unlike anybody else in my own family, Billy picked up.

"Where are you?" Billy says.

"Eclipse Lanes, in Hasbrouck Heights. Look, I need help."

"Don't go anywhere, I'll be right down."

So Billy comes right down, 9:00 Sunday morning, to pick me up. He walks into the building and looks me over. He can see right away that I look and smell so bad that I need to get cleaned up, at least a little, before anyone can even tolerate me.

"Get in the car," he says.

"Where are we going?"

"I'm taking you to your sister's house."

"I can't go there."

"I'm taking you to Patsy's house. Where does she live?"

Billy knew Patsy from bowling, but not well enough to know where she lived.

"I can't go there," I say. "If my brother-in-law sees me, he'll kill me."

"Bobby, you've got to take a bath and change your clothes, man. Where does your sister live?"

"She lives in a different house now, on Mountain Avenue in Pompton Plains."

So Billy starts driving me to Mountain Avenue in Pompton Plains. And I'm terrified.

You see, Patsy's husband, James, was not real crazy about the fact that the last time he and Patsy let me stay there I found $360 underneath some clothes in a dresser drawer and stole it. It was their special stash of rainy day money or something, and James was not a real forgiving type of guy. As far as he was concerned, I deserved the death penalty. I'm serious: If he found me in his house, he would literally have killed me. Not just for the $360 I stole from him, but because he loved my sister and he could see that I had practically killed her over the years. I hadn't been invited to their wedding or nothing.

James was a guy who grew up in Brooklyn and Staten Island, who had a real good job running the lingerie department at Lady Ester in Manhattan. He and my sister had a big house in a nice neighborhood, with a big lawn. Coming over here from my roach-infested world on

Forty-Second Street and the bathrooms at Port Authority was like taking a trip to the moon.

So we show up at Patsy's house. And Patsy opens the door just a little bit until she gets a load of me.

"What are you doing here?" she says, real cold and angry.

"I'm with Billy here. He's from AA," I say.

"I don't care who you're with," she says. "Get the fuck away from my house. James is going to be home in 20 minutes, and if he finds you here, he'll kill you. And you fucking deserve it."

She turns to Billy, who she doesn't seem to recognize.

"Get this pig away from my house," she says. "I don't care where you go, but you better take him with you. I don't want him in my house or anywhere near it."

Then she says to me again, very hostile, "You're lucky James ain't here. He'd kill you."

I didn't back away, though. I kept trying to break through to my sister, who used to love me. But she kept getting angrier and angrier. Finally, she threatened to call the cops unless I went away.

Then Billy broke in.

"Please, Patsy—he's not going to be here that long. He just needs to get washed up a little and get some clean clothes, and I'm going to take him to an AA meeting."

I don't know why. She had no reason to do it. But finally Patsy gave up and let me in the house. She and I, we had a bond that went way, way back. Beneath all the cursing, she was someone who had known me all my life, and really all she wanted was what was best for me. In her heart she was a saint. I had abused her, manipulated her, robbed her, taken advantage of her in so many different ways, and she'd reached the end of her rope. I couldn't blame her if she hated me. But now she decided to take a big chance for me—one of the many times in her life that she took a big chance for me.

"Look, you can come in and take a shower," she says finally, in a softer voice. "I'll get you some clothes. But you better make it quick before James comes home. If he shows up here, you're dead."

"Yeah, I get it: If James comes home, I'm dead."

I came creeping into the house like a sewer rat, trying not to touch anything for fear of polluting it. She laid out some socks, a pair of dungarees that didn't fit, and a sweatshirt. I dunno, maybe they were James's clothes. Then I left my dirty, old clothes behind. And, I dunno, I didn't take a shower—it had been so long, I might not have known how to do it. Maybe I would just melt in there. I also just wanted to get out of there. I didn't belong there in that clean, tidy suburban house owned by one person who hated me and another person who loved me and hated me at the same time. I washed my face, though, trying not to look in the mirror. When I came out of the bathroom, there was a 20-dollar bill laid out on the kitchen table, and Patsy was gone. I think she left that money because she didn't want me to rob her. She'd done what she could do for me. Now she had to get away from me.

Patsy Purzycki: To this day, I believe it was a miracle that I was able to do that—to slam the door in Bobby's face one last time. The first miracle was that Bobby even lived. The second miracle was that I was able to help save him by no longer enabling him, even though nothing in this world was harder for me.

I came out of Patsy's house and Billy was standing in the driveway.

"What are you still doing here?" I say.

"I'm waiting for you."

I got in the car.

"We're going to a meeting," Billy says.

"Well, okay, but don't take me to one of them meetings where there's a lot of people," I say.

"Okay."

"Don't take me to one of them men's meetings."

"Okay."

"Don't take me to one of them step meetings."

"Okay."

"Don't take me to one of them speaker meetings."

"Okay."

See, I'd had some experience with this AA thing, and I was pretty sure I knew all about it. I'd gone to St. Christopher's Inn before—until Brother Pious handed me a bus ticket back to Manhattan. For a little while I even had a sponsor then, a wonderful man, and he just kept trying to convince me to come back to meetings, and he'd say I'd been out on maneuvers and to get started again. Try to get sober again. "Progress not perfection" and all that. But I refused to do it.

"I'm not doing it," I told the sponsor. "I'm not standing up there and telling people I went out and got drunk. That I fucked up. I ain't doin' it."

Stubborn sonofabitch.

So I didn't do it. And what happened was, I went back out again, drinking and doing dope and all the rest of it. My life spiraled out of control, down into one great big blackout again.

But now Billy tells me he's taking me to a small meeting in Montclair, New Jersey. We walk into this huge church—I guess it was also a school—and there are two meetings, Al-Anon on one side and AA on the other side. There is some kind of celebration going on, maybe 250 people there, so Billy and I go to the back of the room and sit down way in the back.

A guy sitting next to me says, "Are you Bob?"

"Yeah, I'm Bob," I say.

It was weird: I'd never laid eyes on this guy before.

He hands me this card that says "Just for Today." The card is this whole list of spiritual tips, stuff like:

Just for today I will try to live through this day only and not tackle all my problems at once. I can do something for 12 hours that would appall me if I had to keep it up for a lifetime.

I lean over and whisper to Billy, "Hey, look. This guy just gave me this card."

"Shut up," Billy says. Then he looks over at the chair next to me. "What guy?"

I look over to where the guy was sitting and he's gone. I mean, he isn't even in sight. He is just gone.

Then the guy who's running the meeting says, "Do we have anybody here for their first AA meeting, or anybody who's coming back?"

"Stand up," Billy whispers to me.

"No," I say.

"Stand up."

"No."

"Stand up," he says, and he grabs me with one hand and just drags me to my feet.

So here I am, standing in the back of this huge room in front of all these people.

If you'd have seen the way I looked, you would have been shocked, with my greasy hair, my infected teeth, bleeding from my nose constantly—the whole miserable package.

"My name's Bob and I'm coming back," I say.

I found out later that usually, when people say things like that in meetings, there's a big round of applause. But not too many people clapped for me.

I sat down and listened to the main speaker, a wonderful guy from Clark, New Jersey, named Frankie D. It seemed like everything he was describing had happened to me. I could relate to everything that he was saying. He'd been homeless, he'd been a bum and a dope addict, he'd had blackouts, and all the rest. Drinking and drugging ruled his life, and he wound up on skid row. But now the guy had something like 5 or 6 years sober, which to me seemed like eternity, impossible. One thing that really stuck with me was that he said he read pages 86 to 88 of the *Big Book* (sort of the Bible of AA) every day. It was about beginning each day with a grateful heart, without selfishness or self-pity, and trying each day to ask God to help. Boy, did I ever need that.

After the meeting, Billy told me to go get a copy of the *Big Book* and that he'd pay for it. I picked up a paperback copy, because it was cheaper, and stuck it in my back pocket.

After Frankie D.'s talk, there was this big party with cake and whatnot and people milling around. I had sores everywhere and a bloody nose, and I could tell that people were moving away from me. It wasn't like anybody was making some big effort to get to know me. But this guy Frankie D., I wanted to ask him more about pages 86 to 88 in the *Big Book*. Also, you know, this seemed like a guy who could understand me and my story. Maybe even a future friend. So I went up to him.

"So what's so important on page 86 of the *Big Book*?" I ask him. "And could you give me your phone number?"

Look: I'm from Jersey. Some people might say I'm a little pushy, but I didn't see any problem with just going up to the guy and asking for what I wanted.

"Aren't you that guy that stood up in the back?" he says.

"Yeah, that's me."

"Well, that book's not going to help you," Frankie D. says, looking me up and down. "AA will not help you—you need to find another way. You're too far gone, man. You need to go somewhere where they can help you, like a psych ward or a detox or something."

I was absolutely shocked. Here was this guy, who'd supposedly led a life like I had, who'd been homeless, who'd been cast out. I thought he was going to help me, but instead he only belittled me. I felt so degraded by what he said to me. I felt like I'd been assassinated. In fact, I carried around that hurt for years afterward, maybe because I was afraid he was right: I really was too far gone, beyond hope. And I thought this guy was going to give me a miracle!

"Billy, take me out of here," I say. "I want to go back to New York."

I walked out of that stinkin' place, and away from that guy who could cram that *Big Book* as far up his ass as it would go.

"Look, Bobby, don't take that too hard," Billy says, following me out of the building, kind of begging. "You shouldn't go back into the City. You shouldn't do that."

"Just take me to the fuckin' bus stop."

"Bobby, please, let's try another meeting."

"Take me to the bus stop in Union City, that's the cheapest ticket to Manhattan—a buck-fifty."

"Bobby, you need to get better," Billy says to me, practically begging. "If you don't, you're going to kill yourself, kill someone else, or end up in an insane asylum!"

"Yeah, well I'd rather do that than go to the rooms of Alcoholics Anonymous. Leave me the fuck alone!"

Billy took me to Union City, and I got on the buck-and-a-half bus back to Manhattan, back to my old homeless haunts, the floor of the peep show on Forty-Second Street, the cellar on Eight Avenue, and all those other places I swore I'd never go back to. But I had my self-respect: I swore I'd never go back to Homeless Louie's rat and roach-infested "room" in the subway, and I didn't. But now the insanity of my situation was really taking hold. It seemed like one day would go by, but it was probably a week; I had no way of knowing. Now I was dragging around the *Big Book* and reading it to myself and to other people, like some demented street preacher. I always wore this old jacket my mom had given me for winter, which was by now as ratty and nasty as the bottom of a dumpster, with my paperback copy of the *Big Book* stuck in my back pocket.

Here I was, this hopeless alcoholic and dope addict, reading the *Big Book* while I was doing crack. Here I was in a bar, reading the

Big Book to some lonely, drunk commuter while both of us were getting wasted. (The other drunk would be paying the bar bill, of course.) Here I was in the peep show, trying to read the *Big Book* to some perv who had come in there to get off.

That book was driving me absolutely insane, because I knew it was the truth. It described my life completely, and I knew I had no other idea what to do. I'd reached the end of the road. I couldn't eat. I couldn't breathe. I couldn't sleep. I couldn't wake up. I couldn't live. I know the book said suicide was not the answer, but I was constantly thinking of ways to kill myself. Still, I'd find myself sitting on the steps of the YMCA or on a park bench on Eighteenth Street, by the projects, talking to other drunks and junkies and reading to them out of the *Big Book*. We'd talk together, we'd be philosophizing and reflecting, while our whole lives went up in flames all around us. Like, who gives a shit what a bunch of bums and crackheads have to say about the meaning of life?

So one day I called my sister Patsy again, collect, as always.

"Please, please don't hang up the phone," I say to her. "I need your help."

"I don't care, Bobby, goodbye," she says.

"Please, Patsy, please."

"Try praying to mommy and daddy," she says. (Both of my parents were dead by then.) "Maybe they'll give you the answer. Don't call this number again."

Click.

Almost everybody in my life had tried to help me, even Tommy Lorenzo, in his twisted enabling way. But I had used and abused everyone, sucked them dry of everything I could get out of them. Other people were just ways of satisfying my own desires. They weren't really people at all. They were just scenery. Now they had all turned their backs on me, even my own beloved sister, and I was alone. Uncle Raymond, of course, had been a fixture in my life for years, sort of a big brother and godfather, but I'd broken his heart and he wanted nothing to do with me anymore. Last time I saw him I'd stolen some money from him and promised to pay it back, but I never did. Uncle Raymond was out of my life now but it didn't matter. John Gotti and the mobsters, my "friends"—they were all long gone, too. (I learned much later, after I got sober, that Uncle Raymond and my sister, at least, were praying that I was not suffering or dead, even though I had no contact with them at all.)

So I prayed to my mother, a woman who had once loved me and who had sort of slowly seeped out of her own body with Lou Gehrig's disease, and to my father, a humble Polish man who had worked various humble jobs his whole life and who had also once loved me, before I broke his heart. I prayed to them from the bottom of my heart because I did not know what else to do.

I was a dead man who could not die—a dead man who could not live.

And what came up in my prayers was the name of Graymoor and St. Christopher's Inn—that place I'd gone to 11 years earlier, where I had acted like such a flaming asshole that the monks had kicked me out after 10 days.

The Graymoor Spiritual Life Center, in Garrison, New York, was a kind of religious retreat run by the Franciscan Friars of the Atonement, a bunch of priests who dressed like John the Baptist, with the brown robes and sandals and all that stuff. Graymoor was sometimes called "the holy mountain," because part of the 400-acre property ran up a wooded mountainside. I think they also called it that because supposedly miracles happened up there.

There was also a homeless shelter and a 21-day program called St. Christopher's Inn on the property. Apparently, the Franciscans had been doing this work since around 1908, picking up drunks and dope addicts off the streets of New York City and carting them up to St. Christopher's for "a cot and three hots" for 21 days. They'd give you a bus ticket to come up there, give you clean socks and sneakers, underwear, sweatshirts, all donated by wealthy people, and your own little locker. You'd get a break from the streets, and food and shelter, for 3 weeks.

In the early days, of course, before AA (which got started in the late 1930s) that was about all they could offer, but now it was a 12 step–based rehab place. All kinds of famous people had gone there to sober up over the years. Wellington Mara (the owner of the New York Giants) and other prominent people would donate all kinds of money to Graymoor every year.

The legend, supposedly, was that once, a long time ago, a little wobbly old man stopped at St. Francis Convent (which was there before St. Christopher's) and asked for a meal. The custom was that, in exchange for a meal, all the bums and homeless people who stopped there were asked to fill two buckets with water from a spring down the mountain. But the sisters decided this old man was too weak to fill the buckets, so they decided not to ask him to do it. When he finished eating and left, the sisters discovered that both buckets were full to the brim. So maybe it was a miracle or something. Anyway, after that, the sisters and the brothers started calling all the homeless people who came there "St. Christopher" (Christ), since it says in the Bible, "Be not forgetful to entertain strangers: for thereby some have entertained angels unawares." That's how it came to be named St. Christopher's Inn.

Well, I kind of knew this story because of my stay up there 11 years earlier. But at that time, I wasn't really paying much attention to any of that spiritual shit. I was just trying to convince Debbie that I was dealing with my problems so she wouldn't leave me. But, you know, from Day One at St. Christopher's, I had this bug up my ass about how my mother's cousin was this big shot in the Franciscan world. My mother's cousin, Father Joseph Benjamin McVey, had actually given a speech in front of the Pope one time. And he lived at Graymoor for the last part of his life and was buried there, in the friar's cemetery. So I thought this made me better than all those bums and losers and crackwhores in the homeless shelter. I was totally different than them, better than them—I was a world-champion bowler and all this other good stuff. In other words, I had a real attitude, and a real mouth on me, too. I hardly went to any of them AA meetings they had up there. I thought they were stupid. Besides, I could see that all the things these people were asking me to do in order to keep Debbie were really hard. They were asking me to actually change my life. And I just didn't want to go there. Fuck that.

So, finally, Brother Pious handed me a one-way ticket back to Manhattan, and I was happy to take it. Fuck them. What the fuck did they know?

But now, the second time I went to St. Christopher's, 11 years later, it was a whole different story. The first time, I may have been an arrogant know-it-all, but at least I had a home to go back to. I had a woman who loved me, or was trying to love me despite my behavior. I was still bowling in tournaments, winning lots of money. I still had Uncle Raymond and other people in my life. Both of my parents were still alive.

But now I was a pathetic, beaten-down, homeless, filthy alcoholic and drug addict who had alienated every single person who had ever loved him or tried to help him. Now I was completely and utterly alone. All of my top teeth were gone. I stunk. I almost never bowled anymore—where was I going to bowl? Forty-Second Street? In fact, I had been beaten down to my knees. I was desperate. I had nowhere else to turn. Only later did I learn that being driven to your knees is a blessing—the beginning of recovery.

So I called Graymoor and asked for Brother Gregory, who I had gotten to know pretty good the last time I was up there. He came on the phone.

"This is Father Benjy's relative—Bobby Purzycki," I say.

"I know who you are," Brother Gregory says. (He obviously wasn't real happy to hear from me.) "What do you want?"

"I need help, Brother."

"I can't help you."

"I've been living on the street for 6½ years."

"I can't help you—we don't want you here," Brother Gregory says. "You're not allowed here. Don't you remember? We tried to help you years ago, and you wouldn't listen."

"Brother, I'm ready to listen now. I'm desperate. I'm dying out here. I want to get better. I need your help."

There was a long pause on the other end of the line. I didn't know if Brother Gregory was about to hang up, or falling asleep, or what.

"When was the last day you drank?" he says.

"When was the last day I was allowed?"

"Thursday."

"Okay, it was Wednesday."

I'm not stupid. I'd been there before, and I knew the ropes.

"When was the last time you did drugs?"

"When was the last time I was allowed?"

"Tuesday."

"Uh, I think it was Monday."

"Well, I'm sorry. I don't have any beds available."

"Please! I don't think I'll make it!"

"I can't help it if I don't have any beds."

"Please!"

Another long pause.

"Okay, be here Monday morning at 8 a.m. and don't be late, because if you're late, I'll give your bed away. And don't show up drunk."

"What do I do until Monday?"

"If you've been on the streets for 7 years, 2 more days won't hurt you."

As religious as those Franciscans were, they could also be very hard-assed. They had to be. They had probably listened to more junkie lies and bullshit than you could imagine. And Brother Gregory was absolutely right to be skeptical of me: Eleven years earlier, when I was up there, I wasn't exactly applying the principles of AA in all my affairs, as the *Big Book* said. In fact, I had basically told AA to kiss my fuckin' ass.

So what did I do when, for practically the first time in my adult life, a little ray of sunshine appeared—some faint hope of survival and recovery and healing? When John the Baptist himself actually opened the door to me, even though I didn't deserve it?

Well, I immediately called Tommy Lorenzo, my best friend, partner in crime, and chief enabler. The guy who always came through for me, helping me out with money, food, a hotel room, dope, booze, whatever. I was totally insane. I didn't want to live no more. I was dying as I was standing there. I figured within 2 or 3 days I'd be dead and that would solve everybody's problem. And as I look back on it now, I don't know why I didn't die that weekend.

I don't know what was going on with Tommy Lorenzo in the middle of all this—he was a guy who kept feeding my addictions, and his own, for years. He could see that I was killing myself, but his way of helping me was giving me money to buy more booze and dope. It was nuts. I know now that Tommy had his own inner demons. It turned out he was gay but tried to hide it from everybody. Anyway, this friendship with Tommy Lorenzo was an incestuous relationship that kept us both permanently sick and addicted, even though, at the time, I think we thought we were having a good time.

Believe it or not, my behavior had gotten so whacked out in those days that finally even Tommy Lorenzo wouldn't answer my phone calls anymore. But at least he picked up the phone when I called him that day to tell him I was going into treatment at St. Christopher's on Monday. I told him I needed a place to stay for a couple of nights, and that I needed some money for, you know, entertainment. So Tommy came over to where I was, and we immediately went out to the liquor store and bought a couple of them liter bottles of vodka, the big ones with the handles; then we went out and scored a bunch of coke. Tommy rented a room at the Kings Inn right off Route 46 in Wayne, New Jersey—a semidive kind of place where people picked up broads and rented a room for a couple of hours. Then he and I got started knocking back all that booze and dope, and when he left, I just holed up in that ratty hotel room and drank and did drugs all weekend, trying to die before Monday came.

Before he left, Tommy told me he couldn't drive me up to Gray-moor by 8:00 Monday morning. So I called my sisters, Jeannie and Patsy, but neither one of them picked up the phone. So I called Billy. And Billy came through, like he always seemed to. He showed up at 6:00 a.m., but he seemed kind of alarmed by my appearance. I was stone drunk, and totally filthy, even though there was a bathtub in the room.

"Listen," Billy said to me, real earnest, "for the first time in your life you got to do what's good for you. Forget about what everybody else says. It doesn't mean a thing. You got to do what's good for you, Bobby."

Billy drove me up to Garrison. I felt terrible. My life was a complete pile of shit and I couldn't even succeed in dying. We stopped for gas on the way and I went into the convenience store for doughnuts or whatever, and I noticed they had these little pint bottles of vodka for four bucks a pop, so I bought one and drank the whole thing within a mile of the gas station.

Billy dropped me at St. Christopher's and I walked in there.

There was Brother Gregory. He wasn't stupid.

"You're drunk," he says.

"Hell yeah I'm drunk," I say.

"Do you want help?"

"Hell yeah I want help. I can't take this no more."

"The last time you came here needing help we extended our love to you and you rejected it. When was the last time you took a bath?"

"Maybe 2 years ago."

"When was the last time you changed your clothes?"

"About a month ago."

I looked down at my hands and I could see that they were black with grime. I was afraid to look in the mirror for fear of what the rest of me might look like.

"If we allow you to come into this program, we're going to watch you very closely this time," Brother Gregory says. "And if you get out of line, we'll hand you a one-way bus ticket back to the City—for the last time. No more chances."

"Okay."

"Okay," Brother Gregory says to the intake clerk. "Sign him in."

So I was in, even though I broke every rule they had about taking people in.

The first night they put you in a sort of intake area, like a quarantine. And in my case, they made me take a shower, and then they sprayed me down with some kind of antilouse shit, to get all the bugs off me and out from under my skin. They sprayed me on the head and hair and arms and legs and my whole body, and the bugs started coming out. They gave me a brush to brush my hair, and my hair was full of bugs. It had been so long since I washed that when my skin came in contact with water, it just kind of shriveled. And, of course, as soon as my body started waking up to the fact that I wasn't drowning it in booze, I started puking, and all this stuff came up in my throat. Look: Of all the addicts and drunks who came in there, I was the worst of the worst. I bet 99 percent of the people who came in there in the condition I was in, died.

I went and found a nurse and told her I wasn't doing too good, that I thought I was going to die.

"We could send you to the hospital," she said very sweetly, "but if we do, you can't come back. All we can do for you here, medically, is to give you some aspirin and some lotion for the sores."

I called my sister Patsy collect, but she didn't answer.

I called Billy collect, but he didn't answer.

There wasn't a long-term bed available for me yet, so they gave me clean clothes and a temporary bed in the intake area called Matt Talbot Hall. Other guys near me complained that they were getting bugs from me. You know, somebody who's living the good life makes a positive impression on other people. Me, I was giving people bugs.

Finally, I crawled into the temporary bed with its crisp, white sheets, but I was scared shitless. Every time I fell asleep in New York, the animals from the street robbed me blind or fucked with me. And a bed felt so strange to me that I could hardly sleep at all. The nurse gave me some pills so I could go to sleep.

The next morning I called Billy again, and he picked up.

"Bill, I think I'm gonna die."

"You're not gonna die," he says (even though there was a good chance he was wrong). "I told your family what's happening, that you've gone into treatment up there. But to tell you the truth, they don't seem to care."

Brother Gregory started to get real concerned about me.

"You need to be in the hospital," he says, "and I'm thinking of putting you in there."

Later that same day, another priest, named Brother Richard, says to me, "You're quadrupally addicted and you've got no chance of living. You belong in the psych ward, but try the AA meeting tonight. I don't think it will help you, but give it a try." (I don't know if "quadrupally addicted" is a medical term, but I sure was homeless, helpless, useless, and worthless.)

But I guess I gradually started returning to the land of the living, or, at least, the half-living. As my strength started to return, so did the sense of guilt about my life. The guilt was killing me. I wrote a letter to Uncle Raymond from St. Christopher's that said:

> I'm in a treatment center trying to save my life and hope-fully some day you can forgive me. I don't know if I will ever see you again. I am getting better, I am not dying on the street, please forgive me.

Uncle Raymond didn't write back. Nobody answered any of the letters I wrote from St. Christopher's. But the fact is, there was no reason for anybody to answer them because it would only interfere with my getting better. If Uncle Raymond forgave me, I wouldn't be helping myself as much as I needed to. Even so, it was a lonely feeling. Nobody was calling me up and telling me to come home.

Nobody.

I came into St. Christopher's on a Monday, and by Thursday I got a permanent bed inside the shelter. There were 106 guys in all, with 22 guys sleeping in bunk beds in each room. It wasn't the Ritz, but it was the best thing I'd seen in a long time—I was indoors, I was safe, and I had my own bed.

So one day I walked to the top of this hill, which is, like, the beginning of the holy mountain. I sat down on this bench up there. I was still just getting adjusted to this place. I didn't know what I was going to do, because everybody had to be assigned a job. You were supposed to work 3 hours a day in this 21-day program, but I couldn't functionally do anything. The only things I really knew how to do well were drink, smoke crack, manipulate people, and bowl. It's not like I had anything useful to contribute to society, or to any other person.

So this priest sat down on the bench next to me. He looked like all the other priests up there, brown robe with a hood in back, sandals with no socks, about 60, balding, no beard, but with some little tufts of gray hair on the sides of his head. Actually, he looked a little bit like Father Benjy.

"How are you doing?" he says.

"Not too good, Father. I still don't know if I'm going to die or not."

"What's bothering you?"

"What about all those people I hurt in my life?"

"It doesn't matter."

"What about all those people I robbed?"

"It doesn't matter."

"What about the lives I ruined—Debbie and my sister Patsy, who stuck by me until they couldn't stand it no more? What about my whole family? Nobody is ever going to talk to me again."

"It doesn't matter."

"Then what matters?"

"God helps people who help themselves."

"That's it? That's your big advice?"

"I understand you were a bowler at one time," the priest says, very gently.

"Yeah, I was a famous bowler. How'd you know that?"

"Father Benjamin told me."

"You knew him?"

"Of course I knew him."

"I could have been the greatest bowler ever."

"Yes, I know that. But what you need to do now is to take all that talent you had from bowling and apply it to the task of getting sober. You have to understand that there's a reason you have to get sober. It's really, really important that you get sober."

"How come?"

"When you get sober, you'll find out. Do what I tell you, and I guarantee you it will work."

"Okay," I say to the old guy. "I'll see you later."

Then I get up from the bench and walk to the bottom of the hill. And I see three old black dudes standing there, fellow patients at St. Christopher's, I guess. And they're laughing their asses off.

"Brother, what are you so happy about?" one of them says to me.

"I got hope," I say.

"Where'd you get that?"

"From that brother up there."

They all double over, laughing.

"You weren't talking to no brother up there—you was talking to a tree! There's something wrong with you, bro. There's nobody up there!"

CHAPTER 9

JACK COMES BACK

NOT TOO LONG AFTER I walked up the holy mountain and talked to that priest up there, another guy who was staying at St. Christopher's, an old guy I'd run into the last time around named Old Man John, came up and sat down next to me. He was very rough-looking, like he'd lived on the streets for a long time. He told me that he'd seen the whole thing—watched me go up to the top of that hill and talk to a tree, and come back with hope.

"What's the problem?" Old Man John says.

"I don't know what to do," I say. "I had this great life, a great family, a great girlfriend, tons of money, a big career, and I wind up here. I'm broke, I'm alone, my body is fucked. I have nothing."

"You want to know how to get better?"

"Yeah."

"You truly, truly want to know how to get better?"

"Yeah, sure."

"Shut up. Don't drink. Go to meetings."

"You're kidding me, right?"

"No, I'm not kidding."

Not too long after this, Brother Richard comes up to me.

"Bobby, I have a problem," he says.

"What's the problem?"

"I know you've been telling people about going up the mountain and having some conversation with a priest who wasn't there. I don't want to hear about this priest anymore. If you continue to talk about the priest, I'll be forced to transfer you to the psych ward."

"Yeah?"

"Yeah. Look: I'm not denying the reality of whatever it was that you experienced. I'm just asking you to keep quiet about this."

"How come?"

"Because I don't want to have to send you to the psych ward. People in detox have delusions. When you came in here, let's face it, you were pretty far gone. You're getting better. But I just don't want you talking about this."

"Okay," I say.

For some reason, even though Brother Richard was Father Benjy's nurse when he was dying at Graymoor, I don't think he liked me. He was hard on me. He wouldn't take no shit from me. The other people up there might be getting their 21 days and going home, but as it turned out, the brothers kept me at St. Christopher's for 67 days. Maybe other people were breezing through in 3 weeks, but I was setting up a program to get a life. I didn't realize at the time that I was the lucky one.

"There's an AA meeting tonight at eight," Brother Richard goes on. "I think you should go."

"I don't think it will help."

"I think you should go. And please, just don't say anything more about what we talked about."

So I went to this AA meeting at 8:00 that night, on the grounds. The speaker was a guy who was an "alumnus" of St. Christopher's. He looked right at me and said, "I once sat where you sit. I looked like you look. I felt like you feel. And finally I walked into the chapel here and asked God to help me, and I haven't had a problem since."

So even though I was in heavy withdrawal from alcohol and shaking like an earthquake half the time, I started to pray. I prayed harder than I had ever prayed in my life. And then I just started crying.

Something way down deep in me was coming to pieces. I was coming unglued. After that meeting, I went upstairs to my little room and climbed up onto the top bunk of my rickety bunk bed, but I was shaking so hard the guy underneath me told me the bed was gonna fall apart if I didn't stop it.

I didn't know what to do, which way to turn. I didn't know what was happening to me. So I crawled out of bed and went downstairs to the chapel. It was, like, 10:30 at night and the chapel was closed and locked, but I found a priest who was like a security guy or something and he took one look at me—a guy turning to pudding—and he opened the chapel for me. And I went in there and did something I had never truly done before in my life. I threw myself down on my hands and knees and humbly begged God to help me, to touch my heart, to lift these terrible addictions and all the fear and pain and lies that was underneath them.

I mean—me, John Gotti's golden boy, the greatest, the unbeatable, the money bowler of all money bowlers, the studliest of studs, the guy with the stacked-heel shoes and the hot-combed hair. Yeah, me—the pathetic toothless old drunk and junkie, the liar and the thief, "Poppy," the 39-year-old 90-year-old, the king of nothing.

Now my whole giant, glittering trophy shelf of ego just came crashing down, all the way down to complete and total surrender. I gave up, completely. I was exhausted by all the lies. I couldn't live this way anymore—not one more minute of living death. I had no choice, no way out. I couldn't breathe. The only thing to do was to go down on my hands and knees in front of God, or die. And since I was already dead, I had nothing left to lose. The strange thing is that when everything is gone, when you've got no more to lose, you're way up. You're starting fresh. It's like you're being born all over again.

Finally, after all those terrible years, I asked God to help me and I truly meant it. I was desperate, beyond hope. And it was the weirdest thing, but suddenly, for about maybe 5 or 10 seconds, everything just stopped. All my pain and troubles, all my stories, all my lies, it all just lifted. For just a flash, I wasn't thinking about nothing. And in that flash there was a kind of presence around me, even though I didn't know what it was. During those few seconds, something new and powerful seemed to touch me.

Look: No Red Sea parted or anything like that. No thunderbolt came down from up high. But for the first time I could ever remember, I felt a power come over me that took away the pain, a power that might actually help me change my life after all them years of phony-baloney trying—trying to change my life without changing my life. I was almost 40 years old and I had been abusing addictive substances every waking hour of my life since I was 18, and suddenly this obsession was lifted from my soul in about 2 seconds flat.

What would you call that? I know what I'd call it. I'd call it a miracle.

I didn't know it then, but this moment would be the beginning of more than 20 years of uninterrupted sobriety—I hope for the rest of my life.

I was still shaking when I dragged my sorry ass back up to my room, but I was a different man. And over the next few days, I began to realize how much I had changed. For one thing, weirdly enough, I already knew all about the *Big Book* of Alcoholics Anonymous, because I'd carried that fat blue book around for years and I'd read the damn thing from cover to cover.

I'd actually preached from it while drunk, to other drunks. I'd sit at a seedy bar on Eighth Avenue preaching to a congregation of one—that other lonely drunk, the guy who was paying the bar bill—and drink and preach all night long. I read that book over and over, to the point where my copy was as ratty-looking and dog-eared as I was. I knew parts of it by heart. But yet, my heart was still completely empty.

I mean, how fucked-up is that?

The problem was—besides the fact that I hadn't stopped drinking or doing blow for a second—I was actually just trying to figure out how to get well without actually quitting. I was trying to find some back door into sobriety without actually putting down the vodka-and-orange-juice and the little vials of sweet poison that were my true salvation. I wanted to change without changing. But it never worked. Or, as it says in the *Big Book*, "half-measures availed us nothing."

Now, though, for the first time in my long fucked-up life, I stepped out from behind the wall of lies into the broad daylight of Truth. Now, for the first time, the long con was over. I had to give it all up. I climbed down out of the pulpit where I had been drunkenly preaching to the world and admitted that I was utterly powerless against alcohol and drugs, that my life was a total disaster, and I turned my will and my life over to a power greater than myself.

Giving up, letting go, turning the steering wheel over to God (or whoever you think is up there), and trying to figure out the next right thing he wanted me to do: That was the key to a new life. That was where I'd find the power to face the day, to help other people, to regain my sanity and stay sober for the rest of my life.

Of course, a person doesn't just change overnight, even if they come to realize this. When you surrender your will, it takes a long time to get better—not 1 day or 2 days or 3 days or a week, but gradually, over the months and years, life just gets better and better. Getting sober doesn't solve all your problems, that's for sure. But it does give you a reason for living, and I didn't have one before.

Later on, when I started reading more of the AA literature, trying to understand what the hell happened to me in the chapel that night, I came across a book that was a biography of Bill Wilson (or Bill W.), one of the founders of AA. Wilson was a real smart guy, a big muckety-muck on Wall Street, but he was also a hopeless, screwed-up drunk. And one day he fell down on his knees and asked God to help him. He had this crazy "white light" experience that to him felt like the presence of God coming down, and it changed him forever. He never took another drink after that.

So after this happened, Wilson started trying to understand what had happened to him, just like I did, and he came across this book by a guy at Harvard University named William James. The book was called *The Varieties of Religious Experience*, and it described all kinds of spiritual breakthroughs and spiritual conversions in all different kinds of religions—the Catholics, the Jews, the Muslims, the Sufis, whatever. Sometimes these experiences really were like a thunderbolt out of the blue (like Paul in the Bible seeing that white light on the road to Damascus), but other times they were just more of a gradual change. The main thing that Wilson noticed in this book was that James said there were three things that almost always came before one of these breakthroughs.

The first thing was catastrophe—the person's life was totally fucked, like mine was. The guy had reached the end of the road.

The second thing was that the guy was forced to admit complete and total defeat. He just gave up, like I did. His way of living had led to a freight train running into a brick wall.

And the last thing was that the guy reached up to heaven, up to some power up there that was bigger than he was. He reached up to God—the one who has power over everything, who can solve all problems because, after all, he created everything. And that's what I did that night in that little chapel at Graymoor, while the security guard waited for this pudding-man to stop crying and shaking and stand up and walk out of there a new man.

If there was one person who was critical to my search for a new life, it was Jack, my first sponsor, a guy I came to consider one of my angels. Jack was a guy who spent 30 years driving a magazine delivery truck, just dropping off bales of magazines at newsstands or wherever. No fancy job or nothing. He talked very slow and to the point and looked straight at you. He never had a problem with the bottle. His problem was heroin. He was a bad heroin junkie for many years until he finally stumbled into the program. (I don't know why he didn't go to Narcotics Anonymous, but he didn't—and AA sure worked for him. By the time we met, he was already 30 years sober.)

Jack had an older brother, George, who was also sober a long time, and they were both tight with Billy. Sometimes Jack would come up with another old guy, Doc. These guys—even though they looked about as ordinary as the guy who comes to unclog your toilet or fix your tire by the side of the road—they were saints.

One thing you learn pretty quickly in the church of Alcoholics Anonymous is that it don't matter for shit what somebody looks like. When you go to meetings, down in some dingy church basement somewhere, you'll see some raggedy beat-to-crap old guy who looks like he's been sleeping in a car (and maybe he has) and he won't say nothing for a long time. But then he'll say something, short and sweet, that will just knock your socks off with its spiritual wisdom. If the whole world blew up and we were all struggling to survive in the rubble and ashes, you'd want that guy—or any of a thousand other people in the program—on your side. Maybe the reason why a lot of the people in the program look so beat up is that they've already lived through the end of the world, like I did. And if the end came again, they'd be the ones that came up to help you.

Without these guys, and especially Jack, I would never have succeeded in getting sober. No way. I'd be dead, and nobody would have come to my funeral, either. I was what they mean when they talk about a "low-bottom drunk," and I think Jack knew what he was in for when he first met me. He and a friend of his had come up to St. Christopher's from his house in Whippany, New Jersey, which was, like, 90 miles away, because they had made a commitment to speak once a month. It wasn't Jack who spoke that night, it was his friend.

So after that meeting, Jack comes up to me.

"Hi, my name is Jack," he says. "I'm an alcoholic and I'm from New Jersey. How ya doin'? Your name's Bobby, right?" (He'd heard me share in the meeting, talking about my personal situation.)

"Yeah."

"How ya doin'?"

"Not too good."

"Yeah?"

"Yeah. I got no family no more, no friends. I wore out the welcome mat wherever I went. I robbed everybody, I ruined women's lives, my family disowned me, I got nobody asking me to come home. I've been on the streets 7 years and I lost everything. I even lost my fucking teeth. My mouth is fucking killing me."

This guy Jack—he's listening and looking at me earnestly, as if he actually cares about what might happen to me. Not like the way I listened to people, which was just pretending to be listening, waiting for my opening so I could start hustling them for food, money, dope, whatever. People weren't really people at all to me. They were just a way to get what I wanted.

"You've got to stay at St. Christopher's until your time is up," Jack says. "Don't leave here early. I know it's bad. I've been there. But things will start getting better if you stick with this program."

"How do I do that?"

"You do it one day at a time. Isn't there a meeting here every night?"

"Yeah."

"So go every night. How long you here for?"

"I'm here for 3 weeks—I got 2 weeks and 5 days left. But then what? Where do I go after that? Go back to the streets? I got no place to go after this." I am practically crying, listening to my own sob story. (Little did I know I was already 2 days into my life as a sober man.)

Jack started coming to see me every Saturday, and he stuck with me for 15 years. He became my sponsor. He helped me understand the *Big Book*, which I had read about 200 times (about half of the time shit-faced on vodka or coke or something else). I met his friend Doc, who still sponsors me today, over 20 years later.

Gradually, things started to change. I wasn't worried about dying anymore. I wanted to learn how to live. And, if I learned only one thing, it was that I could only do this one day at a time.

"God will supply your needs," Jack says. "Just believe this, and you'll be taken care of. The important thing, Bobby, is you need to focus on today, on this one day. Can you do that? Just this one day? You know, like the next 24 hours?"

"Yeah, I think I can do that. So?"

"So you don't have to use the word 'never'—like 'I will never drink again,'" Jack says. "No drunk can do that. I don't think anybody can do that. Just say, 'I won't drink or drug today.' That's it."

"Okay."

"And avoid 'people, places, and things' that will lead you back into drinking and drugging. That'll be easy for you—you're in here, confined. So take advantage of that. Okay?"

"Uh, okay."

"When you find the answer, you'll begin to live in the answer, and then your problems will start to disappear. Okay?"

"Okay."

"Okay, so I'll come back and see you here next Saturday night at five. Okay?"

"Okay."

"Look: I don't want you to call me collect; it's too expensive. I live 90 miles away. But will you trust me to come back next Saturday night?"

I'm standing there looking at this guy I just met, this old beaten-down delivery truck driver who's lived through the end of the world, and for some reason I trust him.

I thought about that thing in the Bible where it talks about "entertaining angels unawares." What the hell. What did I have to lose? I had already lost everything.

"I'm going to give you an assignment," Jack says. "What I would like you to do, if you can do it, is whenever you're sitting around, not working, just get a piece of paper and write down everything that's bothering you. I want you to keep clearing your head out, writing your thoughts down, and then setting that aside. Can you do that for me?"

"Uh, yeah, I guess so."

"Don't read what you write down. Just put the pieces of paper in a cardboard box. It's a 'God box'—when you put the papers in there you're giving your problems over to God. Later on, we can burn the papers or flush them down the toilet. Whatever. They're not your problems anymore."

"One other thing," Jack says. "Don't call nobody on the phone. The phone is a booby trap. If somebody listens to you and maybe even says they forgive you, you'll want to call them back, but they don't want to hear from you anymore. That will just keep you from doing the work you need to do. Okay?"

This really hit home to me. I had called Patsy and told her I was sorry a hundred thousand times. But I wasn't really sorry, at least not sorry enough to change my life. I just wanted money to get high again, or, at least, a little bit of forgiveness so I wouldn't feel so bad and guilty about getting high again. Asking her to please, please, please forgive me was just my way of not doing anything. It was my way of staying the same.

"Okay."

"So I'll see you here next Saturday night at five," Jack says. "You smoke?"

"No."

"You like candy?"

"Yeah, sure."

So Jack buys me some candy, almost like I'm a 12-year-old kid— and actually, inside I am about 12 years old, because when you start drinking and doing dope like I did, your emotional development just stops at that age. Your body ages, but you don't.

Then Jack and Doc leave the building.

For the next week, I just do what Jack told me to do. I don't try to run my own life, I don't try to tell everybody else how to run their life or what pathetic fuck-ups they are, or none of that. I just do what I'm told. It's a brand-new experience for me, because after all, for most of my adult life I'd been acting like I was God, conducting the whole show right down to the weather. And look where it got me. Yeah, that worked out real well!

I go to at least one meeting every day. And I start writing down everything—all my regrets and fears and sorrows, everything I shouldn't have said or done, all the lies I told Debbie, all the lies I told Patsy and Uncle Raymond. In the morning before work and in the afternoon after work, I sit on these benches outside in the hot sun and I scribble away like mad. I keep asking the guy at the front desk for more paper—I use up, like, 50 or 60 pages, filling them with all the shit that's bothering me, which is pretty much everything.

But one day I go to a couple of masses and a meeting and then I realize around bedtime that I have actually gone through an entire day without wanting to leave the shelter. This is incredible to me. (At St. Christopher's, the brothers made it very clear that you were free to leave at any time—you could pick up a one-way bus ticket to Manhattan at the front desk of the inn. I knew, because last time I was told to leave and picked up a ticket at the front desk on my way out.)

One day Brother Gregory sees me sitting there on these benches in the sun writing away and he asks what I'm doing. I tell him what Jack said, and about how he promised to come back.

"Don't get your hopes up," Brother Gregory says. "Honestly. Nobody ever comes back."

But I just keep on writing. For one thing, it helps me to keep my mind off the pain. My teeth and gums are killing me from where they're all infected and stinky. The sores on my body hurt. I am just learning to take showers again, and it still feels strange to have hot water pouring down over my skinny, wasted, junkie body. It hurts. It seems like everything hurts. Even my heart hurts because I can't drink or do drugs and I have to begin confronting what I look like in the mirror, what I have done to my life and all the people in it.

When Saturday night rolls around, I'm waiting in the room where they have speakers come. Five o'clock comes, and Jack ain't there. Five-oh-one. Five-oh-two. Five-oh-five. And then Jack and his friend come rushing in, just like Brother Gregory said they wouldn't.

"How ya doin'?" Jack says, very calm, very slow, very direct.

For the rest of the time I was at St. Christopher's Inn, Jack would drive those 90 miles, each way, every Saturday, just to see me. Can you imagine that? Me, the thieving junkie who threw away a chance to be one of the biggest somebodies anyone ever saw. Just for me.

And Jack kept coming back for me for the next 15 years, until the day he died.

CHAPTER 10

YOU ARE FORGIVEN

DURING MY SECOND STAY at St. Christopher's, I started out working at the intake desk again, where new people would come to check into the shelter in all kinds of conditions, all of them bad.

So one day I heard the bell for confessions, which were held in the chapel at 4:00 on Thursdays, and I got up from the intake desk and went into the chapel. There was nobody there. And then I opened the door of the confessional booth and looked in, and who was sitting there but the priest I had talked to up on the holy mountain that day. (Actually, it was more like a big hill, but they called it a mountain.)

That priest was as real as you or me, as real as that mailbox over there. I could have said, "Let's go have coffee," and he'd have said, "Yeah." And then we would have gotten coffee. Despite what others may have believed, he wasn't some cloud that came down with them little angel wings. He was just a regular guy. In the flesh.

"You're getting me in a lot of trouble," I say to him.

"What are you here for?"

"I'm here for confession."

"Go ahead."

"Bless me, father, for I have—"

"Stop, stop with all that," he says. "Let me ask you one question, and one question only: Did you ever kill anyone?"

"No."

"You are forgiven, and you can forgive yourself."

"Okay."

"And you are forgiven for what that guy across the street did to you when you were a kid."

"Okay."

It was weird: I don't know how he knew about that, since I had never told anyone.

"And you need to forgive that kid who blinded you in your left eye when you were 12."

How did he know this stuff?

"But most of all, you have to forgive yourself."

When he said this, it crashed over me like a wave of sadness. Because I realized I had been drinking to drown my own feeling of guilt for years. I'd been drinking in order to kill myself because of all the terrible memories and feelings I had inside of me. Lots of times I'd even cut myself, hoping that I would bleed to death, but I guess I never did a very good job. But the one thing I had never done was to forgive myself for everything that had been done to me in my life, and everything I had done to myself and to other people. The guilt was eating me alive, but I didn't really even know it.

"And remember what I told you," the old priest says. "Take your talent from bowling and apply it to the task of recovery, and I guarantee you'll make it. I can't tell you how important this is."

So I'm coming out of the chapel, and for the first time in a long while I'm feeling happy. And I run into Brother Richard.

"How come you're not at the intake desk?" he says.

"Well, I heard the bell for confession, and I went into the chapel and I saw that priest again—the guy from up on the holy mountain."

Brother Richard looks at me funny.

"There is no bell for confession," he says. "Bobby, I'm afraid I'm going to have to send you to the psych ward tomorrow. Pack your bags and get ready to go in the morning."

I ran back into the chapel (it was just a little chapel, with only one door going in or out), and I opened the door of the confession booth, but there was nobody there.

The next day, for some reason, Brother Richard never came for me.

Like I said, Jack came up to see me every week, and I wrote a couple of letters to Patsy to tell her what was happening. And from time to time, I caught a fleeting glimpse of the mysterious priest from the holy mountain around the grounds.

Patsy Purzycki: I'll tell you what I think about that priest Bobby saw at Graymoor. He's a spirit. An angel. And at the time Bobby saw him, my brother was literally half-dead. He was not physically dead, but as he said so many times, he was "a dead man who could not die"—someone with one foot already in the grave. He had already begun walking over into that other realm. But because he had one foot in the world of the living and one foot in the other dimension, he was able to cross over to the unseen world, and see this angel that nobody else could see. That's what I think. And, by the way, I have no doubt that the angel was real, because I've seen the miracle that took place in Bobby's life in the 22 years since then. That's about as real as it gets.

Even though the shelter at St. Christopher's was supposed to be your standard 21-day "three hots and a cot"—just a month-long break from the streets for a few of the homeless drunks and junkies out there—I wound up staying there for more than 2 months. There were a couple of reasons for that.

First of all, even though the priests didn't really want me there—who would?—they had no choice but to take me because my ride left.

Billy just dumped me off at the door and took off. So, by their own rules, they were forced to take me. Just their luck, huh?

Second of all, the way the whole system worked was that if you were a resident of New York State, you qualified for a welfare program that would pay for a more long-term program after your 21 days was up. But I wasn't from New York. I was from New Jersey.

So the priests didn't quite know what to do with me. They knew that I was so far gone that if they sent me back to the streets of New York, I was pretty much guaranteed to wind up at the city morgue with a tag on my toe. So they started trying to work the angle of Father Benjy, the Franciscan big shot, to see if, being that I was his relative, I could qualify for some kind of special Franciscan grant or something. I guess they sort of looked on me as a member of the family, a prodigal son returning home or something.

I think part of the reason I wound up staying at St. Christopher's so long was that the brothers were trying to find me a much longer-term rehab to go to, like 18 months to 2 years, and it was difficult to find one that had space available. They tried to get me into St. Joseph's, in Saranac Lake, New York, but there was no room at the inn. No luck at the Salvation Army, or a couple of other places either.

In the meantime, though, I stayed on there at Graymoor, working at the intake desk, watching these poor dazed-looking bastards come in the door straight off the streets. (Of all these guys, though, there was only one other guy that looked as bad as me. I was one sick puppy.)

And from time to time, I would see the mysterious priest that nobody else seemed to see.

At St. Christopher's there were groups and meetings every day, and—since I've never been somebody who knew how to keep his mouth shut—I kept talking about my higher power and also about this mystery priest, this "angel" or whatever he was that was helping me learn how to get sober and begin to live a real, actual life. The one who told me to take all the talent and focus I had from bowling and turn it into the personal power it would take to begin living a new life.

Gradually, though, I started to realize that the other drunks and junkies at St. Christopher's were beginning to look at me like I was a nutjob. Like the whole thing was a joke. Like I was a joke.

"Look at that dude, man—he's a crazy motherfucker!" I'd hear somebody say in a sort of stage whisper behind me, as I was walking down the hall.

"He sees people that ain't there."

"Yo! Seen that priest of yours lately, man?"

Even so, I didn't feel like shutting up about it. I didn't care what those guys thought. Fuck those guys. I wasn't crazy. I saw what I saw. And, after all, if you needed "proof" that the priest was real, how about the fact that he was the main reason I was on the road to recovery, that I had been lifted up to the mountaintop after that despicably sick, terrible life I'd been living on the street. My own awakening was all the proof I needed. What was happening to me was a miracle, and the miracle was real.

The priest had showed me that I needed to use my fierce inner drive to win at life, when winning wasn't bowling a perfect game or buying a new car or a pair of $500 shoes. It was waking up every morning and not being addicted to a person, place, or thing—being free of the obsession to drink alcohol or do drugs, or any of the hundred other things people get addicted to. Spiritual victory—really, the courage to live—was waking up every morning and being free.

Well, anyhow, one Sunday morning when I was still at St. Christopher's, I went to the 10:00 a.m. Mass. All the residents there were required to go, all 106 of us. We must have made quite a sight traipsing into that little chapel, this crowd of tired, beat-to-shit faces, all these misfits and losers and bums, dragging all our failures and mistakes and regrets behind us, like pets. At least we were all freshly showered and had clean clothes on, because there was some kind of a special event going on. There were wealthy donors there wearing nice suits, and ladies wearing dresses. And there was us drunks, who had to look good even if we looked bad. There was also a special speaker giving the sermon that morning, a visiting priest from Brooklyn.

Me and another drunk—Old Man John—walked right down to the front of the chapel and slipped into the front row. I always sat in the front row. That was my general approach to life: Get right in there, don't miss anything. Old Man John looked about as rough as they come. He'd had a couple of 5-year stretches of sobriety, but he always wound up coming back here to give it another try.

The guest speaker from Brooklyn was a big, jolly black guy, a very powerful Catholic missionary. He was huge: maybe 6-foot-5, with a booming voice. His message was a message of hope and Spirit and the nearness of God, very uplifting.

I'm listening to him speak when I notice another priest up there, seated to the left of him—an old guy wearing a baggy brown robe and sandals, with tufts of gray hair above his ears. And—holy shit!—I suddenly realize it's the mystery priest, "my" priest. He looks as real as a loaf of bread; he isn't no spirit flying off the ground. He is just sitting there like an ordinary person, apparently waiting for his turn to speak.

I jam my elbow into Old Man John's ribs.

"Yo! You see that guy?" I whisper to him, pointing to the priest. "That's the guy I've been telling you about! Right up there! That's the dude, bro!"

"Yeah, I see him," Old Man John says, not very impressed. "So what? I always see him. He's around here all the time."

"So you see him! You see him!"

"Yeah? So?"

"So you gotta tell Brother Richard you seen 'im!"

"Shut up," Old Man John says. "I'm trying to listen."

I sort of slump back in my seat, so relaxed and happy that I ain't crazy and that somebody else has actually seen the guy. I can't wait to tell Brother Richard. I start listening to the black missionary priest giving his sermon, and out of the corner of my eye I'm also watching the mystery priest, sitting up there, real as a heart attack, right in front of the whole church. Then, after a little while, the black priest steps down off the low platform at the front of the chapel and walks right up to me.

"Stand up," he says to me.

So I stand up.

"Have you ever seen God?" he asks me.

"Uh, no."

I'm nervous that I got picked out of the crowd—from my experience, that is always bad.

"Yes, you have." And he puts his hand on my head. He's one of these real jolly, hands-on type of guys, with big, damp hands.

"Uh, well I—"

"Your eyes are the windows to your soul. I can see that you've seen God. I have not seen anything like that in years."

Then he takes his hand off my head, walks back to the front of the chapel, and I sit down. Then the black missionary sits down, and the other guy, the mystery guy, gives the whole Mass and the Communion and everything. I sit there watching him and listening to him do it. I can't wait to get out of there to tell Brother Richard what I've seen. So after the Mass, me and Old Man John go out into the vestibule where there's all these fancy people milling around, and I go right up to Brother Richard.

"Brother," I say to him, "I can solve the problem with that mystery man, the priest I keep seeing around here."

"You can, can you?"

"He just did the service for the Mass in there! And Old Man John here seen him!"

Brother Richard kind of pauses a minute, giving me the once-over with his eyes. Then he turns to Old Man John.

"Is that true? Did you see him?"

"Yeah, I seen him. So?"

Just then a youngish-looking priest, maybe 40 or 50, in a brown baggy robe, walks out of the chapel. I have seen him around before—it's a guy they call Brother James.

"That's him," Old Man John says, pointing to Brother James. "That's the guy that gave the Mass."

"That's who you saw up there?" I say, incredulous. "But that's Brother James!"

"Yeah, that's the guy who was up there. That's the dude that gave the Mass."

"But that's not the guy I'm talking about! The guy who was up there wasn't young like him—he was an old guy about 60, with little tufts of hair above his ears. It was a different guy! It was the guy I've been seeing around here!"

And all of a sudden I realize that Brother Richard, Old Man John, and several other people who are standing there are just staring at me, with their eyebrows raised. Like, "What's up with this shit-for-brains?"

"Please be in my office tomorrow at 8:00 a.m.," Brother Richard says to me, very clipped and businesslike, as if I'm in trouble again. But just then the black missionary from Brooklyn comes walking up, and he puts his hand on my head again.

"This is the guy I was telling you about," he says to Brother Richard. "Look at his eyes. His eyes are filled with Spirit. His eyes are cleansed. He looks like someone who has seen the Light."

Me? I'm just standing there, fresh off the streets of the Bad Apple, the guy who's been sleeping on the floor of a peep-show house on Forty-Second Street, with no teeth, no money, no home, and scabs all over his body. Yeah: Like I'm really a guy who's "seen the Light."

But in a weird way, in a way I couldn't explain, I think I knew what he was talking about.

I showed up at Brother Richard's office the next morning at 8:00 sharp. But it was pretty obvious from the second I walked in there that the poor guy didn't know what the hell to do with me.

"Look," he says, "I don't know what to make of all this. But I do know that all your talk about some mysterious angel or priest or whatever may be starting to annoy people around here, including people who are struggling to get sober. It's getting to be a joke. People are making fun of you behind your back. And it very well may be an ordinary delusion of a recovering alcoholic. So I'm going to ask you to put a lid on it. Just don't share these stories anymore, don't mention them to anyone. Please. God loves us and wants us to do His will. But he doesn't very often send down a personal angel to help us along the way."

Well, I didn't know anything about that. All I knew was what I saw. And what I saw was as real as anything I'd ever seen or felt in my life.

Strangely enough, one of the few other people who was talking to me now was my old friend Tony. And Tony just happened to be the last guy I had robbed. I could call him collect, and he'd pick up. Tony agreed to pick me up when my time at St. Christopher's was over, and to take me to wherever it was I was going next. Eventually it turned out that a spot opened up for me at a hospital rehab called St. Clare's Riverside, in Boonton, New Jersey. I'd be leaving in a few days.

Not too long before Tony came to pick me up, I was walking down the road to the friar's cemetery, to pay my respects to Father Benjy and thank him for everything he had done for me. And while I was walking up the hill, a car pulled over. The door opened. It was the priest who ain't there.

"Get in," he says.

"No," I say. This is just getting too weird for me. "I don't know who you are."

"Robert, get in the car."

"No."

"Robert, get in this car, please."

"No."

"Where are you going?" the priest says.

"I'm going to the friar's cemetery."

"Where is that?"

Then I just stop and stare at him, an old guy in a baggy brown robe, almost like a pajama robe, with his little tufts of gray hair and his piercing eyes, staring at me out of the car.

"Who are you?" I ask him.

"It doesn't matter. What matters is that you do what I have told you all along—that you focus all that talent you have, all that intelligence, all that drive, on getting sober. It's very important that you get sober."

Then he closed the door and drove away.

Look: Am I telling you I saw a ghost driving a car? Well, I'm just telling you what happened. I don't know any more than that.

After the priest drove away, I walked up to Father Benjy's grave and stayed there quietly for a while, thanking him. When I turned around to walk away, my foot scuffed something in the dirt, and I leaned over to pick it up. It was a Miraculous Medal, one of these little gold coins made to celebrate the time when a lady named Bernadette had seen the Blessed Mother, at a place in France called Lourdes. They say that if you put this medal in the hands of somebody who's dying, they go directly to heaven. All I know for sure is that when you get a spiritual gift like that medal, you've got to give it away. That's how you get it back. I've heard that called "the divine paradox," and maybe that's what it is.

One other little thing I've got to explain here. Quite a few years after this, I went back up to Graymoor to help with the making of a documentary film about my life, called *High Roller*. This was in 2002. And after I told my story about the mystery priest to one of the main priests up there, he took me into a back hall where there were all these pictures of priests that had lived at Graymoor.

"Recognize anybody?" the guy says.

"Yeah, that's him," I say right away, pointing to the mysterious priest's sweet little face. "That's the guy I saw."

The priest guy pauses a second and then he says, "That's Father Paul Mattison—he was one of the founders of Graymoor. He died in 1940." That would have been 62 years before I seen him. It sent chills up my spine when I heard that.

Later I found out that Father Paul's grave was not in the regular friar's cemetery, but over near where that bench was where I first met him. Look: I know the whole story of Father Paul is pretty whifty. But all I can tell you is that I was there, I'm not crazy, and it happened.

Oh, and there's a couple of other things about Father Paul that I'm pretty sure about. One is that, when he told me how important it was for me to get sober, part of the reason he was saying that was so that you could read this book.

The other thing is that, when I die, I'm going to meet him again.

———————————————

Right after I had that strange meeting with Father Paul (which would turn out to be the sixth and last time I'd ever see him), I told Jack about it. He listened to me in his slow, quiet way. He didn't tell me I was fucking nuts to have seen a ghost driving a car.

"Why do you think they call it the 'holy mountain'?" he says. "Lots of crazy shit happens up there."

Truth be told, Jack was much less interested in ghosts and angels than he was in making sure I stuck with the program. That I do it day by day, and not try to lay out some grandiose plan for the whole rest of my life. Doing it that way was guaranteed not to work, he said.

After a little while we started working on the Twelve Steps of Alcoholics Anonymous, which is where you kind of really put the program to work in your own life. The really, really hard work I had never been able to do.

The First Step, Jack told me, was absolutely critical to everything that would come later. Like all the steps, it was simple.

STEP ONE: *We admitted we were powerless over alcohol—that our lives had become unmanageable.*

"Powerless"? "Unmanageable"? Forget about it. The main thing I knew was that my life had become unbearable, unlivable. If I didn't change, I would die. So for the first time in my adult life I began to look at my life honestly, to confront all the damage, to lift the veil on all the lies I'd told all those years, to other people and to myself, just to survive. All of it, everything, was a lie. All I really cared about, all I ever wanted to do, was get wasted, and then get even more wasted. That was it. That was my whole life. Everything I told Debbie, everything I told my sister, everyone—it was just a cover story so that I could get money to stay high and not have to think about anything, not have to take responsibility for anything.

I heard the saying, "Alcoholics love their childhood so much they want to take yours," and in a way that summed it up. I took advantage of everyone around me just so I could stay in the happy self-centeredness of childhood, just satisfying my own desires. And only now was I beginning to face all the damage that caused. It had been more important to me to get drunk or stoned than it was to work, have a family, have a relationship, reach my potential, have financial stability, help other people, or anything else.

There's a saying in the rooms, "First you take a drink, then the drink takes a drink, then the drink takes you." That's what people mean when they say somebody "got drunk"—the bottle drank them. They were powerless.

Was I aware of this at the time, when I was doing all this stuff? Yeah, kind of. But I didn't give a shit. I just went ahead and did it anyway. Uncle Raymond used to say, speaking mainly of bad stuff, "it only turns into experience once you stop doing it." In other words, if you just keep drinking and lying and doing dope, you're not learning anything, you're not aware of anything, you're doing the same bad stuff over and over. Only after you stop doing it do you kind of wake up to what's happening.

Well, now I'd stopped. Even though my life was in ruins, and my physical health was almost destroyed, at least I'd finally stopped. And that's when the burning pain of self-awareness and shame and guilt started to kick in. Just because you stopped drinking doesn't mean you're "sober"—becoming a genuinely sober person is a long, slow, painful process, and the Twelve Steps, I came to learn, are the key to it. Jack told me that the First Step was so important, and we spent almost the whole 67 days I was at St. Christopher's on that one step. He said I couldn't get much further unless I was absolutely clear on it. He told me that I was in a good position to begin this work—I was sober, if only for a couple of days; I was in confinement; I had the time; there were meetings every day; and the brothers were there to help me.

"I don't know how long it will take," Jack said, "but it will probably take a long time. You need to get the First Step in you, or else you can't go any further."

Every morning I would go to Mass, and all us drunks and junkies and thieves and liars would sing the St. Francis of Assisi prayer (what's also known as the Eleventh Step prayer).

> *Lord, make me an instrument of your peace.*
> *Where there is hatred, let me sow love;*
> *Where there is injury, pardon;*
> *Where there is discord, harmony;*
> *Where there is error, truth;*
> *Where there is doubt, faith;*
> *Where there is despair, hope;*
> *Where there is darkness, light;*
> *And where there is sadness, joy.*

Because I had so much time on my hands, and because it was so quiet there, I had a lot of time to work on my First Step at St. Christopher's. I would sit outside with a prayer book or the Bible, or walk up the holy mountain to that bench where I had first seen Father Paul. I prayed. Other times, I just got sick of the whole thing and started thinking, *Man, I gotta leave this fucking joint.*

One day Jack showed up when I was in one of those moods and he just exploded at me.

"Man, I'm driving 90 fucking miles up here to see you, and if you're not listening, or doing what you gotta do, you're wasting my time," he said. "There is a big change you have to make in your life— it has to be done. If you're not willing to do the work, I'm not coming back. I've got better things to do. But I'll tell you one thing: You go out there again, and you'll probably wind up dead."

Then I started begging and pleading for him not to give up on me, not to leave.

Everybody in my life had left, except Jack and Patsy. Even at St. Christopher's, where there was the biggest collection of crackheads, dopers, and losers you ever saw, even there, people kind of gave me a wide berth because of the way I looked. The only person who didn't treat me like I was nuts was Jack (and Patsy, when she came for a visit). And he was about ready to leave.

So I promised Jack I would ask God to help me find my way to a new life, a new way of living.

I wanted to get off the last train to oblivion. And Jack promised that he would give me another try.

"When you really start to change, other people will see it—there will be no reason to tell them about it," Jack told me.

I was waiting for that day to come, but so far it seemed like it never would.

CHAPTER 11

THE SECRET

ST. CLARE'S RIVERSIDE HOSPITAL in Boonton had a 7-day detox followed by a 28-day rehab. It was kind of a rest stop on my way to a longer-term "behavior modification" program that I would eventually enter. I guess the priests at Graymoor recognized that my shit was going to take some industrial-strength medicine to change.

I had to fight to get into St. Clare's, and I couldn't have done it without Father Paul backing me up. I prayed to him and my Higher Power, and then I went to see the intake lady from St. Clare's. She kept saying over and over again, no, it's not possible, we don't have the beds, other people are already checking in, we can't accommodate you.

"I can't live like this no more!" I begged her. "I got no money but I will do anything you ask!" And I just basically prayed and begged and prayed and begged, leaning on this poor lady with everything I had. It wasn't like I was humble or nothing. I was desperate—terrified of going back out on the streets, dead broke, just when I'd patched together my first few weeks of sobriety. It could all come apart at the first sight of a tiny little glass tube of rock cocaine. "I really need help!" I begged her. "You gotta help me!"

Well, they say that "coincidence is God's way of remaining anonymous." And after banging on this lady's brain for an hour or more, something happened. There was a cancellation or something, or so she said, and suddenly I had gotten in.

There was no doubt in my mind that this stroke of "good luck" happened because I had prayed to Father Paul and to my Higher Power.

Because there ain't no coincidences—just miracles from God.

Now the intake lady was telling me that I could be admitted tomorrow afternoon, and the next morning, first thing, I was sitting there in the waiting room waiting for the next miracle to happen. I was going to make 100 percent sure that I didn't miss my chance.

When I showed up at St. Clare's, I was still crazy, even though I had a string of several weeks of sobriety, the first in memory. Unlike St. Christopher's, this was a hospital-based program, so I was finally able to deal with the nasty, painful infections in my mouth. There were meetings and classes almost all day long, and I started gradually adjusting to the fact that normal people sleep all night, get up in the morning and have coffee, make friends, have normal conversations, take responsibility for stuff, and all that. It was weird.

So one day, about halfway through my stay at St. Clare's, I was in the kitchen making coffee for the group, and I had my back turned when I heard a visitor come into the room. Then I turned around and saw her.

It was Patsy.

"Hi," she says, kind of shyly.

"Hi," I say.

And then she starts crying.

"Oh my God," she says. "It's really happening."

"I told you I'm getting better," I say.

"I can see it."

"How you doin'?"

"I'm doin' okay. You know you can't come home."

"Yeah, I know."

She asked me if it was okay if she brought Jeannie some time, and I said, sure, I'd love to see her. So the next Sunday Patsy came with my other sister, and Jeannie saw me, and she believed it, too. (I had two other sisters, but at the time they wanted nothing to do with me.) I was really coming back into myself after all those terrible years. Patsy later said that all she ever wanted was for the Bobby Purzycki that she knew was in there to come out again. And it was happening. It was almost like Lazarus, in the Bible, getting raised from the dead.

"You know you can't come around us anymore," Jeannie said, repeating what Patsy had said the week before and what I already knew.

I'd done this to myself. I knew I had. Now it was my job to take responsibility for my own life. Maybe someday I'd be allowed back into the circle of the family, but I had a lot of work to do before anything like that ever happened.

It was while I was at St. Clare's that something very scary and painful happened that changed my life. It later became known as "the pizza incident."

One Friday night, I just completely flipped out. I went nuts. I was throwing chairs and tables, bouncing off the walls. People were ducking for cover from all that flying furniture. What set me off was one of them tiny things that isn't tiny at all—those "little" things that can set off bitter arguments, like the ones I used to have with Debbie. The sort of arguments that can get people killed.

What happened on the surface was that, on Friday nights, all of us patients in the program would pool our money and get pizza, and on this particular night I was put in charge of collecting the money. There was a woman named Peggy, a very hard, no-bullshit woman, who was in charge of that shift. She was the boss, and for some reason Peggy was on my case. She didn't like me, and more important, she didn't believe I would ever make it. She thought I was too far gone ever to get my shit together and become a responsible, sober person. She thought I had no shot at redemption. It was like I was already a corpse. I could feel that from her, and even though it was probably a reasonable thing for her to think, it fucking pissed me off. As a result, you know, there was bad blood between us.

So this particular night, after I'd collected the money and given it to her, she accused me of slipping a little bit into my own pocket.

"This money doesn't add up, Bobby," she says, very stern, counting. "Where's the rest of the money?"

"Are you accusing me of shorting the money?" I say to her. "Bullshit! I didn't steal a penny! Look in my pockets!" And I pull my empty pockets inside out to show her.

Look: Nobody else in that room was willing to collect the money for the very reason that handling money was a loaded issue for a lot of these people. We'd probably all been accused of stealing money before, and with good reason. I had decided to take on this job because I was trying to take responsibility, and now I was getting treated like a fucking sneak-thief. And even though what Peggy was saying was not true, she persisted. She really got in my face. She wouldn't back off. And neither would I.

"You're just in my shit because you think I'm a loser and I'll never make it!" I yell at her. "Well, look at you! Making five bucks an hour at some crap job on the drunk ward!"

"You're a thief, and you know it, Bobby! Give that money back, or I'll bring you up on charges!"

And that's when the explosion hit: BOOM! I just went off. Shit flying everywhere. I turned a bed upside down. I knocked over a desk. I just absolutely flipped out. To be unfairly accused like that, and also to be treated like someone who could never get sober, never get well, a homeless addict who would always be a homeless addict—well, it blanked out my brain, it made me so mad.

Obviously, Peggy could have called the front office at St. Clare's and had me thrown out of there after this incident. I was being violent and scary. But she didn't. Maybe it was partly because, after I started to calm down, I started to beg.

I guess Peggy had calmed down, too, so she backed away from a bigger fight and we ordered the pizza. (Later on, believe it or not, Peggy and I became friends and we corresponded for years.) But the thing is this: Like most arguments, it wasn't about pizza, or money, or any of that.

Earlier that same day, a therapist named Judy had about 12 or 18 of us sitting in a circle for a group session. She said you were "only as sick as your deepest, darkest secrets," and we were going to explore some of those. Then she hypnotized us, or tried to; I don't know how that works. It didn't feel like much, but before I knew it, I was waking to some ancient, ancient memories, and they were scaring me shitless. In a way, the therapist tricked me into this. I wasn't prepared for what happened next.

I had gone all the way back to when I was 12 years old, just a skinny, little Polack kid growing up in Paterson and starting to show all this amazing promise at the bowling alley. I was a scared kid who was beaten up and bullied. I was not a fighter. I just got pounded down. Then I got busted in the eye and went half-blind. But that wasn't the scary part.

Right about this same time, there was this older kid who lived across the street, named Joey. He was, like, 18 years old or something, 5 or 6 years older than me. And whenever his parents weren't home and nobody else was around, he would call me across the street.

"Hey Bobby, come 'ere," he'd say. "I got some candy!"

I liked Joey. I admired him. Then he'd lead me into the house. He'd take me downstairs. And then he'd do these sex acts to me, disgusting things, things I'd never heard of. I had no idea what was happening. I just knew I was being kidnapped and forced into hell. There was no way I could get out of it, and nobody I could ever tell. When it was over, Joey would tell me that if I ever told anybody, he'd make me pay. He'd kill my whole family. He'd kill my mom, my dad, and all my sisters. If I told anybody, I'd be a murderer.

So I just put these disgusting memories in a box and decided to bury that box way down deep inside myself where it could never be found. I just stuffed it. (Many years later, when I saw parts of the Jerry Sandusky pedophilia trial, at Penn State, on TV, I started to relive the whole thing. When I listened to the testimony from Victim Number Four, I heard this kid say that Sandusky had threatened him with the exact same words Joey used to threaten me. I knew that kid was telling the truth, because he was telling my story. I felt so sorry for that kid. I knew how alone and messed up he felt inside.)

There was one time that I actually screwed up the courage to tell my dad about it, even though I risked killing my whole family. "Are you sure? Are you sure?" I remember my dad asking me. I could see his face getting red. I was afraid he was going to go charging across the street and rip that kid's lungs out. I actually remember asking him not to go over there, because of what might happen.

Instead, he called the police, and they came to the house to interview me. But when they asked me what Joey had done to me, it was too embarrassing, and I couldn't really describe what it was anyway. I didn't know anything about sex—I was 12 years old. I didn't know what it was. Besides, if it got out in the neighborhood that I'd been messed with like that, I knew it would give the other kids one more excuse to beat the shit out of me. Why would the victim get blamed? Because that's the way it worked where I grew up. So in the end, I finally just told the cops, you know, "forget about it. It never happened." I just wanted it all to go away. The police left and nothing ever came of it.

Eventually, Joey's family moved away, and I never saw or heard from him again. But yet, for all those years, I had carried that secret box, with all those secrets hidden inside. I had tucked it away so deep that I didn't even know it was there anymore. And when the therapist brought it all up at St. Clare's, I just flipped. I went nuts, not because I was mad at anybody, but because I didn't know what to do with the shame.

Patsy Purzycki: When I found out about this later, it really made sense to me. I actually suspected that something like this might

have happened. It's my belief that a lot of Bobby's later problems came from being sexually abused and never talking about it, and also being injured in the face like that. He was traumatized. I see these men on *Oprah* that have been abused, and they have no self-worth, can't do anything with their lives—it's so similar to what Bobby went through. He went from extreme to extreme—he was either the greatest who ever lived, or worthless, nothing.

Jack would come to meetings at St. Clare's every Thursday. We began working on Step Two and Step Three of the Twelve Steps. We actually kind of worked these two steps together, because Jack said they were so related.

STEP TWO: *Came to believe that a Power greater than ourselves could restore us to sanity.*

STEP THREE: *Made a decision to turn our will and our lives over to the care of God as we understood Him.*

Unlike a lot of people in the rooms of Alcoholics Anonymous, I never had any problem believing in God. I grew up Catholic and had accepted Jesus Christ as my Lord and Savior when I was a little kid. But most importantly, I had had a direct experience with God when I was 12 years old, when I was blinded and raped. When I was lying there in that bedroom with both of my eyes covered in patches, not knowing if I would ever see again, I prayed to God to restore my sight, and he did. Same thing when that creepy, little pedophile Joey across the street was raping me—I prayed, and God answered my prayers.

Look: I'm not really a religious guy at all. I didn't trust the priests at Catholic school—they were mean as shit, they beat me with a paddle. Instead, through AA, I was becoming a spiritual person. I've heard it said in the rooms that "religion is for people who don't want to go to hell. Spirituality is for people who have already been there."

As a guy who'd been to hell and back, that's the way I look at it, too. But the program of AA is about God's love for you, and that this

Higher Power will be there for you through everything so long as you turn your will and your life over to him, and try to do the next right thing. That you change your life from being self-centered to being God-centered. Spirituality in AA is not a religion, it's one-on-one contact with someone you can't see, with a Spirit you believe in that protects you always—that helps to ease your burdens and solve the problems you have in your life. It's love in action. It all boils down to: Help others, and God will help you. For me, that's about it.

Even so, the whole process of turning my will and my life over to God was a major, major change. Basically it was like firing my old employer (me) and hiring a completely new one (God).

Jack gently led me to the understanding that I had caused such hurt and pain to people that I loved, like Patsy, that there was a good chance I would never see them again. He also led me to the understanding, in a fundamental way, that I had never even learned to take care of myself, that society had no place for me, and that once my life underwent a dramatic spiritual change from working the steps, life would still be hard for me. Basically, I'd fucked it up almost beyond belief. Even so, very gradually, I realized that my heart was shifting from a feeling of complete uselessness to a sense that I might somehow be useful, not only to myself but to other people. That I could make a positive difference in other people's lives. That I didn't ever have to go back to the streets, or to the nightmare that my life had become. That my life was being transformed because I had met God or his angel, one or the other, and that whether Father Paul was real or not real, I was learning to use the talent I had as an athlete to become a sober man living a useful, spiritual life.

Jack told me that if I stuck with this, he guaranteed I'd make it.

CHAPTER 12

THE GOD BOX

MOST PEOPLE HAVE JUST ONE SPONSOR, but I kind of had three—Jack; his older brother George; and my friend Billy, the guy who always showed up. These guys were my little community. It's quite possible I needed three people because I was so fucked up. Or maybe I was just lucky. Or maybe that's the same thing, in some strange way. I mean, the luckiest thing that ever happened to me was getting into AA, and I never would have gotten there if I hadn't been driven to my knees.

The program that Jack was leading me through now was pretty simple, actually. Some people say you can boil it down to six words.

"Quit drinking. Clean house. Help others."

The "cleaning house" part is the Twelve Steps. That's it. Sounds simple, but it's some powerful magic, that's for sure. And if you do it right, it hurts. Sometimes people will do the steps two, three, four times or more, because every time you do this work, you hurt more, and you feel better as you do the hard work of cleaning up your house. Like it says in the *Big Book*, "We are not saints. . . . We claim spiritual progress rather than spiritual perfection."

So it's a program for people who have failed, who have been humbled, who finally had to admit that they were "powerless over alcohol."

Now I started working on the Fourth Step.

STEP FOUR: *Made a searching and fearless moral inventory of ourselves.*

Oh, jeezus. Like, I was actually supposed to look at that sick, twisted vampire in the mirror, at everything I had become, at everything I had been running from all those years? I was supposed to actually come clean about all the people I done wrong, everybody I'd cheated, lied to, robbed or stolen from? The whole idea of cleaning up the mess I'd made of my life made me feel exhausted, scared, panicky, freaked out, sad, angry, and every other bad feeling you can imagine. It also made me desperate for a drink or a line of coke or a little glass stem of crack. But I couldn't do it. I could not do it. If I did that, I knew that I would go right back to the place I was before, and not long after that I would be dead. And I'd make a pretty scrawny, pathetic-looking corpse.

Jack told me that now was a good time to start using the "God box" I'd learned about before, and to just throw shit in there—things I done wrong, things I was embarrassed about—and give them over to God. It was a relief not to have to carry that shit around anymore. I wrote and I wrote and I wrote, laying out all the stuff I regretted (at least, the parts I remembered) and putting it in the shoebox for God.

Jack pointed out that if I was going to stay sober for the long term, I was also going to have to avoid the "people, places, and things" that I associated with getting drunk and doing dope. Unfortunately, at least for now, that included bowling alleys. Alcohol was so much a part of the sport that at a lot of bowling alleys it was literally built in, with cup holders in the tables right by the lanes. Even though bowling had played such a critical role in my life and my sense of self, my sobriety was a whole lot more important than bowling. (It would be 2½ years before Jack felt it was okay for me to bowl again. And even then, he strongly warned me to be careful about setting foot in a place that was so loaded for me.)

After Jack felt that I'd gotten a handle on the Fourth Step, he told me he was going to lead me through the Fifth Step.

STEP FIVE: *Admitted to God, to ourselves, and to another human being the exact nature of our wrongs.*

But before we got into that, Jack said he was going to take me down to a meeting in central Jersey where he had a speaking commitment.

"Who's speaking?" I say to him. "You?"

"I don't know," he says. "It ain't been determined yet."

So me and Jack and George and Billy drove down to Red Bank, New Jersey, the next night. It turned out, it was a huge meeting—there must have been 300 people there—and Jack was leading it.

After the preliminaries, Jack says, "I brought along some friends of mine, George and Billy and Bob. And our first speaker tonight will be Bob P."

Holy shit, man. I was just a beginner at this. I was shaking all over. But I started speaking anyway.

"Hi," I say. "My name is Bob and I'm an alcoholic. I've been sober since May 6, 1992, and for that I am eternally grateful."

And then I started telling people the whole story—getting raped and blinded when I was a kid, growing up to be a champion bowler, Uncle Raymond and John Gotti and Bobby Cabert, falling down the black hole of addiction, life on the streets, Father Paul and Graymoor, and my first attempts to claw my way up out of the darkness and into the Light.

Jack told me later that his original plan was to have each of us talk for about half an hour. But, I don't know, I just kept talking, pouring out my heart, pouring out my story, and when I finally finished, I realized the time was almost up. Jack told me afterward that I had talked for 1 hour and 20 minutes. Through that whole thing, I could see and hear that the other drunks and druggies in the room were listening intently. I'm sure that in many ways I was telling their story, too.

Anyway, when we climb back into the car after the meeting, Jack says to me, "Congratulations. You've just done your Fifth Step."

"You're kidding," I say. "Really? That was easy!"

"Well, that's the way we do it in New Jersey."

STEP SIX: *Were entirely ready to have God remove these defects of character.*

Now we were starting to move into the realm of miracles—the realm of Father Paul. How was I supposed to remove my own defects of character? I couldn't, really. I could only ask God to do it, or to help me do it. In this process, I used the power of the pen every day, scribbling down these defects of character, putting them in the God box, and asking God to take them away. And gradually, I began to change. When somebody got up in my face, I began to learn how not to retaliate, not to bring up that angry, small, pissed-off alcoholic behavior. To try to step back into a place of calm and serenity.

"Look," Jack said to me, "you gotta do this step work in AA, because in the future, if you get into a tough situation, it will work for the rest of your life. This is about fundamentally changing yourself, not just putting a Band-Aid on a problem."

I started to learn how to do basic life stuff like making commitments, planning ahead, showing up on time, keeping my word. Before, I'd hand you a whole shitload of promises, almost all of them lies, about what I was going to do or not do next week. I didn't realize that making commitments and sticking to them, just like showing up on time, was a matter of integrity, a matter of character. (Character? Integrity? In my former life, I had no idea what those words even meant.)

But now I could say, simply and honestly: I commit to going to five meetings a week. To making coffee before the meeting. To joining a home group. To bringing a meeting to St. Clare's on the first Monday of every month. And, of course, to not picking up a drink or a drug.

My new, changed life also began to appear in other ways. I started trying to be completely honest, which was about as easy as learning to speak Chinese. Helping other people. And, of course, no robbing, stealing, or manipulating, which in my former life came as naturally as breathing. That, in fact, was a pretty good job description of what I spent most of my time doing. Now, everything had to always be on the up and up. I started paying attention to my own cleanliness, to taking care of my teeth, to going to doctor's appointments. As usual,

I sometimes got carried away: I'd sometimes wash myself 30 times in a day, because of all those years on the street. It was like I couldn't wash myself hard enough, or often enough, to wipe away that feeling of shame and degradation.

STEP SEVEN: *Humbly asked Him to remove our shortcomings.*

Again, this is all about miraculous stuff here. Now, instead of waking up someplace with a hangover and almost no memory of what had happened the night before (but with this vague feeling of dread that it was probably pretty bad), I was waking with a sense of actual joy in my heart. At least, some or even most of the time. Just because you're sober don't mean you have no problems anymore. Far from it.

For a lot of alcoholics, getting sober means waking up to the fact that the life you've created is a huge, unbelievable mess, that you owe people money, that you've got all kinds of physical problems or injuries caused by drinking, that your liver is fucked, that you're in trouble financially, that various people hate you (and for good reason), and all the rest of it. The difference is that you're now confronting all this as an honest, sober, spiritual-minded person and not as a thieving drunk and a liar. Now, my greatest joy was thinking of ways that I could help other people without them knowing I did it. (And if that ain't a miracle, I don't know what is!)

The Eighth and Ninth Steps kind of go together, Jack said, so we worked on them almost like a single step.

STEP EIGHT: *Made a list of all persons we had harmed, and became willing to make amends to them all.*

STEP NINE: *Made direct amends to such people wherever possible, except when to do so would injure them or others.*

Oh, man. This was painful. It filled me with shame and remorse to start making this list of all the people I harmed, especially the people I loved that I had harmed. But at least I felt shame and remorse. Before, I didn't feel anything. I just saw a vague outline in front of me, not even a person, just a way of getting money to get high. If I had to lie, cheat, or steal to get the money it didn't matter. Remorse? What was that? But now that I wasn't completely numbed-out by dope or alcohol anymore, I began to feel what I should have felt a long time before.

Man, it hurt. And, one by one, where it was possible, I started making amends to people I had harmed. I'm sure there were lots of people I'd wronged but didn't even remember because I'd been in a blackout.

The biggest people I owed amends to, of course, were Debbie and Uncle Raymond. But I felt strongly that it would be a bad idea to go back to Debbie—who was now married, with children—and bring up all this painful old shit from the past. Besides, her husband might have wanted to kill me. Later, I did happen to see Debbie across a crowded room, and she gave me a dirty hello, like "hi, fuck you," so I knew there was a lot of unfinished business there. And Uncle Raymond—he wasn't looking for me no more, and I thought the best thing was to just stay away from him. So I wrote them all letters of apology, and then I burned them. Put them in the God box. Thank God for the God box.

Other people I was able to apologize to in person. I went to the owners of Eclipse Lanes, where Jackson Gist used to work, and apologized for all my bullshit and arguments and getting drunk during league play. I apologized to Joe Tolvay, a friend in the bowling world that I had borrowed a lot of money from, and then I paid him back. I apologized to Tommy Lorenzo, but he didn't seem to care. I apologized—or tried to—to Tommy's father, Rocco, but he didn't want to hear about it. I apologized to Gene and Al from Lodi Lanes for having to bar me from drinking and doing drugs in the bathroom and for all those noisy scenes with Debbie. I apologized to my friend Adam

Monks and to my friend Tony from Tri-State Telephone. I apologized to this guy named Philly Pauchi from Queens, who had been one of my chief enablers in the old days, but it turned out he was tremendously happy when I got sober. And on and on—there were so many people, actually, that I started writing it all down. Then I started having to take care of all the driving violations I had stacked up. Amazingly enough, I didn't have any DWIs, just moving traffic violations, running red lights, and all that type of shit. But now that I was trying to clean up my own mess, I had to go to 16 to 20 different courtrooms. I had to pay, like, $20,000 in fines. But since I didn't have any money to pay them, the court took my license away for 5 or 6 years, until I could finish the payments.

I was also doing what is known as "living amends"—learning to live my life as a sober person and doing right by everyone in my life as I went along. My general approach to life became: I will stay sober every day and when the time comes to make some past wrong right, I'll make it right.

Gradually, I was beginning to build and live a real life.

Now, over time, me and Jack worked through the last three steps on the list.

STEP TEN: *Continued to take personal inventory, and when we were wrong, promptly admitted it.*

Old habits die hard, as they say, and the job of changing into a new person, changing all my sleazeball, junkie habits into the habits of a sober, honest person would take a lifetime. But you can only do this work one day at a time, trying to pay attention to what you've done wrong and correcting it as it happens.

It ain't easy.

STEP ELEVEN: *Sought through prayer and meditation to improve our conscious contact with God as we understood Him, praying only for knowledge of His will for us and the power to carry that out.*

STEP TWELVE: *Having had a spiritual awakening as the result* *of these steps, we tried to carry this message to alcoholics and to practice these principles in all our affairs.*

Spiritual awakening? To my way of thinking, I had had a spiritual awakening before I even started the steps. I had had a personal encounter with Father Paul, who as far as I was concerned was God's messenger, the burning bush, the parting of the Red Sea, and every other miracle in the Good Book combined. He's the one that started me on the path to sobriety and to a new life.

This book you're reading right now is a big part of the reason I got sober. My story only matters if it can help you, and I think it can. If nothing else, it shows you that if I can do it, anybody can. You don't need no angel—but if you're lucky, maybe you'll get one. Father Paul couldn't have appeared to a less-deserving person than me. But for some reason, he did. Who knows? Maybe it was because I was so undeserving. All I know is that I am blessed.

I know that you are, too.

CHAPTER 13

WELCOME HOME

AFTER ST. CLARE'S, I got transferred to a behavior modification program in Glen Gardner, New Jersey, called Freedom House for 6 months. When I first got there, I had to work in the kitchen, and for the first 14 days, I was in full blackout from society—no contact with the outside world whatsoever. It was like I was entering a new world, a new life. And I began the slow, painful work of trying to be honest with myself, trying to come to terms with the mess I made of things, trying to be sober.

I also started getting some of the medical attention I'd needed for a long time. One of the directors at Freedom House, a wonderful man named Frank, really started to focus on my nightmarish dental problems. He arranged for me to go to a medical center where they gave me enough antibiotics to kill the infection in my mouth, but it still hurt like hell. It turned out that the infection in my gums had spread into the bone. I had to take antibiotics for 6 months to kill the infection, and then a lady dentist had to extract the roots of 12 rotten teeth and then actually break the bone of my jaw to get the rot out. It took 90 stitches to sew my gums back up again. Sure: They gave me Novocain and whatnot, but the pain was unbelievable.

After my bones and gums healed (it took months), the lady dentist spent a few more months molding a partial denture to replace my missing upper teeth. And once that was fitted, for the first time in 6 or 7 years, I was able to eat regular food again, without too much pain.

During those early days of sobriety, there was one other person (besides Jack) that really helped me a lot. While I was still staying at Freedom House, I had a day job working at a dry-cleaning place called Tirpok Cleaners. I'd work in the back all day, folding sheets and towels and whatnot (they had a big contract to do all the laundry for local motels), and the person I worked with most of the time was this wonderful, beautiful, petite old lady named Marie. Marie was in her late sixties, semiretired, and just a lovely, lovely lady. She had been through some rough times in her life. She had known pain and regret. She'd made serious mistakes.

But she also had 18 years of sobriety and a passion for both AA and the spiritual gifts it can give to people. Her passion was to share what she had, to give it away to me and anyone else who would listen to her. "You can only keep it if you give it away," she'd say.

Standing there folding those warm sheets and towels in the back room at Tirpok, Marie talked to me all day long about the program and her experiences and what she had learned in sobriety. She became kind of my First Mother of sobriety in AA. She'd tell me these wise sayings, usually very quietly, that were so profound sometimes it took me a week to grasp what she meant. Like she'd say, "time takes time," and what I finally figured out she meant was that the mess I'd made of my life would take a long time to clean up, but that I had to be calm and patient and, most important, try to change my life one day at a time and not all at once. She told me that all the sadness and regret I had over my failed relationship with Debbie, all the ways I done everybody in my life wrong, would all get straightened out sooner or later so long as I just stayed sober, did the steps, and kept going to meetings. It was so simple even I could understand it. I'd leave work every day feeling so good it was almost like I had been to church. And I thought, I was just folding sheets and towels from the Holiday Inn in the back room of a dry cleaner in New Jersey.

One of the most amazing things to me was that Marie's life and experiences, as a drunk and a junkie and now as a sober person, were so similar to my own. Here I was this smart-ass fallen pro bowler in his forties with all these mobbed-up friends, and there she was this poor, little old lady from Flemington. But yet we had both done all kinds of things we regretted, had woken up out of blackouts a thousand times, had lived lives of supreme self-centeredness, and now we were both having to confront it all so that we would never have to go back there again. The story of addiction and recovery is actually an old, old story that's shared by millions of people around the world. Figuring this out helped me get past this idea that Bob Perry was some kind of unique creation—what people in the rooms called the idea of my "terminal uniqueness"—and was instead just a beautiful child of God, like everybody else.

Marie was folding sheets at the dry cleaners one day when I started feeling really faint and dizzy. I tried grabbing onto the edge of the folding table, but I just collapsed onto the floor. Marie was there when I hit that particular bottom. She called an ambulance, and it came and took me to Hunterdon Medical Center, where I stayed for about 15 hours. Turns out, I'd had a heart attack. A doc at the hospital told me he thought it might be related to my withdrawal from alcohol and dope, and to all the anxiety I was going through. He also said it might be related to all that poison from the infections in my mouth. A couple of days later, after I got out of the hospital, I went to a meeting at Freedom House, had a cup of espresso, and collapsed again with another heart attack. They sent me back to Hunterdon Medical Center, and this time I had to stay there 2½ weeks, first in the ICU. They diagnosed me as having something called pericarditis. The docs told me they found black spots around my heart from all those years of booze, coke, and crack. (How ironic that I had "black spots on my heart.")

Freedom House was only 20 miles from Jack's house, so I got to see him more often. It was while I was staying there that I went to this huge AA convention called the Area 44 Convention. There were maybe a thousand people there, with 24-hour-a-day meetings, speakers, the whole deal.

So I was walking into the dining room for breakfast on my first morning there, and I practically ran into a lady I had not seen in more than 10 years. Her name was Irene, and she had been one of the best women bowlers in the New York area and on the entire East Coast. She was always a lot of fun, but she was also a heavy drinker—maybe even more than me. When she laid eyes on me, it was like her face just lit up.

"Oh, my God!" she says. "It's you!"

"Hi, Irene!" I say.

"Bobby! What are you doing here?"

"Well, I'm in the world of sobriety now. I couldn't live like that no more."

"How long are you sober?"

"Over a year."

I guess Irene could see that sparkle in my eye. Then she broke down, crying.

"I never thought you'd make it!" she says. "I could see it was getting really bad for you, and I prayed for you for years to be in here. And now my prayers are answered!"

Irene told me that booze had destroyed her life and that AA had saved it. She'd been sober for, I think, 10 or 12 years, but she hadn't bowled in years and couldn't even go into bowling alleys anymore because of all the memories, and the fact that booze was so much a part of the sport.

"Where are you living?" she says.

"I'm at Freedom House," I say. "Thanks for praying for me, Irene."

I wasn't exactly a Catholic altar boy anymore, but I knew about the spiritual power of prayer and the power of AA.

Over the following weeks and months and years, Patsy and I began to renew the love and friendship we had once had for each other. The love that—incredibly—had never been lost. She even stood up for me when the guy who started Freedom House, a guy name Fred, started coming after me.

As I've said, I'm not a guy who knows how to shut up about stuff, and in the groups, I'd been telling people about my life, about how I had once been a famous bowler. Well, Fred didn't believe me. He thought I was lying. He thought I was having "delusions of grandeur," or whatever, and that if I was being untruthful and living in this fantasyland, I could never get better. The only thing was, it was all true.

So one day I'm going through some almanac or encyclopedia book or something, and there's this list of champion bowlers from recent years, and there's my name: Bob Perry. So I take the book and show Fred.

"There's my name—right there," I say. "Bob Perry. Firestone Tournament of Champions."

"So?" he says. "That's not even your real name! Your paperwork says 'Bob Purzycki.' You're still lying!"

He'd heard of Bob Perry, he knew who he was, and he was convinced that I wasn't him. I also told people that Tommy Lorenzo had a racehorse that he named Bob Perry, which was also true. But Fred said he was going to throw my ass out of the program because I was a liar, because I was living a lie, and nobody could succeed in recovery unless they were standing in the truth.

Because I didn't have any official form of identification at all, it was really hard for me to prove my point. This was in the days before Google, remember.

Finally, one day, Patsy and Jeannie come to visit.

"I'm getting thrown out of the program," I say.

"Whaddya mean you're getting thrown out of the program? What for?" Patsy says.

"Because they claim I'm lying about being Bob Perry, the bowler."

"Well, how come they don't believe you?"

"I dunno. Maybe I don't look like a famous bowler." (Actually, I never did.)

So Jeannie and Patsy have a meeting with Fred.

"Your brother is living a lie," he tells them. "He keeps telling everybody he's Bob Perry, he shows people Bob Perry's name in the encyclopedia, he claims there's a racehorse named after him. He can't get well if he's a pathological liar."

"Why do you think he's lying? He *is* Bob Perry," Patsy tells the guy. "He's my brother. He's not lying. It's all true."

Eventually the guy was forced to back down, but I think he was embarrassed by the whole thing and he kept being nasty to me. Hey, I couldn't help it if I was Bob Perry, the famous bowler. Or, at least, I *used to be* Bob Perry, the famous bowler. And now I was becoming that person again.

Fred hated that. He really did. He just didn't like me, and now he was being forced to admit that he was wrong. Not long after this, when I had that heart attack, he tried to use it as an excuse to not let me back into Freedom House once I got out of the hospital. He said that because I was indigent, Freedom House might be liable if I had another health emergency. Then he suggested that, once I got better, maybe I could agree to give 10 percent of my earnings to Freedom House, since the taxpayers were paying my way. But I told him that wasn't true—United Way paid $375 a week for me to stay there. They took my paycheck, half went to Freedom House and half went to the bank (to create a kind of forced savings account), and I got $20 a week for spending money. The taxpayer wasn't out a dime. So anyway, we had a dispute that never got resolved.

Before too long, Fred arranged to have my stay at Freedom House terminated. He put my stuff outside the building, and I never saw him again.

Patsy came to pick me up when I left Freedom House. She'd agreed to take me back to her house in Pompton Plains and let me stay there for a couple of days until I figured out what I was going to do next. When she let me in the front door of her house, there was her husband James, standing there. My pissed-off brother-in-law. The guy who had threatened to send me to an early grave if he ever caught me in his house.

"Welcome home," he says, reaching out to give me this huge hug. I mean, you could have knocked me over with a feather.

Then he sits me down at the kitchen table.

"I just want to say, I wish you the best," he says. "I'm here to help you."

This was the same man I had robbed, cheated, and stolen from. And he was, at the time, a sick man. He had prostate cancer and he wasn't doing too good.

"I don't know what I can do to help you," I say to James. "I mean, I know I've done you wrong. I almost wrecked you and Patsy's marriage, and I know you love her. If there's anything I can do to make things right, please tell me. Because I'm just trying to do the next right thing, trying to make up for everything I've done wrong. I'm trying to live my life one day at a time."

And it's a funny thing—a really funny thing, if you think about it—but James later told me that the whole idea of "living one day at a time" was the greatest gift I ever gave him, since he was struggling to face the possibility of his own death by cancer. It really helped him. After all, the stuff you learn in AA is not just about learning how to quit living like a drunk. It's about learning how to live.

There's a line in a blues song I once heard that goes, "If thoughts could kill, we'd all be dead." But, by the grace of God, somehow or another, it's possible for people to be transformed by love and actually change. And if both James and I could change, then anybody can. He turned out to be a wonderful man.

I had gone to James and Patsy's house with the intention of staying for a couple of nights. I wound up staying for a year and a half.

CHAPTER 14

THE ROAD TO HELL

LIVING AT JAMES AND PATSY'S HOUSE in Pompton Plains, with its nice lawn and clean sheets and all the comforts of home, was like getting a second shot at life. I was going to meetings all the time, trying to get my life together, and learning how to live with a "new employer"—God—running the ship.

I made contact with my old friend Tony, whose business, Tri-State Telephone, would set up a whole telephone system for movie and TV sets for shows being filmed around New York. He had a production office on Twenty-Third Street at West Side Highway, on Chelsea Piers. Me and Tony were great friends, so he gave me a job, basically as a gofer. But it was a brutal routine, in which I had to wake up at 5:00 a.m. to catch the bus into the City, get to Manhattan by 6:30 or 7:00, work all day, come back to Jersey, and attend an 8:00 meeting almost every night. And Tony was tough on me, too, even though he loved me. They'd have all this food laid out for the crews—we worked on *Law & Order* and other big shows—and he'd give me a raft of shit if I touched any of it. For a recently homeless person, all them tiny hot dogs and pickles and cheese were practically irresistible. So after 6 months or so, I told Patsy I was looking for another job.

Then one day I ran into my old bowling friend Mike Foti (the guy I won the doubles championship with, back in the '80s).

"There's this guy I know in Union City who owns a bowling alley called New Bowl-Rite Lanes," Mike says. "He knows about you, of course—he thinks you can help with his business, just by being around, being well known, helping people bowl, whatever. He's a Polack, too—C.J. Egnosky. His wife's name is Annie Lord. Great people. They've got this doubles tournament coming up over there, so why don't you enter? Get to know these guys a little?"

So me and my friend Adam Monks go over there to Union City to this slightly seedy bowling alley called New Bowl-Rite Lanes, and we bowl in this tournament and we do okay. I hit it off with C.J. right away. He's a short, thick guy, a few years younger than me, and he's really warm and funny. He shows me around his bowling business, which is very near to a pretty rundown, mostly-Latino area, almost but not quite a ghetto. It is only 2 blocks from Jersey City (this was before the yuppies started invading Hoboken). Most of the people in the bowling alley look like Mexicans or Puerto Ricans to me.

"Whaddya think?" C.J. says.

"Whaddya mean, what do I think?"

"Well, would you want to work here? I can't pay you a lot of money, but I'd love for you to work here. I think your reputation and your knowledge would help my business."

I think about this for a little while.

"I don't know if I can take this job," I say. "Look: I'm sober almost 3 years, and my sobriety is more important than bowling."

C.J.'s face kind of brightens up.

"I know all about that," he says. "I'm sober 8 years. And my sponsor is my wife Annie's dad. He's got 25 years. How does $150 a week sound?"

"Well, that sounds alright," I say. "But you're going to get a lot of slack for hiring me—you know that, right? I used to be pretty famous, but nobody has seen me in years. Nobody knows where I've been. And I'd rather just skip the whole story."

"That's okay," C.J. says. "I can handle that."

So I went to work for C.J. and Annie at the New Bowl-Rite Lanes in Union City. It was sometime during the winter of 1994.

C.J. and Annie were the most wonderful people I'd ever met. Not only were they sweet, funny, and kind, they knew all about the disease of alcoholism, so I didn't really have to explain to them where I had been. They were just the greatest friends a guy could find.

So I started working in the bowling alley, helping to run the pro shop, working the front desk, cleaning the lanes, whatever they needed. And it didn't take me long to notice that C.J. and Annie, my great new friends, were getting robbed blind. See, a lot of it was cash business, because their customers didn't use credit cards much. So I'd see, say, the girl at the snack bar charge a guy five bucks for a hamburger, but only put three bucks in the cash register. She wouldn't ring it up. I saw the same thing happening all over, at the ball rental counter, at the front desk, everywhere except the bar, where a girl named Carol, who was honest as the day was long, was in charge.

I guess I noticed these things because, after all, I had once been a junkie and a thief.

So I went to C.J. and told him what I was seeing.

"Is everybody stealing from me?" he asks me.

"Yeah," I say. "Everybody is stealing from you. Everybody except me and Carol."

You could see C.J.'s face just fall.

I didn't quite realize this at the time, but financially, that bowling alley had become a nightmare for them. They had already lost their home and had to move in with Annie's parents. But they still had all this debt hanging over their heads, part of it left over from a previous business partner who had been stealing from them, too.

Why do the good people, the honest people, get targeted by the crooks? Because they're honest, and it takes them a long time to realize they're getting ripped off.

The long and the short of it was that C.J. and Annie owed something like $57,000 in back rent on the building, and the landlord had started getting heavy with them. He was a guy who worked for the Foodtown grocery chain and owned a couple of buildings. Now he was starting to get nasty with my new friends. Finally he sent over a guy named Jimmy Bozzo. Jimmy was his henchman, the manager of his buildings. He walked like a tough guy and talked like a wiseguy. He started to get real threatening.

"You better come up with the money you owe, or else," he'd say to them. And Annie, she was just this little sweet-faced woman, probably didn't weigh more than 125 pounds, she'd just burst into tears. A lot of the back-rent situation had to do with their deadbeat former partner, but the fact was, the rent was owed and Bozzo was gunning for them.

Finally one day he came into the bowling alley and confronted C.J. I just happened to be standing there, and I saw the whole thing unfold. The situation sort of escalated, real quick.

Finally Bozzo just says, "I want all my money by Monday, or else."

And at this point, I just couldn't help but jump in. I'd seen guys like this all my life. I knew Gotti and Cabert and them guys. And this guy was just a fugazi, a fake.

"Or else?" I say to the guy. "What's the 'or else'?"

"I'm not talking to you, Jack," Bozzo says. "Who the fuck are you?"

"I'm their friend."

"Well, you need to be quiet."

"I'm not going to be quiet. What are you threatening my friends with?"

"Look: This here is none of your business. Keep your nose out of it."

"I work here. They're my friends. How about this? If you got some disagreement, that's fine. We can work it out. How about you come back here on Monday, and I'll bring a friend, and we'll work it out. Okay?"

Bozzo pauses a couple of beats, thinking.

"Well, I don't give a shit who you bring Monday. You just get your ass here and bring me my money."

And Bozzo goes strutting out of there, like a little rooster.

C.J. and Annie were really scared. They weren't used to this kind of stuff. They didn't have the money to pay the guy—so they were freaking out.

"Look," I say to them, "I can help you. I've got an old friend who can help you."

"Yeah? Who's that?" C.J. says.

"My Uncle Raymond," I say.

To be honest, I had never mentioned Uncle Raymond—or John Gotti, Bobby Cabert, or any of them other scary guys—to C.J. or Annie before. I never told them I was actually on pretty friendly terms with some pretty spooky people. I just wanted to help them. I was just trying to be a friend. I never really thought it through, which is what you're supposed to do when you're trying to be sober.

They say the road to hell is paved with good intentions. Well, I never really understood what that meant. But now, even though I'd stacked together 3 years of sobriety and was only trying to help out some friends in need, my whole dark past was about to come back to haunt me, like zombies rising out of the grave in *Night of the Living Dead*.

"C.J.," I say, "it's time to go see Uncle Raymond."

CHAPTER 15

THE RETURN OF UNCLE RAYMOND

DURING THOSE LONG, DARK, EMPTY YEARS on the streets of New York, when I was a dead man walking, a vampire, "nothing but a chemical," as my sister later said, there was one person besides Patsy whose heart was breaking over me, who worried and wondered about me constantly, even though I never knew it at the time. That person was the man I knew as Uncle Raymond. Only me and Bobby Schumacher called Raymond "Uncle," because he did not have any children of his own and always treated the two of us as if we were his nephews. Really, more like his sons.

Raymond was a Polack (his Polish wife hardly spoke any English at all), and he liked it that I was Polish on my dad's side. Like I said before, in those days everybody in North Jersey was pretty much divided into ethnic enclaves, with the Polacks sticking with the Polacks, the Italians with the Italians, the blacks with the blacks, and the gangsters with the gangsters. Paterson wasn't any sort of big, happy family—it was a whole bunch of unhappy families that didn't really talk to each other much.

To everybody else except me and Bobby Schumacher, Raymond was known as "the fat man" or "fat Raymond." He wasn't fat, though; he was just stout, like a fucking oak tree, and strong as an ox. I once saw him tip over a full barrel that must have weighed 2,000 pounds. (This was in the middle of the night on some back road, unloading a truck for a "swag" job—meaning, moving stolen merchandise—but that's another story.) Just through his physical presence, the man commanded respect. All the connected guys used to use the word "weight" to describe someone who was powerful, who was feared. Well, Uncle Raymond was a guy who had weight, and he knew how to throw it around. Maybe they called him "fat Raymond" not so much because he was overweight but because he walked into a room like a fuckin' Mack truck. Uncle Raymond had a scary side, especially when he'd been drinking Manhattans with Seagram's VO, but he also had a very sweet side, too. He loved to help people. There was this thing where you could pay 10 bucks to become a pen pal to a kid somewhere, and he spent hundreds of dollars, writing to kids he didn't even know. He was in the trucking business, and if he came across a farmer that had a load of hay that needed to be moved, he'd do it for the guy for free. He loved doing shit like that.

He also looked after the people that were loyal to him, that belonged to him. People like me. Uncle Raymond and Cabert and Gotti: Their whole way of living was like something out of some ancient time, like maybe a thousand years ago, when all the peasants were protected by a local king or a baron or whatever, and at the same time they feared the guy to death.

Raymond was 17 years older than me, so he was less a substitute father and more like the big brother I never had. He had dirty blond hair, wore glasses, and smoked constantly. When he wanted to tell me something serious, something important, he would shove his glasses down to the end of his nose and peer over the tops of them at me. His eyes were like fucking laser beams.

"Perry!" he'd say, as if he were beating me over the head with a blunt object. "Listen to me!"

And I always listened. I listened because Uncle Raymond was the smartest man I ever knew. Everything I ever learned about the Mob, I learned from him.

At the racetrack, where he loved to be more than anywhere else, Uncle Raymond was like a goddamned Rhodes Scholar. He and his crew—the small group of guys that hung around with him like a school of little fish following a big fish—were known as the best grass-race bettors anywhere. Raymond could consistently take short money—say, three or four hundred dollars—and turn it into 10 or 15 thousand, like magic. He did it by understanding breeding and genetics, things almost nobody understood at the time, by studying the *Daily Racing Form,* by watching and listening and understanding. He was a genius at the track. Back in those days there wasn't too much horseracing on TV, so you had to go to the track yourself. So Uncle Raymond and his crew—a guy known as Tom Bill, who was a cop from Bloomfield, New Jersey; a guy named Skinner; a schoolteacher named Tony Margotta (who was actually Bobby Cabert's nephew); and me—would pile into Uncle Raymond's car and drive to the track together.

When grass season came around, like in April in New York, Uncle Raymond and his crew would go to all the tracks in Jersey: Garden State Park, Monmouth Park, and the Meadowlands; Pimlico in Baltimore; Delaware Racetrack in Delaware; and Philadelphia Racetrack outside Philadelphia. Sometimes we'd even go down to Churchill Downs, in Kentucky, or other tracks down in Florida. One time, I remember, these guys actually won $365,000 at the track. I also remember that, except the money Raymond won, all that money was gone within a couple of weeks. (Uncle Raymond lived modestly, in a modest house, and was never extravagant about anything except fancy meals and booze. When he won big at the track, he handed the money over to his wife, whose name was a Polish version of Maryann that I could never quite pronounce. Then he'd start betting again, as if he hardly had any money at all. The whole thing was a big mind game for him.)

In some ways, I was kind of a gofer for Uncle Raymond, picking up the *Daily Racing Form* and delivering it to his house, going to the track to place his bets if he couldn't make it, and bringing back his money if he won. Later I realized that letting me handle the money like that was his way of testing me to see if I could be trusted. And I could be trusted, at least in those early days before booze and dope took over my life.

Another thing about Uncle Raymond, besides his brains, was his guts. He didn't seem to be afraid of anything or anybody. If you were in a war, you'd want him on your side. He was one of the few people who didn't even seem to be afraid of Bobby Cabert, a connected guy who later became a made man in the Gambino crime family. Raymond was the only one who could calm Cabert down when he got all riled up and drunk and angry and dangerous. "It's no good to be angry," he'd say to Cabert, and then he'd just get up and fucking leave. He didn't care. He wasn't scared, even though Cabert—who was his best friend—could be about as scary as any human being could be.

When you "belonged" to Uncle Raymond, like I did, you knew you were being looked after, not just by him but by his whole crew and all these other people who knew him—older men you might never even know were keeping an eye on you, making sure you were safe. I felt loved by him (and, sometimes, dominated and controlled by him, especially when I was fucking up).

Uncle Raymond was a guy who grew up in New Jersey and had been in "the rackets" his whole life without once ever getting arrested. Being in the rackets just meant figuring out how to make money on the street, sometimes legally but usually illegally or semi-illegally, without getting caught or resorting to real serious violence. Yeah, sure: Cabert and other people Raymond knew were in the Mob. Shit, half the people I grew up with in New Jersey at that time were connected.

But Uncle Raymond wasn't in the Mob. He was a rackets guy, not a Mob guy.

What Uncle Raymond actually did for a living was drive trucks that picked up or delivered stuff to foundries, scrapyards, and dealers all up and down the East Coast. He also sometimes brought shrimp and seafood up from the Gulf. But there was sort of a sunny side to this business—a legal side—and a shady side, and I think most of it was on the shady side. Like he'd run a truckload of scrap metal down to some foundry in South Carolina or Alabama or wherever. And after he'd unload the truck, he'd look around for something to carry back, so he wouldn't be running an empty load back to New Jersey

"Hey, what's in all them barrels over there?" he'd ask.

"That's the scrap metal they scraped out of the furnaces," some guy would say.

"How about if I take those barrels off you for 500 bucks?"

And if the guy agreed, they'd make a cash deal on the spot, no papers or nothing (since the guy didn't actually own the stuff, of course), Uncle Raymond would load up the truck, and then he'd "run the road" all the way back to New Jersey—getting around all the weigh stations on the interstate by taking back roads, which he knew like the back of his hand. Back in Newark or Hoboken, where he knew all the scrap dealers, he'd sell the load to some guy and triple his money because he bought the shit for pennies on the dollar.

Uncle Raymond always said there was a million dollars in junk—scrap metal, auto parts, even dirt—and he always seemed to be able to find it.

Uncle Raymond would also sometimes get these swag jobs, and I'd sometimes go along to help, in the dead of night, on some back road somewhere. Raymond would pay me right away, in cash, of course, and I would immediately forget that any of it had ever happened. I had a really lousy memory that way. I knew that what I was doing wasn't legit, but I always made a day's pay—and good pay, too (a lot of times even more than I could make bowling)—working for Uncle

Raymond. Raymond used to like to say he was in the iron and steel business.

"My mother irons, and I steal," he'd say.

One time Uncle Raymond went down to Arkansas or somewhere, and he needed a load of something to bring back. Turned out one of the big businesses down there was rice, so he wound up coming back with something like 30,000 fuckin' pounds of rice. So he figured out a way to sell this rice to all these Chinese restaurants in Bergen and Hudson Counties for six cents a pound (after he'd bought the shit for two cents a pound or whatever).

So one night I'm delivering this truckload of rice to this Chinese restaurant called Jade Fountain in North Arlington (one of Bobby Cabert and Uncle Raymond's favorite hangouts), when all of a sudden this black car pulls up in the alley behind the restaurant, where I've got the truck parked.

Some guy jumps out, and I can see he's got a long gun, a rifle or a shotgun or something.

"You no deliver rice!" he yells, pointing the thing at me.

"What are you talking about, 'Me no deliver rice'? Listen, you don't know whose rice this is."

"Me no care. You no deliver rice!"

"Listen, man, you need to put that gun down," I say. "I'll be right back."

So I go inside, where Uncle Raymond and Cabert are sitting in a booth, getting wasted on Manhattans made with Seagram's VO, their favorite. (Half the time, he and Cabert would get so wasted at Jade Fountain that they'd start having these vicious arguments, and then they'd have to call a cab to get them home.)

"Listen, Raymond, you need to come outside," I tell him. "I got a problem."

"What problem?"

"There's this fucking Chinese guy looking to shoot me, okay?"

So Raymond and Cabert step outside.

170

"What's the problem?" they ask the guy, who is not waving his gun around anymore.

"You no deliver rice to Chinese!"

"You know whose rice this is?" Raymond says. "It's my rice." Uncle Raymond is about twice the size of this little Chinese dude. "Who you work for?"

"Harry Moon. He the owner."

"Well, why don't we get Harry Moon and have a little sit-down over the rice," Raymond says. He calms the guy down, and later everybody goes down to Canal Street in the City and meets with this Chinese Mob guy. "You not allowed to sell my people rice," he says.

"Why not?" Uncle Raymond says.

"Only Chinese sell rice to Chinese."

"Well, how about if I sell it to you instead of all these restaurants, and then you sell it to them," Uncle Raymond suggests. "I'll give you a good price. But there's just one thing: You've got to buy it all."

The Chinese Mob guy takes a minute to think about it. You can just see the wheels turning in his brain.

"No problem," he says finally. "You give me good price, I take it all."

So the next time Uncle Raymond took a truckload of scrap down to Arkansas, he came back with, like, another 30,000 pounds of rice. He delivered it all to this Chinese guy in New York. A few weeks later, he came back from Arkansas with another truckload of rice and delivered it to the guy. Then the next time, I got the job of driving this truck filled with 15 tons of rice to the guy in New York. When I got there, he came out, and he was yelling at me.

"No more rice!" he shouts.

"You said you were gonna buy it all," I say to him.

"No more rice! Tell your uncle, no more rice!"

The Mob guy had enough rice by now to last him 3 fucking years. And he'd learned an important lesson: Don't make deals with Raymond, especially after you tried pushing him around.

After all those years living on the street, and during the first years of my recovery, Uncle Raymond had been gone from my life. Although I thought about him all the time, in all the years since my life disappeared down the dark hole of addiction, I had seen Uncle Raymond only once, and that time just by accident.

At the time, I was still living with Patsy and James, working for Tony in the city. One weekend I took the cheap bus to the Meadowlands, and I was walking along the rail down by the track and there was Uncle Raymond sitting in the front row, wearing a Frank Sinatra hat and smoking, as always. This huge block of a man, full of power, with the *Daily Racing Form* folded under his arm.

"Perry!" he yells, in that gravelly, growly voice. "How ya doin'?"

"I'm doing good, Raymond," I say, genuinely shocked and also happy to see him.

I was a little bit on edge, too, because of all the people I had done wrong when I was on the street, and all them blackouts. I wasn't entirely sure I hadn't done Uncle Raymond wrong.

He gets up off the seat—he's graying, I notice, and he's gained weight—and he walks toward me. He gives me this big hug, and then we chat it up a little. I tell him, among other things, that I have been sober 3 years already.

"If you need help, come and see me," he says, very close and earnest, just as we're parting. "I love you. I'm proud of you. Please let me know if you need anything."

I remembered that encounter at the Meadowlands when C.J. and Annie started getting in trouble at the bowling alley, and that's why I decided to go see "the fat man," a man I once loved more than my own father. C.J. and I drove over to Raymond's modest little house in North Arlington. I asked C.J. to wait in the car and knocked on the door. Uncle Raymond's wife answered the door. She had always loved me.

"Bobby here!" she shouts. "Bobby here!"

Then she reaches out and grabs my face in her hands.

"Oh, my God, you're beautiful!" she says.

I was clean and sober, dressed nice, and I even had teeth. It was great to see her after all I'd been through.

Uncle Raymond had this downstairs room all fixed up, with an easy chair and a TV and everything. It was like the lion's den, nice and safe and cool down there. So I went downstairs and there was Raymond, sitting there like the La-Z-Boy king. He'd gained enough weight that I guess he would have had trouble getting up the stairs. He beamed when he looked at me.

"Perry!" he says. "How ya doin?"

He always said that. We chatted it up, and after a little while I get around to the reason I came.

"I need to talk to you," I say. "I've got a problem. See, I'm working in Union City at this bowling alley owned by a couple of friends of mine, C.J. and Annie. C.J.'s a Polack."

"Yeah, I know—New Bowl-Rite Lanes," he says. (Uncle Raymond always seemed to know everything, at least everything that was happening to people he cared about.)

"Well, this little sawed-off fugazi wiseguy named Jimmy Bozzo is really leaning on them about a bill for back rent. It's for, like, $57,000. They're shittin' bricks over this, Raymond. They don't have no money. They already lost their house. And the thing is, most of it is left over from a crooked partner they had, a guy who was robbing them blind."

Uncle Raymond is glaring at me over the tops of his glasses, just burning into me with his eyeballs. You can see his mind working, calculating.

"So the debt is legit?"

"Yeah. But it's not even their fault. C.J. is the best friend a man could have—he's 8 years sober, and he's helping me save my life."

"So whaddya want me to do?"

"We just want you to tell this guy to back off. Get him to leave us alone."

"What do I get out of it?"

"You get to help me. And I think C.J. would pay you for your help."

"Why does this guy Bozzo, or whatever it is, think he's somebody?"

"This guy thinks he's everybody. He won't back off."

Uncle Raymond looks me over, considering.

You know, he loved me, he considered me almost like a son. He was happy to see that I was cleaned up and sober. He could see that I cared for these people. And C.J. was a fellow Polack.

"Okay," he says finally. "Bring this guy C.J. by to see me."

"He's waiting out in the car."

So I went out there and brought C.J. downstairs, and the two of them really hit it off.

Finally Uncle Raymond says to me, "Okay, make the meeting."

"How about Monday morning, 10:30?"

"Fine. But I gotta go get somebody."

"Who?"

"Nicky the Plumber."

Nicky the Plumber was, like, 70 years old, a half-ass wiseguy. He was about as threatening as, well, a 70-year-old plumber. But he was part of Raymond's crew, a guy who was on the inside of Raymond's world, who knew where all the bodies were buried (so to speak). I really don't know why Uncle Raymond wanted him to come along. But, unfortunately, the fact that he wanted Nicky the Plumber to come along reminded me of something I wasn't really admitting to myself. Let's face it: The only reason I had suggested that Uncle Raymond get involved at all was because he knew the guy who knew the guy who knew the guy. He was connected. He was scary. He had "weight." He could help C.J. and Annie, innocent parties, by threatening the shit out of this guy Bozzo, not personally, but through the guy who knew the guy. It was like Bobby Cabert once said to me: If the Mob comes after you, you'll never see it, and you'll never feel it. It will just get done.

Uncle Raymond wasn't going to off the guy, of course, but he was going to figure out a way to put a hurt on him—maybe a big hurt—at a distance. My dilemma was this: I had been sober 3 years. I had admitted that I was powerless over alcohol and dope, that I had completely failed to live my life without the help of God. I was walking on this new path, a path of honesty and integrity and helping others, a spiritual path. So what the fuck was I doing dragging in a connected guy to threaten somebody over an unpaid debt? By doing this, I was reaching back into my dark past. I was bringing all the old ghosts back to life. But now I was pushing all this down into the memory hole, the blackout hole, and trying to forget about it. I was just trying to help a friend, I told myself.

Little did I know I was about to begin one of the darkest chapters of my life.

CHAPTER 16

THE DEAL GOES DOWN

SO THEN THE MOST amazing thing happened.

The deal went down, and I wound up a hero. No shit!

Uncle Raymond and Nicky the Plumber have a meeting with that little prick Bozzo at the bowling alley at 10:30 that Monday morning, as planned. When Bozzo shows up, he's in a bad mood, and he don't want to hear nothing about how we're going to make no deals. He just wants his money, or he's going to throw C.J. and Annie out on their ass. But then Uncle Raymond and Bozzo walk into the bar—it's got them swinging half-doors, like one of them old-time saloons in the Wild West movies—and I can hear them talking and then the talking turns to laughing, and when they come out an hour later, it's like they're old Army buddies or some damn thing.

"How youse guys doin'?" Bozzo says, all jolly, when he walks past me and another guy standing there at the front desk. I'd never heard him talk like that before.

"Uh—we're doin' okay."

"See youse tomorrow!" he says to Raymond, like Raymond is his long-lost chum, and then he goes swaggering out in that little sawed-off tough-guy way he had.

I was totally shocked. But it turned out, these guys all got along great. They had friends in common. They knew the same neighborhoods. They worked out a deal about how C.J. and Annie could pay back the debt, in small payments, over time, even though the business wasn't doing well and it would be tough and slow. But nobody was getting heavy or making threats or anything. Everybody was happy. Bozzo was happy, C.J. and Annie were happy, Uncle Raymond was happy, and I was happy. I felt useful. C.J. had a friend, and everything was going to work out.

Like I said, I was a fucking hero.

Or so I thought.

About this same time, in the winter of 1995, I ran into my old friend Tommy Lorenzo at the racetrack. At least I saw him at a distance, standing at the rail with that good-for-nothing kid Steve that he was always with now. Steve and I didn't get along at all—I knew what he was up to, trying to suck up all of Tommy's family money, and Steve knew that I knew. In fact, me and Tommy had had a big argument over Steve, and for a while we weren't speaking to each other.

I had also figured out that Tommy had a big secret (or, at least, he thought it was a secret). He and Steve lived together, and they weren't just roommates. Tommy was gay. But I still loved him and cared about him, and it shocked me and saddened me to see that now, even at 50 yards, standing there in the broad daylight, Tommy looked absolutely terrible. He was only 10 years older than me, but he looked old enough to be my father. It turned out that Tommy was dying of AIDS—in fact, he only had a few more months to live. I was convinced Steve had AIDS and gave it to Tommy. I felt really bad when I saw Tommy looking like that. I loved him. He had been my best friend.

Tommy and I had had a big fight over one other, more important thing, too. By then, I was 3 years sober, and I had tried to help Tommy get sober, too. One time I actually drove him up to St. Christopher's Inn and dropped him off, but he left that place so fast he actually beat me back home. Another time, I helped him get sober 5 days, and one other time, he made it 30 days, but he always went back out. He just didn't have the heart for it.

"You gotta get sober," I said to Tommy one time.

"You gotta leave me alone," he replied.

In the old days, of course, Tommy Lorenzo and I had been like Butch Cassidy and the Sundance Kid—two alcoholic addicts who were thick as thieves, feeding on each other's addictions to booze, crack, coke, or whatever else we could get into. Then I sobered up, and Steve moved in with Tommy. And Steve didn't want me coming around no more. I tried to warn Tommy that Steve was no good, but he was sick and he wasn't listening. As his death got closer, though, Tommy and I became real friends again. And we were still friends— real, true friends—the day he died.

I went to Tommy's funeral with my sisters Patsy and Jeannie. Just as I was walking into the front room of the funeral home, I walked past my old flame, Debbie, who was leaving the building with her husband, Ron. I caught her eye for just a second, and we just kind of nodded but didn't say anything, because there was too much pain and anger between us. I wished I could reach out and touch her, tell her I had changed so much since those days when I had done her wrong, when we lived together in that little apartment with Jackson the dog, but I couldn't. It was like trying to reach across the Grand Canyon. She was such a great woman, and I lost her, along with all the other joys and treasures I lost. In that moment, it seemed like my whole life was just a story of loss and regret and mistakes.

There was one other person I was afraid I might run into at the funeral home, and I did. That was Tommy's dad, Rocco, who was very old at the time, in his late eighties maybe. When he looked over at me from across the room, he might as well have been blasting my ass with a submachine gun. Rocco was a mean, old, nasty guy, and he hated me, because Tommy and I had gotten into such trouble together. I think he also hated me because, at the end, Tommy was still doing drugs and I wasn't. But I walked up to him anyhow. He was sitting there in a chair with some other members of the family.

"I'm really sorry about Tommy," I say to Rocco. "You know, I loved him like a brother."

And Rocco gets right up in my face and snarls, "You're the reason my son is dead!"

"I'm the reason?" I say, genuinely surprised. "The reason Tommy is dead is right over there," I say, pointing across the room at Steve. "Your son was a grown man and he made his own choices. And he got AIDS from that kid over there. I didn't have nothing to do with that!"

But Rocco wasn't listening. I guess he was kind of blind with grief.

"Get the hell out of this funeral home!" he snaps at me.

"Okay, if that's what you want, I'll do that. But I loved Tommy, and I still do. I'm as sorry as anyone that he's gone."

And I left.

After Uncle Raymond and Nicky the Plumber helped C.J. and Annie straighten out the mess their finances were in, Raymond came back into my life again. I loved having Uncle Raymond back in my life. I admired him more than any other person I ever met. To me, he was part big brother, part mentor, and part God.

He and Nicky the Plumber would stop by the bowling alley almost every day, just to chat or to have a couple of Manhattans at the bar and watch the action on the lanes. Uncle Raymond would sit there on a barstool in a cloud of blue cigarette smoke, this huge, powerful man, just surveying the world like Santa Claus, and Nicky would sit beside him, pretty soon drifting off to sleep. Nicky the Plumber was old and kind of feeble by this time, and he was always nodding off.

Meanwhile, C.J. and Annie had asked me to supervise cleaning up the third floor of the building. When they took over the place, they'd done some big renovations downstairs, where there were 16 lanes. In the process, they had stored some big piles of lumber up on the third floor (where there were also an additional eight lanes).

So now they wanted it cleaned up.

I went up there and looked the situation over—this huge, dimly-lit room, like a cavern, with piles of junk everywhere—and I realized I'd need maybe four or five of them huge dumpsters, like they have at construction sites. I'd need the big kind, the 30- or 40-yard-long ones. And I knew exactly who to ask. He was sitting right there, nodding off at the bar.

See, Nicky the Plumber might have been old and about as scary as a Chihuahua. But he was connected—big time. He'd been part of the New Jersey rackets, and the Mob, his whole life. Uncle Raymond was best friends with Bobby Cabert, and Nicky the Plumber was best friends with Cabert too. Cabert and Nicky went way, way back. Nicky the Plumber really did know where all the bodies were buried— because, as it happened, Bobby Cabert was now in federal prison, sent there as a result of various convictions, including a couple of murders he had committed for the Mob. But he was also in prison because of his involvement in the mobbed-up garbage business in New York and New Jersey. If anybody knew where to get a couple of construction-size dumpsters, it was Bobby Cabert. (Even though Cabert was in jail, he could still get stuff done.) Nicky the Plumber was also part of Uncle Raymond's crew—part of his own little army. None of these gangsters worked alone; they worked as a family, an entourage. And Nicky was in the thick of it.

So I asked Nicky the Plumber if I could maybe get a couple of them big dumpsters in here. He said, no problem, and he went and asked Cabert about it. And before you know it, three or four giant dumpsters got delivered to the vacant lot outside the bowling alley— for free. Normally these things rented for, like, $400 or $500 apiece. But they just appeared, like magic, and so we started throwing shit out the third floor window into these dumpsters, and then the shit got hauled away, and the city never gave us no trouble at all. It was really like magic. Or so I thought.

Look: You gotta understand something. Part of the code of ethics of that place and time, and being around connected people, was that you never asked questions. What am I, some kind of fuckin' novel writer? You just had to know enough not to ask. You also had to be trusted not to say anything, especially if you got arrested. Maybe that's why Bobby Cabert had always liked me—I could be trusted, and I never asked any questions.

One time Raymond and I were talking about all our adventures, about me delivering a mysterious package to some guy at a junkyard, about swag jobs on back roads in the middle of the night, and Uncle Raymond said, "We oughta write a book!"

Then he thought a second, and laughed. "Nah—they'd kill us!"

It was like that. The biggest virtue was: No questions. The second biggest virtue was: Shut the fuck up. (And by the way: The only reason I feel safe telling you this now is that all those other people are dead.)

So, even though I knew Cabert was really in the Mob, and probably had done all kinds of bad shit, all I really knew was that he was never anything but nice to me. I might have heard about stuff he supposedly did, but I never saw him actually do any of that shit, and I could kind of push that away in my mind. Bobby Cabert was just Bobby. He was my friend. I helped him, he helped me.

But some of the dirty details about Cabert had already come out. It was a few years earlier that a guy named Salvatore ("Sammy the Bull") Gravano became the highest-ranking member of the Mob to rat out his partners in crime. He was what they call an underboss, directly beneath John Gotti, who was by then boss of the whole Gambino crime family. Gravano had been involved in a whole bunch of mob hits, some of them ordered by Gotti, and he sort of blew the lid off the Gambino family and a lot of other people in that world. (Boy, if anybody needed the Witness Protection Program, it was that guy!) His trial, in Manhattan federal court in 1993, made all the papers, of course.

One name that came up repeatedly during his testimony was Bobby Cabert. After Gravano fingered Cabert as the triggerman in the murder of Francesco Oliveri (and for his participation in other crimes), Cabert was arrested, convicted, and sent to a federal penitentiary, where he lived out the remainder of his days on Earth.

In spite of Gravano's betrayal, loyalty was Bobby Cabert's big thing. He was the most loyal person I ever met. If you belonged to Cabert, he would protect you no matter what. That's one of the reasons why, even after he went to trial and got sentenced to federal prison, I kept running little errands for him, making sure his mail got to him in prison and shit like that. He'd call me at the bowling alley collect, through a third party, thinking that would throw the feds off, but it didn't.

One day Cabert asked me to get this computer to his daughter, and nobody knew where she was but me, so I got it to her. I felt that there were times when Cabert had helped me out, so I felt like I owed it to him to help him out as well. I could see that he was in a terrible situation, facing life in prison. But eventually C.J. and Annie told me to stop taking Cabert's calls at work; I guess mainly because it was interrupting my job, and maybe because they knew who I was talking to (and who might be listening in).

But for all kinds of other reasons, I finally just said to him, "Look, Bobby, I can't talk to you no more."

"I understand," he said. "But thanks for helping me anyhow."

I thought that was the end of it.

Actually, though, it was just the beginning.

CHAPTER 17

RULE NUMBER ONE: DON'T ASK NO QUESTIONS

RIGHT ABOUT THAT SAME TIME, Tommy Lorenzo's younger brother, Ray, walked into the bowling alley one day. I'd known Ray and Tommy's other brother, Ronnie, for years—they were a warm, close-knit family, and during my bad years I'd even spent a Christmas or two at their house. (In the bad years, there was no reason to go to my own house, because I'd just be thrown out.) I was also tight with Ray's teenage son, also named Tommy, who I was teaching to bowl. Ray had always been good to me, helping me, loaning me money, and whatnot. But there was one other thing I remembered about Ray when he walked in that winter day in 1995: Tommy had told me several times never to trust his brother.

"I need to talk to you," Ray says to me.

"What's the problem?"

"My dad needs your help."

So I'm thinking, *I'm supposed to help Rocco, the guy who threw me out of my best friend's funeral?*

"Well, you know that guy Dr. Richard and them? They're no good. You remember that $50,000 my brother loaned them guys?"

I remembered the loan, because Tommy had told me about it before he died. There was this sort of nutjob vitamin doctor named

Dr. Richard (pronounced "rish-ARD") who had supposedly come over from Europe with all these miraculous holistic medicines and vitamins, stuff that could cure Alzheimer's and also lameness in horses, and he had actually moved into the Lorenzos' house because he was trying to treat Tommy's mom, who had Alzheimer's, and also Rocco and Tommy's old Aunt Mary, who had helped raise the kids. It was a house full of old, sick people and this nutty vitamin doctor.

I was suspicious of the whole situation, but I wasn't too close to it, because at that point I was forbidden to go to the house because Rocco thought I was using Tommy to get drugs (this was before I got sober). But one day Tommy told me that the family had loaned this guy Dr. Richard and his partners $50,000 to help start a holistic health and vitamin business in New York.

"Yeah," I say to Ray, "I remember Tommy telling me about that."

"Well, the guy moves out of the house, goes to New York, sets up this business, and now he's got a big, successful vitamin business in New York, on Fifth Avenue and Twenty-Third Street. But when my dad calls the guy to get the loan back, the guy just laughs at him. He borrowed the money 7 fucking years ago. But he claims he paid the money back to Tommy before he died. You know, my dad's an old guy. It scared him. And he needs the money. He wants his money back."

It was not like I went around advertising it, but everybody around the bowling alley knew I had some very influential people in my life. People with connections, people with "weight," like Uncle Raymond and Nicky the Plumber and Bobby Cabert and John Gotti and them. Ray knew I was close to all these people—people who could get things done, sometimes in broad daylight, sometimes in the dark of night. I figured that was why we were having this conversation.

"Could you help us, for Tommy?" Ray says, kind of pleading.

"What makes you think I can get the money?"

"I know you know people. Go talk to your people. See if they could help. We'd pay them for their help. And one more thing. My father says that if you help us, he'll forgive you about what he said to you at the funeral home. He's very sorry he said that to you."

"I'll see what I can do," I say. "I'll let you know."

So now I had a lot to think about. This was a complicated debt, not like the last one, which was just about money. Settling up this debt had to do with restoring my best friend's father's honor. It had to do with me getting Rocco's forgiveness, setting things right between us. It had to do with helping out Tommy's family, who had been wronged, and trying to set things right with them about all my past evil deeds. It had to do with doing a personal favor in memory of Tommy, who I had loved. And, of course, it had to do with getting this phony-baloney quack doctor to pay back the 50 grand he stiffed Rocco for. Only it wasn't 50 grand no more. If you added 10 percent interest for 7 years, it was a whole lot more.

But I think, really, what made me want to get involved in this situation was that Ray was laying a big guilt trip on me. I was so sorry for the mess I'd made of my life, and being thrown out of the family I once considered almost like my own, that the chance to make things right again seemed worth whatever risk there might be.

So I make a pilgrimage back to Uncle Raymond's house in North Arlington, get let into the front door by his wife, who squeals something in Polish and grabs my face, and go downstairs to Raymond's basement throne room.

"Perry!" Uncle Raymond growls. "How ya doin'?" He's so heavy now he don't even bother to get up out of the chair.

By this time, I had a fabulous relationship with Uncle Raymond. We only lived a few blocks apart, and I'd see him all the time. I'd go make bets for him at the track, and when he'd win, which was often, I'd go by his house and give him the money. I would give him every penny of the money, too, because now I was trying to live in integrity and honesty. It was almost like all the lost, dark years, the years of addiction and homelessness and spiritual emptiness, had never happened. I was just Bobby, the talented, trustworthy kid from the neighborhood who loved to go to the track for his uncle.

So I explain the situation to Uncle Raymond. I tell him all about Tommy's brother's situation, and Rocco, and Dr. Richard. Uncle Raymond just listens quietly—calculating, analyzing—while I lay the whole thing out. His eyes narrow.

This was a man who had lived most of his life on the shadowy side of the law, but who had never been arrested even once. He was so smart that suspicion had almost become second nature, like an instinct.

He asks a bunch of questions about the specifics of the situation, where this guy Dr. Richard lives and works, whether Ray and Rocco could be trusted to pay him if he collected the loan, and so on.

"Is the loan legit?" he asks, which is what he always asked.

"Yeah," I say. "I think so. That's what Ray says."

"How much money is involved?"

"Well, the original loan was $50,000, but the loan is unpaid for 7 years, so it's a lot more."

Uncle Raymond stares at me, his eyes narrowing.

"Well, let me have a meeting with Tommy's brother," Raymond says. "I have to think about this."

So a meeting gets set up at the bowling alley between Ray Lorenzo, Uncle Raymond, and Nicky the Plumber. The three of them meet at the bowling alley and go into the bar through the swinging doors, just like before. They have a long conversation in there, without laughter, that lasts a long time.

I stay outside, at the front desk, waiting.

Finally, they come out and Ray leaves the building without speaking to me. Uncle Raymond takes me aside. He seems a little troubled.

"I don't know about this. I don't know if I want to do this. Not because of Tommy—I loved Tommy. I just don't like the deal. I have to think about it. I have to talk to my brothers about this."

One of Raymond's brothers, Chet, was a hopeless drunk with something like 10 or 20 DWIs. Raymond spent a fortune trying to get him sober or keep him sober. His other brother was named Stanley, but Raymond called him "Stoshu," which I guess was some Polish thing. These two brothers were like Laurel and Hardy, one fat and one skinny. Anyway, Uncle Raymond always consulted with his brothers whenever a deal made him nervous or didn't seem quite right. And I guess this was one of those deals.

I never asked any questions, of course. (Like, "What deal?") But afterward, Ray Lorenzo told me that Uncle Raymond had asked for a fee of five or 10 grand for collecting the debt, and he wanted it paid up front before he sent his boys to collect the money. Ray got mad at this, but in the end, he wound up agreeing to it. Uncle Raymond had also told Ray that, if anything happened—if anybody got arrested—he would pay the legal fees. I also knew, without being told, that Uncle Raymond would have to ask permission from whoever the guy was that "owned" the territory at Twenty-Third and Fifth. I really knew nothing more than that, and I didn't want to know nothing more. I only agreed to be the guy that collected the money. The bagman.

So sometime after that, Uncle Raymond and Nicky the Plumber paid a little visit to the nutty vitamin doctor's office on Fifth Avenue. It was a Sunday afternoon. I don't know what happened. I wasn't there. All I know is that later that afternoon, Uncle Raymond walked into the bowling alley with a check for $6,800 from Dr. Richard, made out to Rocco Lorenzo.

So a little while later, maybe a week, I got the job of going into the City to collect the next check. I decided to take this guy Louie along with me. Louie worked in the bowling alley and he was this big, hulking kid, a former high school football player. I wanted him to come because he was kind of intimidating. But he also wanted to go because, without being told, he was sort of putting it together that this was a mission to collect dirty money. And he was all starstruck about gangsters, like he was in *The Godfather* fan club or some shit.

So me and Louie take the train into the City, catch a cab over to Twenty-Third and Fifth, and take the elevator to the 19th floor. We come out into this sort of open office area, and there's a receptionist sitting there. I ask for Dr. Richard, and he comes out from a back office. He don't look like no fancy-pants doctor from Europe. He just looks like an ordinary guy. But, I don't know, I had been around Uncle Raymond long enough to be able to almost smell it when something ain't right. And something ain't right. Out of the corner of my eye, I'm noticing this guy sitting there in an easy chair, kind of pretending to be reading a magazine. And there's another guy on a ladder putting medicines or whatever up on a shelf.

"How ya doin'?" Dr. Richard says.

"Good. Have you got the payment?"

"Yeah," he says, kind of cheerfully. "Who do I make it out to?"

"Rocco Lorenzo."

But as he's writing the check, I'm thinking, *This guy is entirely too happy about writing this check*. When he's done, he hands it to me.

"I'll see you next week," I say, and me and Louie walk out of there.

Well, the guy gave me the money and nothing bad happened, so maybe there was nothing wrong after all, I thought. Ray and Uncle Raymond were getting paid. Rocco was getting his revenge. The dude was coughing it all up.

Man, I felt like a big shot again. I was using my connections to come through for Tommy Lorenzo and his brother and his father. I was scaring the shit out of the bad guys, just like in the Old West. But deep down I knew I shouldn't be doing this.

I was supposed to be working on my sobriety, not turning into a gofer for the Mob.

I knew it was wrong. I just didn't know how wrong.

When I got back to the bowling alley, I handed the check over to Ray Lorenzo. And he gave me a hundred bucks for my effort. A hundred bucks to hang my ass out over the edge. No shit. But I was starting to feel worse and worse about the whole thing. It stunk, and I knew it. I opened up to my sponsor about it. Jack always put it to me straight.

"Bobby," Jack said to me, "You can't be in AA and be in the Mob."

Which, when he put it that way, was like, duh.

But by this time, I felt like I was in too deep to back out. I felt like I'd made a deal with Uncle Raymond and Ray Lorenzo and I needed to hold up my end of the bargain.

So a couple of weeks later, I went back into the City to collect the next payment from Dr. Nutjob. But by now, the "wrong" bells were ringing all over the place.

The night before, a Tuesday night, I had to pick up Louie over by the Lincoln Tunnel, and he was just bawling like a baby.

"Man, what's the matter?" I ask him. He looks at me like a scared rabbit, like somebody that just got caught at something.

"A friend of mine just died," he says.

Then, a little while later, I drop Louie off at the bowling alley, and I run into his mother, and she just looks at me and shakes her head.

So the next day I have to go into the City to pick up the next check, and I ask my friend Dominick, the cop, to go with me, but he says he's busy. So I call ahead to tell Dr. Richard I'm coming, take the train to Manhattan, catch a cab over to Twenty-Third and Fifth, and go up to the 19th floor. When the elevator door opens, there's a sort of chain-link fence with a gate you have to walk through, like if there's some construction going on, but I couldn't see any construction going on. And I notice that same guy, sitting in that same easy chair, like a store dummy, and that same guy, up on a ladder, putting medicines on a shelf. When Dr. Richard comes out of the back office, I tell him I want cash, but he says he only has a check, so he writes me a check and I leave—quickly. I get on the elevator but I only go down to the 15th floor. I get off, go over in a corner and rip up that check into tiny pieces. Then I walk all the way down to the ground floor. Something's up, and I know it. Something just ain't right.

Then I walk out into the street. There's one of them little deli stands there, so I buy a banana and a Diet Pepsi. I start to walk down the sidewalk, but out of the corner of my eye it looks like when I take a step, the whole street moves with me. So I walk across the street, and it seems to me like a whole bunch of people cross the street with me. It's like one of them Broadway musicals. On the other side of the street is a guy standing there, apparently trying to catch a cab, but he isn't trying very hard, and when a cab stops, he just motions the cabbie to keep moving.

"Don't you want this cab?" I say to the guy.

"Naw, not now," he says, which was weird.

So I open the back door of the cab and all of a sudden that guy and a whole chorus line of other people come to life. The guy and a couple of other huge guys slam me into the back side of the cab, and I can feel the barrel of a gun sticking in my ribs, another one at the base of my neck, and another one in my ass.

"Bob, if you move, we will blow your fucking brains out," a guy growls at me. "Where's the gun?"

"What gun? I don't have a gun!"

"Where's the gun? Give me the gun or I'm gonna blow your fucking brains out!"

"I ain't got no gun! I ain't got no gun!"

So then the cab driver, some little Pakistani guy or whatever, he starts to freak out.

"Don't shoot! Don't shoot!" he starts yelling. "Please, please! Don't shoot me!"

"Get that fucking cabbie outta there or I'll blow his fucking brains out, too!" yells one of the cops (or whoever they are).

Somebody yanks the freaked-out driver out of the cab.

"Bob, we know who you are," the cop says to me. "Your name is Robert Purzycki. We know all about what you are doing here. Now where is the gun?"

"I ain't got no gun, man!"

I can feel somebody snapping handcuffs around my wrist, behind my back. This whole thing, the vague fear and dread I've been feeling for weeks about this, all these suspicions I've been having, it's all come to a head. My whole life has come to a head in this terrible moment.

I'm spread-eagle against the cab, with cop cars everywhere, and these huge guys sticking guns into me from all directions. Crowds on the sidewalk stop to watch, briefly, then they move on. It's New York. People are busy.

"My name is John Triolo," one of the guys says. "And this is my partner, Louie. We're from the New York office of the FBI."

CHAPTER 18

THE END OF HOPE

"WHERE'S THE CHECK?" this guy Triolo is yelling. "Where's the check?"

He and these other feds have me slammed up against the cab, stuck full of guns.

"What check?" I say. "I ain't got no check!"

"The check you just picked up from that office on the 19th floor. The check made out to Rocco Lorenzo for 68 hundred dollars."

"I don't have no check—look in my pockets!"

But I knew these guys had me cold. I knew I was cooked.

"You have the right to remain silent," Triolo says, "but you're coming with us."

By now I was shitting bricks. The feds had me in handcuffs, and I had to pretend not to know what I knew. Then again, I did not actually know everything that had gone down. It was only later that I found out what had actually happened. Somebody—possibly Uncle Raymond himself or, more likely, somebody working for him—hung the nutty vitamin doctor out the 19th floor window of his office and threatened to drop him if he didn't pay.

"I'll pay! I'll pay!" the doctor yelled. Then they pulled him back inside. But then he changed his tune. He said he wouldn't pay. So somebody—whoever it was—stuck a .45 down the guy's throat and threatened to blow his brains out if he didn't pay, just like in the movies. That was not just extortion (trying to extract money by the threat of force). That was extortion involving deadly weapons, with direct links to organized crime. And because I'd crossed state lines (from New Jersey to New York) to collect the check, it was also a federal crime.

That was about as serious as it gets.

So the next time somebody showed up at Dr. Richard's office— that would be me—the New York Organized Crime Task Force had been notified and they'd staked the place out.

I'd always been able to talk my way out of jams, but there was no talking my way out of this one.

The feds shoved me into a car and then they took the handcuffs off. And all of a sudden, they were nice as hell. It was like the FBI was my big brother. Triolo said, "Yeah, you're probably a little nervous right now, but it's going to be okay."

They took me underground somewhere around the Brooklyn Bridge, to a place called One Federal Plaza, down what looked like a private tunnel into some building. We seemed to be going way down underground. We got out of the car, and they put me on an elevator back upstairs somewhere. Finally I was in this windowless room.

"You can make a phone call," Triolo says.

"Okay."

"Who you gonna call?"

"My friend C.J., and my AA sponsor."

I'm thinking, *Jesus, how am I going to explain this to Jack?*

"No problem," Triolo says. (I found out later that they knew I called my AA sponsor all the time because of the phone taps. I mean, how weird is that?)

So I call C.J.

"C.J., look, I've been arrested. It's a long story, but I'm in some kind of federal building downtown. Could you call Jack and just tell him what happened? And where's Patsy?"

"Patsy just left for Italy," C.J. says. "She told me she's gone 28 days. Are you okay?"

"Well, I'll let you know."

Click.

Patsy. She was the one person, throughout my whole life, who never gave up on me—even when she was telling me to get the fuck away from her door. She always believed in me, always remembered the kind, decent person who was down there inside me, no matter how much I might have looked like a drowned, toothless rat. Patsy, more than any other single person, was the one who always loved me. But now she was unreachable for almost a month. (In those days, of course, there were no cell phones or Internet, and she hadn't left an itinerary.)

So then Triolo starts going through my wallet. He pulls out card after card and holds each one up 6 inches from my face.

"Who's this? How do you know this person?" he says. "Who is this person? Who is this guy?"

One card is from a guy who owns Guess jeans—I know him because he sometimes came into the bowling alley. Another is from the pro shop in Florida. On the back a name and phone number is scribbled: Paula Carter, wife of one of the greatest bowlers in the country, a guy I knew. But I'm sweating bullets now, because I'm pretty sure I've also got that card in there with Bobby Cabert's prison number on it, and possibly even John Gotti's. Finally, Triolo comes across Cabert's card. I had actually written "Bobby Cabert's prison number" on the card.

I'm trying to think fast. But then I think, the feds are going to figure this out even faster. Why lie? (Later on, a guy in prison tells me, "When the feds arrest you, they've already put all the pieces together. If you're lying, they know it. So don't.")

"Bobby Cabert," I say. "Robert Bisaccia."

I have to say, these federal agents were terrific. They didn't rough me up or nothing. They were aggressive but polite. They walked a fine line. You don't have to worry that the United States government is not keeping you safe. But even so, it was obvious that I was in deep, deep shit. This wasn't going to end in 10 or 20 minutes. I wasn't going home tonight.

Triolo makes a phone call, and pretty soon another guy shows up in the room where I'm getting hung out to dry.

"Do you know who I am?" the guy says.

"No, I don't know," I say.

"I'm the guy that locked up John Gotti."

"What's that got to do with me?"

"That's what we're trying to find out."

Then he whips out a photograph. It's a picture of Bobby Cabert.

"Do you know this man, Robert Bisaccia? You may know he's now serving a life sentence in federal prison."

He just stares at me, like his eyes are drilling a hole in my forehead.

"Mr. Purzycki, why do you have this man's prison number written on a card in your wallet?"

"Well, I knew him from Paterson, from the bowling alley. He wanted to know what was in the newspapers while he was in prison," I say. "So I'd mail him the papers." (I knew it was kind of lame. But it was true.)

"Look, can I go home?" I say, figuring it's worth a shot.

"Yeah, if everything goes right, you can go home."

"I think I need a lawyer."

"Okay, we'll get you a lawyer."

So they escorted me through these doors down this little corridor where there were seven cells in a row. They put me in the last cell, all by myself, and I sat there for, like, 5 hours. It was freezing cold. I just sat in there, freezing my nuts off, thinking about how bad this whole situation could get. I had 3½ years of sobriety, and here I was in federal prison. I mean, this place was worse than Alcatraz—at least there you could see the sky. Here there was no sun or sky. I was deep underground, like I was already dead and buried. It would take an atomic bomb to break out of this place. I looked down the long hall and I could see that the floors had been scrubbed sparkling clean. I suddenly realized why. It was because that was what I was going to be doing for the rest of my life.

Finally, Triolo's partner, Louie, came and let me out of my little freezing cage and took me down the elevator again, to an interrogation room or something. I might as well have been 10 miles underground. Then Louie brought me lunch, a turkey sandwich and two Diet Cokes. Man, was that sandwich good. It was the only good thing that had happened to me all day.

Then this public defender came in.

"What's going on here?" he says.

"Can I talk to you?"

"Yes, I'm your lawyer."

"Look, this whole thing is about a debt, a legitimate debt. This guy owed a family $50,000, and we tried to collect it. All I did was pick up the money."

"You got any priors?"

"I got one unpaid traffic ticket from Oceanport, New Jersey. By Monmouth Park Racetrack. A hundred and twenty-five bucks."

"That's it?"

"That's it."

"Well, this looks really simple. We'll go in front of the judge. I don't see any problem with you posting bail. We'll call you after you're done eating."

Before I went in front of the federal judge, in a little underground courtroom like a bomb shelter, I got a little bit of good news. Somebody—I found out later it was Uncle Raymond—had hired me a lawyer, and a good one. His name was Allen C. Marra, and he was one of the most prominent, influential lawyers in New Jersey. He was a medium-size man, maybe 5-foot-11, in his early sixties, with black hair tinged with gray. He was wearing a beautiful suit, but he didn't look like a mobbed-up lawyer. He looked like a business executive who demanded respect.

A US marshal leads me into the courtroom, in shackles, and sits me down beside Allen Marra.

The US attorney, a guy named Ramsey Clark, says to the judge, "I would like to hold Mr. Purzycki for 3 days—72 hours, to prepare the charges against him."

"What are they, in brief?" the judge asks.

"Your Honor, Mr. Purzycki is a capo for the Gambino crime family and I can prove it!" Clark says. "He is capable of ordering a murder with a snap of his fingers—and that will happen almost immediately if you release him. When he was arrested he had the prison number of Robert Bisaccia in his pocket. As you know, Robert Bisaccia is now in federal prison for nine Mob-ordered murders. His activities were recently described in testimony in federal court by Mob underboss Sammy the Bull Gravano."

Holy shit! This guy had me halfway up the ladder of power in the most ruthless organized crime family in New Jersey. I was, like, stunned. And I suddenly realized—duh—that even though it wasn't true, I'd been living right on the edge of all that for years. I could see where somebody could make a case against me. Hanging around with Gotti and Cabert and Uncle Raymond had seemed glamorous and exciting. But there was a reason why I was never supposed to ask any questions.

"What say you, counselor?" the judge says to Allen Marra.

"These charges by Mr. Clark are preposterous," Marra says. "Mr. Purzycki is an upstanding member of society. He has an apartment and a job at a bowling alley in Union City, New Jersey, and has been a nationally ranked bowler. His entire criminal record consists of a $125 parking ticket."

The judge thinks this over for a little while.

"There are enough questions concerning your case, Mr. Purzycki, that it's easier for me to hold you than release you," he says. "You will be remanded to the Manhattan Metropolitan Correctional Center for 72 hours. This is not like jail, Mr. Purzycki. You'll be okay."

𝔚arrant for 𝔄rrest

𝔖outhern 𝔇istrict of ℌew 𝔜ork

August 15, 1995

United States of America

v.

Docket No.: **95 MAG. 1672**

Robert Purzycki,
a/k/a "Bob Perry"
a/k/a "Frank."

To: United States Marshal or any other authorized officer. YOU ARE HEREBY COMMANDED to arrest the
above-named person and bring that person before the
nearest available magistrate to answer to the charges
listed below.

DESCRIPTION OF CHARGES:

Extortion

Leaving the courtroom, I happened to see Ray Lorenzo, surrounded by fabulous lawyers in expensive suits. I found out later that his lawyer was Anthony Martone, one of the greatest criminal lawyers in New Jersey, a guy who had represented Cabert. I knew very well that Ray had access to a lot of money from his family's businesses, and he was going home no matter what the bail was set at.

"You're going home, aren't you?" I say to him. "You're gonna make bail and go home?"

"I don't know nothing," he says. "I told the feds I didn't know you."

"What the fuck did you say that for?"

He was trying to lie his way out of this—pin it all on me. He wasn't owning up to what happened on his end. After all, the whole thing happened because I was trying to do a favor for him!

"You're gonna fuck me, aren't you?" I say.

He didn't say nothing, but I knew it was true. With all that family money he had, he was going to make bail and go home to sleep in his own bed. I had no money, and I was going to be stuck here in this 8-by-10 icebox, maybe forever.

When I get back to my cell, a guy says to me, "You make bail?"

"Nah. They're holding me for 3 days."

"Yeah, ha ha," he says. "You're never making bail. Nobody ever makes bail in here. Welcome to your new home."

Shortly after, I was transferred to what they called "MCC" (Metropolitan Correctional Center), onto cellblock Five North.

Everywhere I went outside the cell I'd be in handcuffs, accompanied by a US marshal. When you were in federal prison, the US marshals owned you. They'd lead me through doors that had to be unlocked when you walked through and locked again behind you. They took all my clothes, which I didn't mind. But what I did mind was that they also took my favorite necklace, which I had been wearing for years. It was just a piece of rope, like a shoelace, but on the end was the Miraculous Medal I had found in the graveyard at Graymoor.

All I knew when I found it was that it looked incredibly old and beautiful and seemed kind of religious or something. But later Patsy found this book that explained the meaning, history, and power of the medal. I put it on a string and around my neck and never took it off, just feeling all that power, like the power of Father Paul, the power that had changed my life.

Now I had to hand it over to some guy at check-in at MCC, and maybe never see it again. The guy gave me a baggy, brown outfit (which looked a little bit like the robe Father Paul always wore), one pair of underwear, two pairs of socks, and these ridiculous blue boating sneakers. Like I was going boating?

"Is there anyone in this facility who would want to hurt you?" one of the marshals asked, apparently trying to decide if I needed to be put in my own cell.

"No, I don't think so."

I was given a sheet and a pillow and ushered into a tiny cell with a bunk bed, a toilet, a small locker, and a roommate—this huge, intimidating-looking black dude whose name, I later learned, was Tyrone.

"What you in here for, robbing old ladies?" Tyrone says.

I don't say nothing. I'm trying to think fast.

"Whassamatter, you don't want to talk to me? I don't like fucking white people."

"Uh, no se habla Ingles. Me no speaka English."

"Hahaha—you funny guy!" Tyrone says. "You okay."

But I wasn't okay.

I thought, *I'm never going home. I'm stuck in this sinking cell with this creepy dude forever.*

I fell into this little routine, where every movement I made was watched by armed guards. There was a pay phone on Five North, so every chance I got I stood in line to use the phone, to try to figure out what was going on "out there." I talked to C.J. again, briefly, and he told me Uncle Raymond and Nicky the Plumber had been arrested; he also told them I'd been arrested.

The bad news was I got sent the charging documents—this big stack of papers laying out the state's case against me. I only had to read the first page to know things had gone from bad to worse. It didn't matter how polite John Triolo was, or how tasty the turkey sandwich they'd served me was. I was screwed.

And to think I had almost succeeded in breaking free of my past! The encounters with Father Paul and my slow, steady return to the land of the living, to sobriety and integrity, had led me to a real, actual life. And now this. Sitting here in this cell on Five North with nothing but a bunk bed, a locker, my blue boating shoes, Tyrone, and a charging document with all the details about how the United States government was throwing the goddamned book at me.

If I ever needed my Higher Power, and Father Paul, it was now.

CHAPTER 19

"I LOVE YOU, YOUR HONOR!"

YOU HEAR PEOPLE TALK about "Club Fed," and how easy it is to serve time in federal prison. Well, forget about it. Those people don't know what the fuck they're talking about. It's the agony, the mental torment, that kills you. And security? Listen, this ain't like no *Escape-from-Alcatraz* type thing, where at least you see the sky through the bars. Here, you're buried alive, like you're in an upside-down skyscraper stuck underground. You might as well already be dead. In fact, in a way, I already had a tag on my toe, like one of them unidentified corpses at the city morgue: It read, 857435757. My prison number.

The worst thing of all was the hopelessness, the believing that I would never be going home. That I would never sleep in my own bed again. All those guys in there told me I would never make bail, and I believed them. Whenever I tried to call my lawyer to find out about my case, he was busy or out of the office. He was basically telling me to fuck off. C.J., Jack, and (after she got back from Italy) Patsy took my calls. Uncle Raymond also took my calls, but then he got put in jail, too, and I didn't hear from him anymore.

I almost wished I could drink or do drugs again, so I wouldn't have to face the possibility that this was my new home, maybe for the next 30 years: Five North, at the Metropolitan Correctional Center in Manhattan, a stinking shithole which I shared with murderers, drug dealers, thugs, and criminals of all kinds. And this place wasn't like no minor leagues of petty crime, like a state or local lockup. This place was the NFL of crime.

One of the guys who was behind the 1993 bombing of the World Trade Center, this huge Arab guy, was there. Guys from the Irish Republican Army were there, including one of its leaders, a guy named Peter McMullen, who I got to know pretty well. Supposedly there were quite a few guys in there who had killed more than 10 people. And there were some big-time nonviolent criminals there, too, like this guy Eddie who used to have a chain of discount electronics stores in the Northeast called Crazy Eddie—he had all these TV ads where the guy would say, "His prices are insane!"—well, he was in there for owing $15 million in back taxes or something.

Gradually, I started to slip into the monotonous routine of incarceration in the federal system. Besides meals, there wasn't much to break up the boredom of "doing time" (even though, strictly speaking, I wasn't doing time, just waiting until my case came up). One thing was the "count." Every day at 4:00 p.m., all prisoners in the entire federal system nationwide had to be counted over a 30-minute period. So if you were working in the prison library or the infirmary or the kitchen, you had to return to your cell for the count.

Every once in a while, there was also what they called "PC movement," meaning that a prisoner in protective custody was being moved through the cellblock. One of the marshals would yell "movement!" and even if the prisoner was down on the first floor, and you were on the fifth (like me), you had to go to the back of your cell and not look. That's because people under protective custody—like, say, Sammy the Bull Gravano—were in serious danger of getting killed by people in there.

There are four levels of incarceration in the federal correctional system: "camp" (for some white-collar guy who embezzles money at work), "medium security" (for more serious crimes), "maximum" (for really scary, dangerous people), and "supermax" (where people like Gotti and Cabert got sent).

Not too long after I arrived at MCC, I got sent to another hold-over facility, called Otisville Federal Correctional Institution, about 2½ hours upstate from Manhattan. Otisville was a medium-security facility. The big advantage of Otisville over MCC was that they had a prison yard where you could actually see the sky and the sun. The exercise area (which had a basketball court, a handball court, and a track) was surrounded by a 15-foot barbed wire fence, with another 15-foot barbed wire fence outside that, which was electrified at night. There were also guard towers, with armed guards in them, staring down at you, just like in the movies. The guards watched everything you did. If you were out there sunbathing, you lost your privileges. If you were talking to too many people, you got reported.

Being in the yard was a long ways from freedom, but at least I could get out there and smell the dirt and the trees and the rain a couple of times a day. I kept clear of almost everybody in there. I learned not to talk to people. I'd just walk around and around and around (25 times around the yard made a mile).

The best thing about Otisville was that, every once in a while, I got a visit from Patsy. The bad part about Otisville was that if you were sent up there it meant your case was a long ways off. It was a holdover facility for people pending trial. They made you get a job or go to a GED class while you were in there. The rest of the time you were in your tiny cell, or released into a larger enclosed "compound," or sometimes into the outside yard. That was your life: The compound, the yard, the cell. Waiting, waiting, waiting.

But just in case you were getting comfortable with incarceration, the marshals would do this thing called "diesel therapy." It was to break you down, drive you nuts, maybe make you talk. Say around 10:00 at night on a Thursday, a guy would come to your cell and tell you to pack all your shit up in a 12-by-12 box. You would try to pack all your stuff in there, but you couldn't fit nothing much more in there but your underwear and socks. Then they would take you downstairs into another bullpen, or holding area, where you'd have to wait until 12:30 in the morning. Then, one person at a time, you'd have to take all your clothes off, and another guy would make you bend over to see you don't got a knife hidden where the sun don't shine. Then you'd put on some different clothes and you'd get loaded on a prison bus for the two-and-a-half-hour ride down to MCC. When you got there, you'd get stripped and examined again, and taken to another cell. By this time, you'd have probably missed breakfast. You'd be held in this cell until 10:00 at night, and then some guy would come to get you and it would start all over again. And this would go on for days, until you were so exhausted you couldn't even see nothing.

Look: I had seen the charging documents, and I knew very well that the case the government was throwing at me was serious. Very serious. But did I really belong in there with those murderers and terrorists? I kept trying to get some answers from my lawyer about this, but he didn't return my calls. I couldn't say that I blamed him: I didn't have any money, like Uncle Raymond or Ray Lorenzo did. I was just your average, run-of-the-mill inmate in federal lockup, an unlucky guy lost in the shuffle.

From time to time I would get through on the phone to C.J., who told me that Uncle Raymond and Nicky the Plumber were out on bail. He said they'd been seen at the racetrack, like nothing ever happened. I found out they'd hired that same heavy-duty lawyer, Anthony Martone, and he got them out on bail in a couple of days. Uncle Raymond had finally gone to prison—but only for 48 hours or something. Yet I was still stuck here with the crooks and the creeps, staring out at the world through bars.

I wound up spending about half my time at MCC and half at Otisville. MCC was the worst. I was trapped there in my little coffin underground, where there was no daylight, no birds chirping, not even the sound of traffic, just the sound of some asshole on Tier Five playing bad rap music, or the jangle of keys locking and unlocking doors, or jail cells clanking, or every now and then the sound of a cue ball cracking a rack on the little pool table, which was the only thing inmates on Tier Five North were allowed to do to keep from going crazy. Part of the day, they'd open up our little area so we could crawl out of our cages into the larger cage. You couldn't get the newspaper. You couldn't exercise in your cell. You couldn't really do nothing, except die. You couldn't even die fast, because you were constantly being patted down for knives or whatnot.

I did not know if I would ever walk free in the daylight again.

And sitting there in my miserable cell, C106, Five North, I had way too much time to think. And more and more, I kept thinking about Bobby Cabert, my old friend, a guy I once thought of as the big brother I never had. It was Bobby Cabert, I had come to believe, who was the main reason I'd wound up in this tomb out of reach of the sun. It was his prison number on that card in my wallet that helped the feds link the two of us together.

I thought about the first time I met Cabert, at a racetrack in New Jersey with Uncle Raymond. This was about 20 years earlier, in the early '70s. I was around 20 years old at the time, a real hotshot (or so I thought). And I thought the world Uncle Raymond was introducing me to at the time was fabulous. That was the word: "fabulous." The fact that there was this shadowy world just beneath the surface of everything, all kinds of things that were never spoken about, the fact that these men were powerful and influential and feared—I thought it was just glamorous and enticing as hell.

And Bobby Cabert, more than any other single person, seemed to personify the dark glamour of that world.

Little did I know at the time where it would all lead.

In a federal holding facility, they give you nothing but a sheet, a pillowcase and a pillow, a thin blanket, and a towel. They also give you this crappy, little locker, and I had all my stuff in the world in there—one extra pair of underwear and a change of socks. Oh, and one other thing: Even though everything is slick as a whistle, in that locker there are roaches. When I'd reach into that locker to get my other pair of socks, the roaches would go skittering away like criminals caught in the act.

Real glamorous.

It was December 21, 1995—4 days before Christmas. I'll never forget the day. I had been in federal lockup for seven months (even though it seemed like 7 years). It was a Thursday, like any other Thursday in the eternity of life behind bars. All that hope I got from Father Paul up on the holy mountain was almost gone. I was just trying to survive. Why, I don't know.

For the past 7 or 8 weeks, I'd been in holdover upstate at Otisville. The big payoff was visits from Patsy, and a couple of hours of sunshine a day. That's what passed for Christmas in the federal correctional system.

I called Allen Marra, my lawyer, and for once he picked up. (I had asked him earlier if I should call him "Mr. Marra," and he said, "No, call me Allen.")

"Allen, could you call the judge and ask her to keep me in Otisville for the holidays?" I say to him. "I gotta see my sister Patsy."

"No, I can't," Allen says.

My heart just kind of dropped. I was going back to the tomb.

"No," he says, "I can't keep you in Otisville."

"How come?"

"Because you're going home tomorrow."

It was like time stood still. I couldn't even breathe.

"What?" I say, figuring there was some mistake.

"I said you're going home tomorrow. You got bail. They gave us bail. Make sure you're on the list to come downtown, because you're going home tomorrow. Congratulations!"

When I get over having a heart attack and a nervous breakdown, I say to Allen, "What happened? What changed that all of a sudden we got bail?"

"Well, I have to say that it had a lot to do with a phone call from a friend of yours—Robert Bisaccia. Bobby Cabert. He was able to convince the US attorney that you don't belong in there."

"Bobby Cabert?"

"Bobby Cabert."

So it was Bobby Cabert, my old friend, the gangster, the guy whose prison number got me in here in the first place—it was him who was getting me out. Even though he was in federal prison for life for being a hit man for the Mob, he had achieved a kind of redemption by freeing me. He would eventually die behind bars, but now he was trying to do a good deed before he went down.

"How much was the bail?" I say to Allen.

"A million dollars, secured, Bobby. Your sister Patsy and her husband James put the deed to their house up. And both of them also signed a cash bond for about $200,000 each."

I could hardly believe what I was hearing. Since this was a federal charge, when you put up bail, it ain't no 10 percent, like for less serious charges. My sister and James had to come up with the whole amount, putting up $400,000 cash and putting their house at risk. If I jumped bail, they would lose it all. I knew James had a good job, but they didn't have that kind of money. Who did?

What they did have, despite everything I had done to them, was love for me.

Love!

When I hung up the phone, these indescribable feelings just swarmed over me. How could anyone love me that much? And, you mean—I wasn't going to spend the rest of my life in this hellhole? You mean—I was going to sleep in my own bed, in my little apartment in Union City, where my sisters had been paying the rent in the hope that I might come back? Like—tomorrow night?

One thing I had to remind myself: Keep this to yourself. Guys who are about to be released are a target in prison. If I blabbed about it, it wouldn't be the first time some loudmouth with his walking papers wound up knifed in the shower. So I didn't tell nobody except Peter

McMullen, the Irish Republican Army guy, who I had come to like and trust. He was the one who had kept saying to me, "What the hell are you still doing in here? You don't belong here."

And I guess he was right.

So that whole day I kept checking to see if I was on the list, but I wasn't. I started freaking out. I called my lawyer back.

"Just tell them to keep checking," Allen said. "Don't get nervous."

It was a little while later, around 2:00 p.m., that they told me I was on the list. Shortly afterward, I was taken by bus down to MCC in Manhattan, and the next day, around noon, I was taken into the courtroom of Federal Judge Miriam Cedarbaum.

And there, sitting in the courtroom, was my amazing, long-suffering, saintly sister Patsy and her husband James, who had risked their whole financial future on me. Judge Cedarbaum explained the terms of my bail, which was that I had to stay in the Southern District of Manhattan and nowhere else without permission, and that I had to report regularly to my federal parole officer. The federal extortion charge was not being dropped, of course; I was just out on bail until the charge could be resolved.

Okay, so I wasn't completely free, at least not yet. But in my heart, I could never remember being happier.

"Can I say something to you?" I say to Judge Cedarbaum, after she finishes talking.

"Yes, Mr. Purzycki?"

"I love you, Your Honor!"

"I love you, too, Robert," she says, laughing. "But you need to get downstairs and do your paperwork if you want to go home." Then she adds, just as I am leaving, "Good luck, Robert."

"Thank you!" I say.

Lord knows I needed it.

CHAPTER 20

GANG NIGHT

GETTING SPRUNG FROM FEDERAL PRISON is like being one of them cave bats flying out of the darkness into the middle of the day. You keep blinking, but it takes you a long time to get used to the sunshine. You don't trust it. You're not sure it's going to last. And usually, it doesn't.

Because the fact is, I wasn't really "free" at all—I was only out on million-dollar bail, like one of them old-timey prisoners dragging around a ball and chain, looking for some dude with a hacksaw. I may not have believed I had done anything seriously wrong—after all, I told myself, I was only trying to help out a friend. But in the eyes of the law, I was a guy with direct ties to the Gambino crime family, who had been involved in an extortion plot involving deadly weapons. I mean, that don't sound too good. I had been told that I might be looking at 3 to 5 years in federal prison. And all for a hundred fuckin' bucks!

When I got out on bail, one of the first things I did was fire my lawyer because I couldn't afford him anymore. I went in front of Judge Cedarbaum and asked for a new lawyer, and she assigned me Maurice Sercarz, a top-notch criminal lawyer who took my case pro bono. I was really blessed. Maurice was a gift from God.

It's almost impossible to describe what living with this hanging over your head feels like.

By now I was going on 5 years sober, but like a lot of people in early sobriety, I found myself having to face the wreckage of my past life without the benefit of drugs and alcohol. There were lots of times when I was just about dying to get drunk or wasted, just to blank it all out. But by the grace of God, the fellowship of AA, and the presence of an old Franciscan monk who may or may not have been real, I didn't go there. The main thing was that, if I broke bail, my sister and James—two beautiful angels that I did not deserve—would have been on the hook for a million dollars. I would have broken them, financially. I would never have forgiven myself (and they wouldn't have, either).

So I stayed and suffered through it, trying to rebuild a real, actual life instead of a fake life built on lies, self-pity, and self-centeredness. I don't know what else to call that except a miracle.

They say you can't keep your sobriety unless you give it away, so part of my daily practice was to sponsor other alcoholics, to try to get them on the right road, try to show them that there is a way out—an escape from coke, smoke, and booze. Even so, a lot of the people I sponsored early on died. Alcohol, as the *Big Book* says, is "cunning, baffling, powerful," and the people it has killed would make a mountain. But you just do your service work, helping people where you can, making coffee and setting up chairs for meetings, being sensitive to when people are hurting or in need, trying to do the work of the angels if you can. Sobriety isn't something you own, it's a gift you are given, and you have to give it back.

Of course, you can't fuck up your life as bad as I did without there being some consequences. The day after I got out of prison, I went back to see C.J. and Annie at New Bowl-Rite Lanes in Union City. They had been some of the closest friends I ever had. C.J. was the best friend a guy could ever want. He was in the program 8 years, so besides the fact that he was a Polack, we had always had a lot in common. C.J. and Annie had welcomed me with open arms when we first met.

But when I came back from my little shoebox-size cell in the federal big house, everything felt stiff and tense between us. Jokes kind of fell flat. Something was "off." But C.J. and Annie were nice enough to offer me my old job back, so I went back to running the pro shop, helping to keep the lanes clean and conditioned, working to build up the leagues and so on, but there was no getting around the fact that because of what I had done, C.J. and Annie had had their whole world seriously rocked. I was different, too: I was older, sadder, more suspicious, and pretty close to completely broke.

When I was in prison, I used to call C.J. quite a lot (you can only make collect calls from in there, and C.J. took my calls for a while before he got fed up with it). Well, apparently the feds had the phone tapped. What they were really interested in was collaring the bigger shots than me. They actually thought I was a capo in the Mob, when I was really just a pathetic recovering-alcoholic bowler and former homeless crack addict who was doing somebody a favor for a hundred bucks.

So one day C.J. gets called down to the federal building in Manhattan to be interrogated by the FBI. (He later told me he wasn't even really nervous. He was completely innocent, so what was there to worry about? Believe me, even if you're totally innocent, if the FBI wants to interrogate you, you should be really fuckin' nervous.)

So C.J. goes downtown and the feds get him in a room and they spread a bunch of photographs of these mobsters on a table.

"Where do you fit in this picture?" they say. "How high up the ladder do you go?"

C.J. couldn't believe it. Here he was this chubby Polack who ran a bowling alley in Union City, and they thought he was Michael Corleone or some damn thing. It was a joke.

"You ain't got a ladder high enough!" C.J. tells them, busting out laughing.

The feds didn't think this was terribly funny, though. And they started showing up at the bowling alley—two or three clean-cut guys, who would play three games of pool in 4 hours, maybe drink a Pepsi because they'd show up at a time when the bar was closed, and just kind of sit around looking to see who came in and out.

"Yeah, we had some more pool players in today," C.J. would tell me over the phone when I called in from prison.

"Look, Bobby," he'd say, more nervously, "I'm telling the feds everything."

"Go right ahead," I'd say. "I got nothing to hide."

I can understand why this really rattled C.J. and Annie's cage. And it was all because of me, because I tried to help them and instead dragged a bunch of mobbed-up thugs into their life.

It was like my whole past life was a disease, and it had spread to their world.

The bowling alley had turned out to be a nightmare for them in other ways, too. It was located in a pretty poor neighborhood, and nobody who came in there had any money. Business had been so slow, even before this whole mess with the Feds, that C.J. and Annie had sold their house and moved in with Annie's parents just so they could keep the lights on. But there were still more unpaid bills—huge ones—I don't know how much money, but enough to hang over their heads like one of them science fiction monsters in the movies. Every time I talked to C.J. on the phone, I could hear the stress in his voice.

When I got out of prison and went back to work at the bowling alley, I could tell that all this debt was eating away at him. But I also knew, from learning to live as a sober person, that sometimes taking on other people's problems as your own is a terrible idea. That's part of the meaning of the Serenity Prayer, which we say at every meeting: *God grant me the serenity to accept the things I cannot change, the courage to change the things I can, and the wisdom to know the difference.* It's about knowing where to draw the line of your own responsibility, identifying exactly what it is you're responsible for, and, on the other hand, what you're not responsible for.

Even so, almost as soon as I went back to work at Bowl-Rite, I began to notice that there was this crowd of kids, almost all of them

Hispanic, anywhere from 8 years old to their late teens, early twenties, who used to come into the bowling alley after school and just stay there until dinnertime or later. For some of them, I don't think there was a dinnertime. I guess a lot of businesses would have told these kids to scram, because they didn't spend any money. But I got to talking to them, and I could see that a lot of them were good kids who'd gotten a bum rap in life. A lot of them came from broken homes, the mom working long hours at some crummy job, maybe the dad in jail, nothing much for them to do after school except smoke dope and get in trouble.

I saw myself in these kids. I knew where they were headed. I knew what it was like to feel unloved, to feel abandoned by the world, to feel lost, to be on the wrong road. So they'd come into the bowling alley in the afternoon, and I'd let them do their homework there. Then I'd let them bowl a few games and give them some tips about the finer techniques of the game. Some of these kids had a real gift for the game, like I had. I felt that helping them gain confidence at something might even help to turn their lives around.

Helping these kids like that made me remember what it was like when I was a kid growing up in Paterson, when the bowling alley was about the only safe place in my world. It was also about the only place you'd see whole families—mom, dad, sis, junior, Fido, whatever. Well, at Bowl-Rite there might not have been whole families, but I wanted to make sure there was a clean, safe place for these kids to come. I wanted them to feel that same feeling of safety and security that I felt there, growing up.

I didn't tell these kids about my sorry history, being homeless, being in prison, and they never asked. To them I was just an older guy who showed an interest in them, a kind of father or uncle figure that they probably didn't have at home. I saw in them the children I never had.

I got real fond of a kid named Jeffrey Butler, who was half black and being raised by a single mother (his dad was in prison). I took care of him and his brother Eddie, whose nickname was Spanky, like they were my own kids. Spanky was only 5 or 6 years old, but he came to the bowling alley every day and I watched over him, kept him safe, kept him in line. Spanky was a great two-handed bowler at such a tender age. (Much later, after he was grown, Spanky told me that if it hadn't been for bowling, he'd probably have turned into a street kid.)

Then there was Havie, who was a tough gangster kid. But when you broke that shell, you learned that inside he was a sweet youngster who was actually extremely bright. And there was a good-looking Puerto Rican kid, an extremely bright kid, who went by the name of Melrock.

Melrock came to me one day and asked if he could have a job. "Sure," I said, pointing at a troublemaker. "Throw that kid outta here."

So he threw the kid down the stairs.

Melrock was not only a good bouncer, he was also a fabulous graffiti artist. I had him paint a skyline of New York on the wall of the bowling alley, and it was so good that not too long after that we changed the name of the bowling alley to Skyline Bowl.

Then there was Paul Stamos and Dustin (C.J. and Annie's son) and a whole pack of others. As time went on, I hired more and more of these kids to work at the bowling alley, and I paid them whatever I could (not very much). I must have had 10 of them on the payroll at any one time, cleaning the lanes, being porters, cleaning the restrooms, working the front desk, whatever.

A lot of these kids, it turned out, had ties to the local street gangs, like the Latin Kings, the Ñetas, or the Vatos Locos. Then there were other kids with ties to the Crips and the Bloods.

But the thing was this: I knew these were basically good kids. And, once I started showing them how, it turned out a lot of them really liked to bowl.

So what happened was that I decided to start having Gang Night at the bowling alley. The rules would be that there were no guns and no fighting allowed. If you wanted to fight, you had to go 3 blocks away. And I got the cops to agree that there would be no arrests at the bowling alley, either. It would be like one of those demilitarized zones in wartime, a bowling DMZ, a safe place where the kids could go at night and not have to worry about getting hurt.

There was a cop named Dominick DiPinto who worked in the gang unit of the local police force, and he worked nights at the front desk at Bowl-Rite. The rule for Dominick and his cop friends was, hands off. Sometimes Dominick would take pictures of the kids, and the kids would just goof for the camera, like it was a joke. You were safe there, no matter who you were or what you had done.

Annie was a great promoter, and I met another lady in AA who was a marketing expert, so the three of us started really targeting the Hispanic community, who didn't usually bowl too much. We sent out coupons and postcards and promotions to Union City, Jersey City, Hoboken (where there's a lot of gangsters and yuppies), and nearby areas. I went out and talked to schools and camps, inviting all the kids to come.

The first time I put out the word that we'd be having Gang Night at the bowling alley, nearly 400 kids showed up. It was amazing. These kids came in and bowled 1,400 games in 5 hours. All 24 lanes were filled all night.

But by a couple of weeks later, 200 kids had dropped out. The reason was they didn't have any money. So I started letting a lot of these kids bowl for free. We offered them prizes, and had a little banquet at the end of the year. Jeffrey was a regular 12-year-old phenom, just like I was, and Dustin bowled a 300 game when he was only 14. So bowling, which in a way had been my downfall, became a kind of salvation for a lot of these kids.

Eventually, I gave up the apartment Patsy was paying the rent for while I was in jail; stayed with Patsy awhile; and then rented a nice little studio apartment within walking distance of the bowling alley, at a place called the Washington Park Towers. Now I had a decent place to live, and a job I liked, and people who needed me and depended on me. I even had kids, for the first time in my life. Things were looking up.

Financially, though, it was always a struggle to keep the bowling alley solvent, even though we were now the center of the universe to a whole bunch of semihomeless Hispanic gangbangers. I was working at the bowling alley all the time and doing everything I could to help the business pull up out of the shithole it was in. I walked to work from my apartment every day, and went to AA meetings after work almost every night. Every other week I went to Hoboken and took the PATH train into Manhattan to the federal probation department. Man, I'm telling you: I stuck to the terms of my probation like glue, because I had no intention of going down that road again. Even so, I knew it still might not be enough to save me from serving more federal time.

Then one day C.J. sat me down for a talk.

"Look," he says, "I want to make you a deal. Me and Annie— we're getting pretty burned out on running this place. How about if we just sell it to you? The sale price would be a steal: $1. We'd sell you the bowling alley, the whole schmear, for a buck. But, see, you'd also have to agree to take on everything, including the bad debt we got. You'd buy the business, good and bad. If you can turn it around, you could make some real money. That's the deal."

I thought about this overnight, and the next day I told C.J. I'd do it. I just knew I could make it work.

Now I focused my whole attention to trying to turn the damn thing around. I was well known in the bowling world; I had a national rep. Maybe because of that, and because I did everything I could to build the business—built up leagues, had special promotions, and so on—things started picking up pretty quickly. People started coming into the bowling alley again. I was starting to reach into my pocket and find money there instead of lint.

I even started attracting some celebrities. I got to know Robert Menendez, the US senator from New York, and his son, who would come in to bowl. Lawrence Taylor, who used to play football for the New York Giants, would come in. Ray Allen, an NBA star whose girlfriend lived nearby, came in sometimes. And there was that MTV host, Downtown Julie Brown, who would also come in quite a lot.

C.J. went to work for another bowling alley, one of our competitors actually, and Annie decided to stay on as an employee, working for me. So now, for better or worse, I was a business owner—practically a member of the Chamber of Commerce. Me, the guy from cellblock Five North, was almost an upstanding citizen.

Being in charge of the leftover bad debt was like learning to be a grown-up, taking responsibility for mistakes. As business picked up, I started making regular payments on the old debt, chiseling it down week after week. Because it was easier, I started paying the rent every week, and some months I'd add more than 4 weeks. Once I could afford it, I got C.J. and Annie health insurance, and I gave Annie a raise. And I told them both, if the business ever climbed out of the hole and got sold, I'd give them a piece of it. After all, they had helped to save my life.

By this time, all the mobbed-up guys who had once been so much a part of my life were gone, and they had also left my mind and my heart. They wound up where they belonged, I guess. Bobby Cabert, convicted of federal racketeering charges and sentenced to 40 years, would eventually die of cancer in prison (in 2008). I never spoke to him again. The feds had nailed John Gotti, the "Dapper Don," after years of trying. He was convicted of murder, loan-sharking, bribery, tax evasion, and a few other things and sentenced to life in prison. He wound up dying in the federal prison in Springfield, Missouri. I was just glad the feds never found his prison number in my wallet!

CHAPTER 21

HIGH ROLLER

IT WAS CHRISTMASTIME, 1996, and I'd been out of prison for a year. I was sober, and an almost-respectable member of society. I'd been a business owner, and an employer, for the past 7 months. I was even a mentor to kids. Imagine that! My past criminal history and links to a murderous crime family? It was nobody's business but my own. Look: There are plenty of people in America with a past they'd rather forget. But this is a country of second chances. So I figured I'd take mine.

The thing that seized my attention now was the Super Bowl High Roller tournament in Las Vegas—the biggest-money bowling tournament in the country. The top prize was $100,000. The tournament started out as the "High Roller," in 1981, but in the early 1990s, it was renamed the "Super Bowl High Roller," because it was the pinnacle of my sport. Twice a year, in January (right around the time of the Super Bowl) and July, the Showboat Hotel and Casino and the bowling equipment manufacturer Brunswick sponsored this glitzy tournament in Vegas that attracted all the top bowlers in the country. All the big professional bowling tournaments were in Vegas, but the Super Bowl High Roller was the big kahuna, the biggest of the big.

Because of the prize money, and all the other ways of winning money in Las Vegas, the Super Bowl High Roller drew almost every single top bowler in the entire country—and from lots of other countries also. The incredible Mike Newman. Chris Barnes, a fanatical guy who bowled, like, 10 or 12 hours a day and was ranked number one in the world at the time. His approach was as smooth as silk. Pat Healey, the three-time World Cup Amateur of the Year. "Rudy Revs," from Long Island, who curved that ball better than anybody, even me. Joe Vita (his real name was Joe Buenavisto), the great money bowler from Texas. David Haynes, Chris Hayden, Willie Willis. Mike Mullin, a leftie who bowled for St. John's University and later became World Bowler of the Year. I mean, forget about it!

According to the rules of the tournament, these guys were all amateurs, but a lot of them would later go on to become some of the top pro bowlers in the country. Winning the Super Bowl High Roller was not just about winning the biggest purse. It was also about winning the biggest honor in bowling. It put you in the permanent record books. The finals of the tournament were filmed on tape delay and broadcast nationally the next day on ESPN, ABC's *Wide World of Sports*, and an affiliate of Prime Sports Network.

The main idea of the Super Bowl High Roller was simple: It was a tournament where, if you lost, you were out—no second chances, no second rounds, so long, see ya later. Since the tournament had a full field of 2,048 entrants, it was like starting out with 2,000 gunslingers in the Old West. If you lost the duel, you were dead. And as the tournament went on, Main Street in Dodge City would get knee-deep in bodies. Anybody, even the greatest bowlers in the world, sometimes have a bad match. But in the Super Bowl High Roller, that doesn't matter. In order to win, you had to win all 11 of your matches in a row.

Actually, I was pretty familiar with the whole drill of going to Vegas for the tournament, because I had entered six or seven times before. Back in my drinking and drugging days, I'd go out there, cocky as hell, with my hot-combed hair and major attitude, convinced I could win it all. And for the first few games, I'd do great. There were lots of ways to make money without winning the whole tournament, too. For example, you could bowl what they called "sweeps"—two games together—and if you won them both, you'd win a couple thousand bucks. I'd go out there and win a few sweeps, almost as a warmup to the big tournament.

Then I'd start drinking. Or, more accurately, I never stopped drinking, from the moment I got there to the moment I left. I'd get smashed out of my mind for, like, 7 days straight. When I was younger, alcohol was like fire in my veins, and I just became unstoppable, unbeatable. When I knocked back a few glasses of vodka-and-orange-juice and stepped up to the line, I was like Wild Bill Hickok, scattering them pins with a hit dead square in the pocket, one strike after another. One time I won 5,000 bucks on the first day I got out there.

Back then, in the 1980s, I had turned into an old, slow, sloppy drunk, and I'd be drinking all night and all day long at the tournament. I had a drink in my hand at all times, from Day One through the whole event (or, at least, as long as I lasted). I'd drink at the bowling alley, in the bars, in the casinos (where if you bet a dollar you got a free drink), at the craps tables. I'd drink socially and I'd drink alone. I'd wind up in my hotel room at 3:00 or 4:00 in the morning, drinking and puking.

Sure, there were some big-time bowlers who were falling-down-drunk alcoholics, and a lot of bowlers did dope, but I'm pretty sure I broke some kind of world record for alcohol and drug abuse. I was the Super Bowl High Roller of addiction.

Me and Vegas never really agreed with each other. Alcohol jacked up my game at first but then destroyed it, and I'd wind up on an eastbound plane headed back to Jersey with a bad hangover and a dwindling stash of cash in my pocket, an early loser knocked out of the tournament before it even really got started. I felt like all this great promise that I had, or once had, this chance to touch my inner greatness, this chance to reach my dreams—well, fuck it. You just flush the toilet, crawl back into bed, cover your head, and try to forget about your life. Having big dreams only made you feel worse.

Maybe tomorrow would be a better day.

Except that it wouldn't be.

One thing I didn't quite realize at the time about all this was that my troubles were not exactly my little secret. I had become so well known in the bowling world when I was younger that when I started my long, ugly downhill slide and then vanished completely from the bowling scene for more than 7 years, everybody in the bowling world knew about it. Everybody knew my story, even though I never told nobody nothing myself. Even the FBI knew my story.

So anyway, that January of 1997, I decided I was going out to Vegas and I was going to win the Super Bowl High Roller. I wasn't just going to compete. I was going to win the damn thing.

Sure, I'd been there before, but now this was a new day. For the first time, I'd be going out there sober and focused. I put my head into the laser-focus of winning, however far-fetched it might have been. I was convinced that I was capable of doing it. I remembered (as just one example) that time when me and Mike Foti broke the American Bowling Congress record with a team series of 1,639. I threw 22 consecutive strikes—30 strikes altogether out of 36 frames—for a total score in three games of 845. Man, I was hot! And I knew I could do it again. (At the time, I'd been homeless!)

In my usual in-your-face New Jersey way, I figured I wasn't going to make no big secret about going out to win the Super Bowl High Roller, so I told everybody and invited this whole entourage to come along. I told the league bowlers who came to Bowl-Rite on Friday nights—this was, like, 120 people—that I was going to buy them all shrimp when I won. C.J. and Annie and their son Dustin decided to come along for the ride. Paul Stamos, Melrock, Chris Haden, Jimmy Mack and his brother Tim, all great younger bowlers in their twenties, they came, too.

But my favorite kid that came was Jeffrey Butler, who was 12. Jeffrey was an extremely smart kid, and a really talented bowler. He and his mom lived right next door to Bowl-Rite, and he practically grew up there. His dad was in prison, and his mom was raising him and his little brother, Spanky. (Between me and Bowl-Rite, C.J. and

Annie, and the parents of some of the kids, we came up with the money for the trip.)

Jeffrey Butler: My mom said if my grades were alright, I could go. So I went. Man, it was surreal! Getting out of school and going to Vegas to watch the biggest bowlers in the country compete! I remember we all squeezed into a room at a hotel called the Stratosphere that had a roller coaster on the roof.

I think my mom understood that being with Bob, and hanging out at the bowling alley, was about the safest place I could be—and I'd be safe in Vegas, too. The neighborhood around Bowl-Rite (where my mom and I lived) was pretty rundown, and 99 percent Hispanic. So the bowling alley was kind of a safe haven for me. I was there every day, learning from Bob and watching what he did out there on the lanes. And he was amazing! I had heard all that stuff about him living on the streets, and being a dope addict and all. But I didn't care about that. To me he was just a good bowler, and a great guy.

Me and C.J. and Annie and the kids wound up staying at the Stratosphere Casino, Hotel & Tower, on the strip, because I knew a guy there and he comped us the rooms. The kids were nuts about this place because it was, like, a zillion stories tall, brand-new, and up on the roof was this enormous tower and a crazy-ass roller coaster. (Amazingly enough, it was called the High Roller.) The kids thought this was the coolest thing they had ever seen.

Going out to Vegas with this whole entourage, even though a lot of them were kids, was almost like the old days when I came sweeping into that big-money match against Ruby Red, in Belleville, New

Jersey, with John Gotti and Uncle Raymond and the whole mobbed-up crew. Except now I was sober, legit, and nobody I was with knew a damn thing about the Gambino crime family except what they had read in the papers.

Compared to all the other times I went out to Vegas with stars in my eyes, this time I had one huge new thing going for me. I was sober. If I sat down at the bar, it would be to have a club soda with lime, not five Manhattans.

I'd always been convinced that if I could stay straight, I could win the Super Bowl High Roller. Now, with more than 4 years of sobriety and constant contact with my Higher Power and Father Paul, I believed that I could succeed. I believed that I could make my dreams come true. This time—I don't know—I just had a good feeling about the tournament from the very start. (Of course, there were 2,000 other great bowlers who might have had the same feeling!)

But, realistically, I also realized that this would probably be my last chance to win this star-studded tournament, something I had dreamt about, and repeatedly attempted, for like 20 years. For one thing, I was in my midforties, and bowling is like anything else—you start to lose your chops as you get older.

Oh, and there was this other little tiny thing hanging over my head—a little tiny thing about the size of one of them 40-yard dumpsters Bobby Cabert had sent over to Bowl-Rite. Patsy and James had posted a million-dollar bail to get me out of federal prison. But the extortion charges had been winding their way through the federal court system and were about to come before the judge. In fact, the way everything was working out, if I made it to the finals of the Super Bowl High Roller, I might have to skip the championship round and hop on the red-eye back to the Newark airport to face the music. (I had to get special permission from the judge to leave the state for the tournament.)

Maurice had warned me that I might be facing 3 to 5 years in prison. And if the judge gave me 5 years, by the time I got out, I'd be practically 50, and way too old to compete at this level.

So, bottom line: This was my last chance.

Then there was this other problem. Bowling, like golf, is a game of intense concentration. It all comes down to that instant when the ball is released, either from your fingertips (in bowling) or the club (in golf). It's like Zen: The whole thing comes down to one moment. But how was I supposed to beat all the other superfocused bowlers in the United States if half of my mind was worrying about going back to prison for 3 to 5 years? How was I supposed to block that out of my thoughts?

When I got out to Vegas, I met Eddie Baur, who was an old friend and an executive of the American Bowling Congress. Eddie had given me a free spot in the tournament (normally, the entry fee was around $1,200 for three people). I had introduced Eddie to Brad Edelman, who ran the event. They were glad to see me there, and they were nice enough not to mention what everybody knew: That I'd been way, way down and out, but now I was back.

Just before my big trip to Las Vegas, a lady named Joan Taylor, who was one of the metropolitan sports writers at *Bowlers Journal* magazine, decided to do a feature story about me. She came to the bowling alley to interview me, and the last question she asked me was, "Do you think you'll ever win again in bowling?"

"If I stay on the road, and stay sober, no doubt I'll win again, including the Super Bowl High Roller," I told her.

So this story, titled "To Hell and Back," came out in February 1997, right around the time of the tournament (which ended February 1), and it looked like I was predicting that I was going to win. Which was a pretty ballsy thing to do. But I was pumping up my confidence, against all odds, like a prizefighter talking trash about his opponent. In a way, I was just covering up my fear.

The only place in Las Vegas big enough to handle 2,000 bowlers at the time was the Showboat Hotel and Casino (which also happened to be the cosponsor of the event). The place was huge, with lanes 1 to 70 on the left side, by the casino, and 36 more lanes on the lower level. Before the tournament actually began on Saturday, I bowled a few sweepers to get a feel for the lanes. Jeffrey sat up as close to the action as he could get, just watching every move I made. He was like my right-hand man.

"Are you gonna win?" he'd ask me.

"What, are you kidding? Of course I'm gonna win," I'd say. "Forget about it."

"You don't look like you're gonna win," he'd say.

"Shut up, Jeffrey," I'd say.

I'd decided to use these new balls made by the Storm company called Thunder (which was black) and Lightning (which was purple). In fact, these were the very first high-performance bowling balls not made out of rubber, but some kind of synthetic material. This was the beginning of a whole new trend in bowling—synthetic lanes, fiberglass kickbacks, synthetic balls—that gave everything a big bounce and made a lot of noise.

Thunder and Lightning rolled really well when I bowled a couple of practice games. I decided not to bowl any more sweepers, like the old days, because I had my sights set on winning the whole tournament, and I needed every ounce of concentration I could get. I wasn't going to be rolling up a few grand here and there by winning sweepers, then slinking off someplace to get wasted. I was going to blow into this place like Captain America and win the whole fucking thing.

On Saturday afternoon, I bowled my first match, and going into the 10th frame, I was up by 18 pins. But, I knew that if I threw a bad pitch, I could still lose. So I got up to the line and threw three strikes in the 10th, boom, boom, boom. The other guy, a great bowler from Ohio, was furious, because he knew he'd had a chance to win at the end but I stopped that.

Jeffrey Butler: Bob was very superstitious. You had to draw a lane out of a hat, so he let me draw the number for the first match, and after he won, he had me draw the number for the rest of the tournament.

The second day of the tournament, Sunday, I didn't have to bowl, so I spent my time watching everybody else. Nobody had the "look" I had, which meant I was playing in the middle of the lane, and Thunder and Lightning were beautifully matching the lane. The next day, I won my second match easy.

Whenever I finished my matches for the day, I went back to my room at the Stratosphere and called Patsy. Calling Patsy was like touching home base in all this craziness. She was my center, my anchor. But—it was weird—when I called, Patsy kind of seemed to already know what had happened that day. She was thinking about me all the time, and praying for me like crazy. She was praying harder and harder. She told me she had gone to the cathedral to see the statue of Our Lady of Fatima and prayed to the Blessed Mother for a miracle.

"Bobby," she tells me, almost crying, "I just know you're going to win!"

When she tells me that, I almost start crying, too. And I'm not even drunk.

"Patsy," I say, my voice trembling, "I think I'm gonna win it! I can feel it!"

"I know it," she says.

I also told Patsy about that other little problem I had: That the finals were on a Wednesday night, but I had a sentencing hearing in New York federal court on Wednesday. (Yeah, I know, it doesn't really make sense: Why would I go out there expecting to win if I knew I couldn't finish the tournament? But that's the way my mind worked in them days.)

So I called Maurice, my lawyer, frantically.

"I'm doing great—I just won my first match," I say to him.

"That's great!"

"But I got a problem."

"What problem?"

"I'm supposed to be home Wednesday for the sentencing hearing. But the finals are Wednesday night."

"Look, who's the lawyer, you or me?" Maurice says.

"You," I say.

"Okay, so relax and let me take care of it. I'll try to get the judge to delay the hearing. I can try to get a continuance. You just concentrate on winning."

"But Maurice—I'm really worried. I'm out on a million-dollar bail—if I don't show up on time, my sister, my brother-in-law, all these people who helped me will lose a fortune!"

"Bobby," he says, "just concentrate on winning. Let me take care of the rest."

Meanwhile, I seemed to be getting some help from upstairs—way upstairs. I was engaged in a constant prayer connection with my Higher Power. And I also prayed to Father Paul, the old monk who didn't exist, with his long brown robe and his tufts of gray hair and his laser-beam eyes. Talk about a guy who was connected! He had told me that if I used all the focus and concentration and talent I had used to become a champion bowler, if I focused all that on my quest to become sober, I could succeed.

Now I prayed for the power to use that focus to win this national tournament, for the benefit of everyone who loved me and believed in me. I prayed that I could stay in the moment. I had to bowl this tournament one frame at a time, just like alcoholics learn to live one day at a time. I prayed that I could keep everything "in sync," in the pocket, in the rhythm. I prayed that I could win.

The fact is, though, if I made it through the field of more than 2,000 bowlers and got down to the final 32 or even 16, I would be up against some of the best players in the world—top amateurs, a lot of whom would later go pro. Beating even one of them guys would take a sky-blue miracle. Of course, I had one big weapon that I never had before in all the times I had come out to Vegas: sobriety.

I had a couple of other weapons, too. I had Patsy. I had my Higher Power. And I had Father Paul.

Patsy didn't care what kind of hotshot opponents I had coming up. She just kept sending all those good vibes my way. They say big miracles can happen in the program, and we both were thinking that this might be it. This might be what we've been waiting for. The stage was set for something fabulous to happen.

It was so great to know that Patsy believed in me and was praying for me, and that I also had all these supporters by my side in Vegas. Even so, look: This was the biggest bowling tournament in history, and there were so many accomplished bowlers out there that any one of us could have won. It could be that the difference between who won and who lost was prayer. There was a side to this glitzy tournament—a side to life, I guess—that was all about the intervention of angels.

Meanwhile, over the course of 2 days (Monday and Tuesday), I bowled six matches and won them all. Four solid hours one day, 5 solid hours the next.

Look: When you're 44 years old, bowling against a guy in his twenties—especially if it's your third or fourth match of the day—the younger guy has the edge. You've got to rely on your skill and command of the game, saving up your energy, using experience instead of strength and your ability to psych the other guy out. Luckily, I was in a state of continuous prayer to my Higher Power, and it seemed like I was running off a battery that never ran out of juice.

Tuesday morning I bowled a guy from Oklahoma who thought he was great. I figured it was going to be a tough match. Eddie Baur told me during practice to use Thunder, the black ball, so I did. I got a spare in the first frame, then I threw six strikes in a row and the game was over in the seventh frame. Mr. Oklahoma bit the dust.

That day, Tuesday, I had to win four matches to keep going. And by now, I was mentally moving deeper and deeper into the winning mode, praying to my Higher Power and to Father Paul to keep my focus.

I won my next two matches—boom, boom—and then, in order to make it into the top 64, I drew a guy named Mark Dyson, who was, at the time, one of the hottest amateurs on the planet. But this guy was a real loudmouth, and the night before the match, I heard him running his lip about what a hotshot he was and how he was going smoke everybody out there (including me). I got up in his face about this—he just fucking rubbed me the wrong way—and we got in a pretty big argument. He was drinking a lot, and I saw myself in him—the trash-talking alcoholic, so full of himself he has no idea how he looks or sounds to other people. It's funny how the things that irritate you the most in other people are the same things you hate in yourself.

So there was definitely some bad blood between "the Diceman" and me before this match.

I drew lanes 5 and 6, with Jeffrey's help. Jeffrey sat down close to me, in the settee area, which was this big half-circle of padded seats a couple of steps down from the main level of the bowling alley.

"Can you beat him?" Jeffrey whispers.

"Watch me," I say.

"You don't look like you can beat him."

"Shut up, Jeffrey," I say.

Eddie Baur had told me, again, to use the black ball, and I threw a strike in the first frame and a spare in the second. I made the sign of the cross before every frame I bowled. I don't know, maybe that was pissing Dyson off, but on the third frame the guy got up and threw, and only clipped a couple of pins. It was amazing. Bowlers at this level never fuck up that bad.

In the third frame, I got up and I whispered to myself and to my Higher Power, "If you're ever going to throw good, do it now!"

I threw a strike, and Dyson was toast.

CHAPTER 22

MANIFESTING A MIRACLE

BEFORE I KNEW IT, I had made it into the top 64. Man, I was on a roll. I knew I was going to do good. I felt that I might even be able to grab the brass ring. This was the furthest I had ever got in the Super Bowl High Roller before. In the past, if I even got to the top 128, I'd collect my $2,000 or $3,000 and then I just wouldn't show up for any more matches. I'd be down at the bar, having a heart-to-heart with the bartender and getting wasted—wasting my promise, wasting my potential, wasting my life. I'd also be hustling the guy for money.

I didn't know it at the time, but by this point in the tournament, I was developing a fan club down at the federal building, back in Manhattan. It was 1997, and some people were using this newfangled thing called the Internet so they could follow the tournament. And an amazing number of judges and lawyers there liked to bowl, so it had gotten around the courthouse through the grapevine that Robert Purzycki, inmate #857435757, the defendant in the Mob extortion case, was doing real good out at the Super Bowl High Roller in Las Vegas. So all these judges and lawyers and FBI agents were starting to follow the action, and rooting for me. Who knows? Maybe some of them were even betting on me. Now even the guys that arrested me—agent John Triolo and his pal, Louie—were rooting for me. They wanted to see me do good. They wanted to see me make something of myself.

Can you imagine that?

But my most important fan was Maurice.

"Look, Bobby, I got some news," he tells me on the phone. "The judge granted you a continuance. You don't have to be back here until Thursday morning, 10:00. So if you win Wednesday, you'll have to get on the red-eye back to New York for the hearing the next morning. But you've still got time to make the finals."

"Wow! How'd you get the judge to do that?"

"Didn't you know you got a fan club at One Federal Plaza?"

So now, if I did succeed at getting into the finals, I wouldn't have to drop everything right when I got to the top. The fact that a federal judge would allow a continuance on an extortion case because the defendant was bowling in a tournament in Las Vegas—I mean, how amazing is that?

By Wednesday, I had made it into the final 32. There was nobody left but the world-class bowlers. But the only one I was worried about was Pat Healey, who was considered the top amateur in the country at the time. He was up next on my docket.

In the years leading up to the 1997 tournament, Healey had racked up an amazing string of victories. In 1991, he was a Gold Medalist in both doubles and trios at the FIQ World Championships (the international bowling federation, going up against bowlers from around the world). In 1991, 1992, and 1995, he won World Cup Amateur of the Year. In 1995, he won US National Amateur Champion. And in 1995–96, he won World Amateur Bowler of the Year. Et cetera.

He was also 28 years old, and I was 44. You'd be surprised how physically taxing competitive bowling can be—all the stress and pressure, especially. Also, while I figured this was my last shot at glory, Healey was in his prime. Which put a lot more pressure on me. And, of course, not to mention the fact that my body had been dragged through the agonies of hell by all those hard years on the street. In a tense, close fight, all that damage would count against me.

Whoever won this match, me or Healey, would make it into the final 16. I knew very well that I'd have to use all the power and skill and cunning I had learned over my whole life to beat this guy. Plus a tip of the hat from an old monk.

"Can you beat him?" Jeffrey whispers to me, as I'm getting ready to approach the foul line.

"Forget about it," I say.

"I'm not sure you can beat this guy," he says.

"Shut up," I tell him.

I am lost in concentration but having trouble getting into rhythm with my Higher Power.

I decide to start out using the purple ball, Lightning.

And in the first frame, I throw a strike—beautiful, powerful, and very loud. My trademark. Eleven more of those and I'll be fine. Then Healey follows with a strike that's just as powerful and just as loud. Perfect, flying down the lane bed and exploding the tenpins like a bomb.

Among all the different styles of bowling, Healy would be considered a "stroker"—a guy with a high backswing and a smooth-as-silk follow-through. A guy with a lot of accuracy. "Spinners" are bowlers who spin the ball like a top, which can be real effective because of high performance bowling balls. "Heavers" just throw that bitch up the lane as hard as they can. And "crankers" just "grip it and rip it," giving the ball the most power and rotation of any bowling style.

My own style is pretty unique—I'm a stroker with a big breaking ball. I have a very high backswing and then I snap it hard on the back end. My dad had a high backswing, so maybe I copied it from him, but nobody else copied it from me. I have no imitators.

I'm watching Pat Healey's supersmooth approach and delivery, and I don't know what it is, but suddenly I start to lose it. I lose my concentration, lose my nerve. I start thinking to myself: There's no way I can beat the three-time World Cup Amateur of the Year. Who am I trying to kid? Just a few years ago, I was sleeping on the floor of a peep-show house on Forty-Second Street. I was hustling some lonely commuter for a drink in a bar just so I wouldn't have to face up to my miserable life. Why did I ever think I could do this? I can't do this. Back on the street: That's where I belong.

When I had been out here for the High Roller a couple of times when I was homeless, I took my two grand in winnings (or whatever) after I got knocked out of the tournament, hopped the red-eye back to LaGuardia, and caught a cab to . . . where? Where was I going? Where did I live? I'd go to a bar I knew, or a bowling alley, and find somebody to hustle so I could get something to drink, something to eat, someplace to sleep for the night. That's who I was: A grifter. A hustler. A bowling bum.

By the fourth frame, Healey is leading by 42 pins. He's leading because he's better than me. The fact that I'm here at all is a joke. I'm not a championship bowler at all. I'm a junkie and a drunk. Who let me in here?

"You're not winning," Jeffrey whispers, helpfully.

Then a great bowler named James Mack sits down next to me on the semicircular settee. He can see I'm getting rattled.

"Relax," he says, very soothing, very quiet. "Concentrate. I think you should switch balls and move inside."

So I take his advice, exchanging the purple ball for the black one, Thunder, and focusing on firing it closer to the center of the lane.

I make the sign of the cross.

I ask for help and power.

I beg for mercy from my Higher Power, and from Father Paul.

And then I throw a strike.

And another strike.

And another strike.

Boom, boom, boom!

My rhythm, and my game, is roaring back. Boom! I'm getting better and better. Then Healey throws two more strikes. Then I throw another strike. Then, in the ninth frame, Healey misses a ten-pin. It's an incredible blunder—for Healey to miss something like that is practically a miracle. I get up in the ninth frame and throw a huge, powerful strike—just hook the crap out of it and torch the pins, clattering them all over the place. Now it's come down to the very last frame. Either one of us could win this thing now. But for me, the task is huge: All I need is to throw two strikes in the 10th frame. In other words, I have to be perfect.

If I throw the first strike, I'm still in the tournament. If I don't, I'm out—heading back to New Jersey with my tail tucked between my legs like all those other times. I get up and address the line. I make the sign of the cross. I ask for Father Paul's blessing. I throw—and it sails down the lane and just kills those pins. A strike, powerful as a punch in the nose.

The bowling alley explodes in applause.

I don't know what's happening, really, because when the great, near-perfect Pat Healey gets up and throws, he leaves a tenpin standing—again.

"Concentrate," James whispers to me, as I'm getting ready to walk up to the line.

"You can win," Jeffrey whispers.

"This is why we came out here to the Super Bowl High Roller," I whisper back to them both. "This is what I've been living for."

Then, silently, to my Higher Power and Father Paul, I whisper, "Don't fail me now."

I need this last one to stay alive. If I miss, there will be no hurrah. I'll be going home to face the judge and maybe 3 to 5 years in a tiny cell where the lights burn all night and there is no sun, no quiet, and every move outside my cage involves locking or unlocking a steel door.

"It's time to play the game," I whisper to myself. "Win this one, and I'm down to the final 16. Miss this one, and I'm forgotten."

The moment the ball leaves my fingertips and goes sailing down the lane, my whole life flashes in front of me. The whole thing—all my great promise as a kid, getting blinded, getting raped, overcoming it all to become a superstar, all my perfect games, Uncle Raymond and John Gotti and Bobby Cabert, getting hit by a cab and almost crippled, pain and pain pills and alcohol, the dark night of addiction and all those terrible years on the street, the six apparitions of Father Paul, Jack and the steps, the gradual return to the light, then getting arrested and spending 7 months in federal prison, and now this, the Super Bowl High Roller, the pinnacle of my promise.

I throw the ball so hard it goes sailing down the lane like a black missile—a thunderbolt, spinning down those 62 feet, 10 inches of hard maple. It's arcing sharply to the right, almost to the gutter.

"Hook," I whisper. "Hook!" And just then the ball hooks hard and blasts all 10 pins across the pin deck. It makes contact just behind the headpin and—kaboom!—the pins explode, like a collapsing house in a hurricane.

By now the whole bowling center is watching, and they break into wild applause. For a second, I don't even dare to breathe.

Then I hear it, all around me: Wild applause and cheering and wolf whistles. I've beat Pat Healey, the number-one amateur in the world. At least for one frame and one game, I won. I beat him.

Healey doesn't take it well. He throws a temper tantrum, just like a little kid, throwing his bowling ball down the lane.

"Why are you mad?" I say to him. "Are you mad because you lost to me and I'm not any good? Are you mad because I'm more than 40 years old, and an old man beat you?"

He just glares at me.

"Well, you didn't get beat by no dog," I say. "I'm one of the best bowlers who ever lived."

Finally he cools off and comes over to me.

"Congratulations," he says, holding out his hand. "That was a great match."

And after that, Pat Healey is a total gentleman. In fact, for the rest of the tournament, he's right there beside me, rooting me on.

After I beat Pat Healey, I am into the final 16. And I'm on a roll. I beat a great bowler from Kentucky. Then I'm in the top eight, and up against John Dillard, who just bowled 266 and is the Hudson

County Bowler of the Year. I actually know him—he's from my hometown of Paterson, and we usually root for each other. But this time, I throw 10 spares in a row, like a machine, and he never has a shot. In fact, halfway through the game, he throws a bad ball. He loses it.

I hope it don't sound too egotistical to say this, but I think he threw a bad shot partly because the myth of Bob Perry got to him. He didn't believe that he could beat me, and that destroyed his game, just like self-doubt had nearly destroyed mine in my match against Pat Healey. So much of any game, from baseball to pinball, is about what happens between your ears. And this time my mental game beat the crap out of his mental game.

By now, I know that I actually have a shot at winning this thing—not just the happy talk I have been telling myself. This is no bullshit, no trash-talking, this is for real. I am on national TV, in a bowling alley so quiet you can hear a pin drop, focusing with every ounce of my concentration until the moment my ball shatters those tenpins and they go clattering down the lane. I know very well that I might never have any more chances to win "The Big One." I know I have to dig deep and let my talent come out, just like Father Paul said. I know this might be the last time I will be able to actually reach out and touch my dream.

Sure: I am experienced, I have the chops, and I know how to take advantage of breaks and mistakes other people make. And if they don't make mistakes, I know how to outperform them. But the thing is this: The most important thing I am doing here is spiritual. In my heart, I am imagining myself performing to my greatest ability. I am remembering everything Father Paul told me.

I am manifesting a miracle.

And I am bowling for everybody out there. I am bowling for everybody who never got a chance to bring their dreams to life. I am bowling for everybody whose second chance never came. I am bowling for all those alcoholics and junkies and crackheads down on Forty-Second

Street, guys who could have been something but somehow got sucked down by their disease. I am bowling for C.J. and Annie, who lost everything they had and yet still stuck by me. I am bowling for my sister Jeannie. I am bowling for my kids—Spanky and Jeffrey and Junior and Dustin and Melrock. I am bowling for everybody who ever believed in me, who ever thought I was the greatest in the world, or that I could have been. I am bowling because I want to show them that they can reach higher than they ever thought they could. This is the day for me to prove that everyone's dreams, not just my own, can come true.

And, most of all, I am bowling for Patsy. If anybody ever deserved to be made a saint, it's her. Patsy never gave up on me, never lost faith in me. Even when Patsy was telling me to get the fuck out of her house, in her heart, all she wanted was for me to come back to myself, to overcome the demon that was possessing me, and become what I could be—to reach the point in my life that I had reached this day. And when push came to shove, James and Patsy had put up the money to get me out of jail—they laid everything they had on the line for me.

Now there are only four of us left in the tournament. If I win the next two matches, I win the whole enchilada—a 10-gallon trophy cup with great big handles on it, a check for $100,000, and the honor of being a role model for everybody in my life. Now they roll in the big TV cameras and lights (as if I'm not nervous enough already). This is what I have waited for my whole life. Now all the judges and lawyers and FBI agents can watch and so can Patsy and my other sisters and everybody else who has completely written me off.

Next up is a guy from Kansas. I've never heard of him, but he's got incredible chops—at the time, he had more sanctioned 300s than anybody else in the American Bowling Congress. Now there are, like, hundreds of people watching in the bowling alley, not to mention these glaring lights and TV cameras. I feel like I'm on the set of *Let's Make A Deal*.

The guy from Kansas starts out with a strike. I don't throw a strike in the second frame, leaving a 3-10 split. It's crucial that I make this, or I could be down 30 pins. I make the split, turning the match around. Then he throws a strike, misses a spare, and from there it is an easy coast to victory. Now there is only one match to go.

Now, if I was a gunslinger, I'd have beat every other gunslinger in town except one. And the last guy standing, besides me, is Chris James, a guy from Springfield, Massachusetts—a phenomenally gifted bowler. You go down to your local bowling alley and watch a bunch of guys in the local league, and they all bowl kind of the same. But once you get to the highest levels of the sport, you see guys who just look different. Their whole approach, their swing, their delivery—it's like the difference between Tiger Woods and your local duffer. There's no comparison.

Well, this guy Chris James is one of those guys.

To have any chance of beating him, I have to put myself into a winning frame of mind, with 100 percent of my focus on the task at hand, just like Father Paul said. Not thinking about what's for dinner or the other guy throwing two strikes and I'm down 43 pins, or the condition of the lane surface, or whether or not I have the right ball for the lane, or whether the ball is hooking like it ought to, or any other damn thing, even the possibility of a federal prison sentence hanging over my head. I know that when I bowl good, I am as good as anybody in the world.

And on this particular day, bowling the final match against Chris James, I am *better* than anybody in the world. I am unstoppable. And then I get a break. After the fifth frame, they stop the match for a commercial break. And after the break, Chris James gets up and he throws a bad split, 6, 7, 10. It's almost impossible to throw that for a spare. And he doesn't do it—the ball goes right over the nose of the head pin, but still leaves two pins standing. So by the fifth frame, he's down 25 pins. All I need after that is to throw a clean game, and the next four frames I throw spare, strike, spare, strike. He throws a strike in the ninth frame, but by then it's too late.

When I get down to the last frame, I know it's practically over. I make a sign of the cross. I say to my Higher Power and Father Paul, "This strike is for everybody—my mom and dad, Annie, C.J., Jeffrey, everybody. If I'm gonna throw it great, let me throw it now."

I throw. The ball sails down the lane, makes a beautiful hook into the pocket, and the tenpins shatter in every direction. A strike. A beautiful strike. I've won.

For everybody.

The whole place explodes in applause, and 50 or 60 or 70 people come pouring down onto the approach, hugging me, clapping me on the back. I can hardly believe what's happening. All my kids come crowding up, and C.J. and Annie. Even the guy I just beat comes up and shakes my hand (he probably doesn't feel too bad, because the second-place finisher gets 50 grand).

I can tell you one thing: A lot of people were crying, because everybody knew what I had gone through in my life. They knew what the tournament meant to me.

A little while later there's an awards ceremony, and Eddie Baur hands me that enormous, shiny trophy cup, and a check for a little over $112,000 (which was the grand prize plus some other money I won).

Not bad for a homeless crack addict with no teeth from Forty-Second Street.

I only had one regret: That Patsy could not be here to share it with me.

It's only a couple of hours later that I get on the red-eye back to New York. I arrive at LaGuardia at 6:15 in the morning, and there's a federal probation officer waiting for me. He takes me over to One Federal Plaza, in Manhattan, and a little while later I'm standing in the hall with Mr. Rodriguez, my PTI guy (pre-trial intervention), when a couple of very important-looking federal judges come walking by.

"Are you the guy we let go to Vegas?" one of the judges asks me.

"Yes, sir, Your Honor."

"And you won?"

"Yes, sir."

"Good job!"

When the judge walks away, I say to the PTI, "Who's that guy?"

"One of the top judges in the Southern District of New York."

So, you know, that was good.

Even so, the contrast between today and yesterday is like the difference between yes and no. Yesterday there was screaming and yelling and trophies and TV cameras on the Las Vegas strip, and thrill rides on the 108th floor. Today there is only serious, silence, and scary. After all, Judge Cedarbaum seems like a nice lady, but she has the power to send me back to federal prison for 5 years—which, considering my damaged condition, could be the rest of my life.

I really don't know if winning the Super Bowl High Roller—going out into the world and showing I could make something of myself— had anything to do with it. All I know is that when I went in front of Judge Cedarbaum later that morning, she decided to cut me a break. She didn't send me back to my high-security shoebox at MCC or Otisville. She gave me supervised release, and I began to honorably serve out my federal parole, which I finished a couple of years later, with no problems.

There's no way to express what a relief that was.

When I came back home to Union City, to the wild applause of everybody at the bowling alley, I paid off some debts, gave some money to C.J. and Annie, gave all the kids a couple hundred bucks (which was probably more money than they had ever seen), and of course, I bought everybody shrimp. I bought myself a TV and a VHS player. And I gave the kids a few short words of advice (which I give now to you, too):

"Never give up, no matter what."

A couple of months later, there was another honor.

It was a vote by some of the big-name sportswriters who covered bowling. Every couple of years they would give out this award to people who had been through some real tough shit—a heart transplant, cancer, personal difficulties—and then returned to the sport of bowling, and to life. They hadn't given it out for the past 3 years.

But that year, they decided to give the award to me.

It was called Comeback Bowler of the Year.

Which, I gotta tell you, almost made me choke up. The last thing in this world I wanted was to go back to those dark, lost years on the street, and I couldn't think of any award that I'd be happier to get. For better or worse, I couldn't think of any award I actually deserved less, either. Because my "comeback" from the gates of hell wasn't anything I had done myself.

It was a miracle made manifest.

EPILOGUE

"We have been called to heal
wounds, to unite what has fallen
apart, and to bring home those
who have lost their way."

–ST. FRANCIS OF ASSISI

WELL, HERE IT IS 15 years after that incredible night at the Super Bowl High Roller in Las Vegas. I'm 63 now, and my life has been a roller coaster of good fortune and bad, but the main thing is that I have maintained my sobriety for 23 years. Man, it's a miracle! Believe me, if I can do it, anybody can.

You know what's one of the main keys to my spiritual transformation? Helping other people.

It wasn't too long after the tournament that my sister Patsy and I set up a little nonprofit business in an old train station in Pompton Plains, New Jersey, called the Last Stop. Our business was to sell (at no profit) a whole line of spiritual books from Alcoholics Anonymous and Hazelden. People would come into our store in such pain and suffering—they'd be lonely, they'd be lost, and even their friends and family (if they had any) didn't know how to help them. And since I'd pretty much gone as low as you can go without actually dying, I was able to help them by using my own experience. I was paid in the spiritual satisfaction of seeing somebody else get help. Patsy knew about the sorrow of addiction from the point of view of a scared and angry family member, so she could talk to people whose kids or spouses or friends were in trouble, too. That was her service work.

Me and Patsy would have kept doing that work, but we got shut down (the city of Pompton Plains took the train station by eminent domain, because it was supposedly of historical significance). Afterward, we tried to set up shop in a church around the corner, but we lost 80 percent of our "business," so we quit.

Patsy Purzycki: Last Stop was the most wonderful, fulfilling thing I ever did in my life. If I could do that, just help people, for the rest of my life, I'd be happy. I loved to see people who were down and out come into our recovery store and read some literature—not even buy it, just sit there and read it at the table and chairs we put out—and then come back again and again and start to get better. That's what made my heart sing.

One time a dirty-looking guy came in and he said, "I was told I could get money here, and maybe get a place to stay for the night. I just got thrown out of the place I was at."

"Let me call my brother Bobby," I told him. "He's bowling in Vegas, but I think he'll help you out."

So I called Bobby in Vegas.

"Bob, I got this guy here with no place to stay. What should I do?"

"Tell him there's an AA meeting right next door at 7:00 tonight. Tell him to ask for Tom, and he'll give him a place to stay. Ask him what else he needs."

The guy told me he was starting a new job in the morning, but he looked like hell, so I told him I'd take the extra clothes he had with him and wash them and give them back to him in the morning. And I gave him $20. I knew Bobby would want me to do that. So the guy went next-door to the seven o'clock meeting, and Tom gave him a place to stay. In fact, Tom told him he could stay as long as he needed to. In the morning, the guy stopped by the store and I gave him his clean clothes and he went off to his new job, whatever it was.

This kind of thing happened all the time—you could say that was our "business" at Last Stop, even though we never made any money at all. I know for a fact that we got over 400 people into treatment centers, so our business was a big success, spiritually speaking.

A few months later a nicely dressed man stopped by the store.

"You don't remember me, do you?" he said.

"No, actually, I don't."

"I'm the guy you loaned $20 to." And he handed me back the money.

He'd gotten a job, gotten sober, turned his life around. And I can't tell you what that makes you feel like inside. I feel like this is what I'm here for. Not to support everyone in the world, but just to do what I can to help those I can. This is what I'd love to do my whole life. To me, this is what spirituality is. I grew up very Catholic, going to Mass and all—I still go to Mass, and I'm still a Catholic—but I don't believe a lot of the crap they hand you, especially the guilt part. What it's really all about is helping other people, just like my father used to do. Love in action. It's as simple as that.

At the time we were running Last Stop, I was living with someone who was totally against what we were doing. He thought we were giving away money to bums, feeding their bad habits, making them dependent. But I didn't care. This was my calling. This was what I was doing with my few days on this Earth. This was God's mission for me.

And Bobby was the very same way. One thing about Bobby—whenever anybody called the store in need, anybody at all, he dropped everything and went to help that person. There are some people in my family who still have no clue how deep Bobby's recovery has been. But I've seen it in action all these years, and I know it's for real.

One time we were stopped in traffic in New Jersey and a bum came up to the window asking for bus fare. I didn't know if it was really for bus fare, but I gave the guy $5.

"What was I supposed to do?" I asked Bobby.

"You were supposed to give it to him," he said.

Me and Bobby—we live a thousand miles apart now, but we talk on the phone two or three times a day, and have for the past 20 years. We're soulmates. And I know he would do exactly what I have been doing in my job as a clerk at a grocery store in Clearwater, Florida, where almost everybody is on food stamps and people are really hurting. The other day this little old black lady came into the store, and she put down her last two food stamps and 71 cents. She needed 73 cents, but she didn't have it. I asked her how long it was until her next check, and it was quite a few days away—she'd be hungry by then, even though she wasn't complaining. I gave her $10, and she was so grateful, but I only wished I could have given her more.

You know: There's that passage in the Bible where it talks about helping strangers because you might be helping "angels unawares." You never know who you're helping. But one thing's for sure: You're always helping yourself. You can feel it in your heart. Because God is not in heaven. God is inside you. And if you can find that inner source of power and serenity, you will know how to live a blessed life. And He is in there if you look for Him.

After that, I went down to Texas and opened a bowling center with some partners, but we got hammered by a hurricane and driven out of business. Then I decided to see if I could win the Super Bowl

High Roller again, so I spent a long time getting my chops back, and then, in 2008, I returned to Vegas and fought my way to the finals in front of a standing-room-only house. In the 10th frame of the final match, my finger slipped and I left an almost-impossible split—the 2 pin and the 10, at opposite ends of the pin deck. My opponent jumped up and started yelling "Yes! Yes!" because the odds of hitting a 2-10 split are astronomical. So I got up, threw the ball like a friggin' heat-seeking missile, and wasted both pins. The place went wild. I had won my second Super Bowl High Roller.

I actually made it pretty far in the tournament in 2009, too, but by then my health was coming to pieces and I didn't have any stamina left. I had developed cancer of the prostate, and at the same time, I was struggling with diabetes, brought on partly by all those years on the street, and all those years of alcohol and drug abuse.

In 2012, I decided to leave Las Vegas and move to Charlottesville, Virginia, where I live now, for a couple of reasons. First, I could get great cancer treatment here at the University of Virginia hospital. But, second, I wanted to write a book about my life and my friend Howard Barnett, who'd grown up in Paterson, thought he could help me. It was Howard who put me in touch with the great writer and journalist Stefan Bechtel, who helped shape and craft the book you're reading, and asked me a million questions to bring out the details.

Stefan wasn't there the day something kind of incredible happened at the bowling alley, but Howard was there and so was Steve Holmberg and two other league bowlers. They saw it happen. We were bowling at Kegler's in Charlottesville, an old house with wooden lanes. We were practicing, you know, because I was thinking about maybe bowling in a league if my cancer and diabetes would let me. The Storm company had sent me this new 14-pound orange-and-green ball called Frantic, with holes drilled especially for me by a guy in the pro shop in Vegas named David Haynes, a great bowler. It was around 6:00 or so and I threw the ball and got a strike.

Then I got another strike and another and another. It felt so good and easy just to be having a great time bowling. My timing was great and I wasn't thinking about anything—not even counting. I was in the zone. And I just kept striking and striking and striking. There was no ego involved, nothing to prove, nothing like that. But every time I threw, I struck. Well, it turned out the other guys were counting. And before too long, the whole bowling alley stopped and everybody was watching me: 28, 29, 30, 31, 32. Strike after strike after strike. So finally I got to 35—one strike away from three perfect games in a row, a "900 series," an almost-impossible feat in bowling, the big kahuna, the 4-minute mile.

And I remembered that story Mike and Larry Stella told, about how one time years ago when I was a homeless addict, I walked into Wallington Lanes in Jersey, about 2:00 in the morning, and threw a 900 series while drunk, then threw my arms up in the air and yelled, "I'm the greatest fuckin' bowler in the world!" and walked out.

I was an empty man, and shouting that out to the world meant something to me then.

But now, none of that meant anything at all. I was a sober man, a whole man, with nothing to prove to anybody. I was just throwing a few balls for fun. I sat down and started taking off my bowling shoes, 'cuz I didn't have nothing to prove. But Howard and them started ragging on me, urging me on, so I put my shoes back on, stood up, grabbed my ball, addressed the line, and threw my 36th perfect strike in a row. It really didn't mean anything to me. It was just 10 pins falling over. I didn't yell or scream or shout. I just took off my bowling shoes and walked away. The funny thing was, when I came back a little while later somebody had stolen that ball. But I didn't care. Like Father Paul was always saying, "It doesn't matter."

At the end of the day, after all I've been through, what would I say to anybody who is reading this? I'd say dreams do come true, no matter how old you may be and no matter what has happened to you in life. Keep moving forward no matter what happens. Never give up. Don't waste time on regret, even though that may take time. After all that happened to me, I have no regrets today. I'm done with regretting. The best thing I can do is to stay sober so I won't do stuff I'll regret later.

If you're struggling with the disease of alcoholism or drug abuse, don't forget—this disease wants you dead, but it will settle for misery. People in the rooms say, "First you take a drink, then the drink takes a drink, then the drink takes you." It totally consumes you. And the only reason I'm alive today is because I got sober, don't drink, go to meetings, and help others. It's pretty damn simple, really.

A couple of things that have been helpful to me is to make a list of five things to be grateful for, every day, and either write them down or just remember them. It says in the Bible that "the grateful heart sits at a continuous feast," and I know what that means. Another little thing is to write down all the shit that's bothering you, crumple it up, and burn it. My old sponsor Jack used to say that 90 percent of the things that you *think* aren't actually happening. So you can just crumple that stuff up and throw it away—it never existed in the first place. You gotta get rid of that self-pity and self-centeredness shit— that stuff will get you drunk again. And never, ever forget to thank your Higher Power, who loves you, protects you, and will save you from your own stupidity if you let him.

Like Father Paul told me, "God helps those who help themselves." I believe that, because it's true.

If you'd like to contact me directly, you can do it by sending a note to bob.purzycki@facebook.com. And you can watch the documentary film that was made about my life, *High Roller: The Bob Perry Story*, on iTunes (or just Google it).

God bless!

Bob

ACKNOWLEDGMENTS

ALL THEM MOVIE STARS get to thank people when they get their Academy Awards, so I'd like to thank people, too. I'd like to thank my sisters Patsy and Jeannie Ambrogio and Frank Ambrogio for never giving up on me, and my brother-in-law James Spadafora. I want to thank the men who helped me stay sober—Jack, Billy, and George—and also my current sponsor, Doc. I'd like to thank Howard and his wife, Beth, who are the greatest friends a guy could ask for. I'd like to thank C.J. and Annie and all the kids from the bowling alley—Jeffrey Butler, Jimmy and Timmy Mack, Chris Hayden, Melrock Castillo, Spanky Penafiel, Dustin. Also, my friends Ed Baur, Steve Chiarella, and Rocky Salemmo. And I'd like to thank all the thousands of people who live one day at a time in the rooms of AA.

Bob, Stefan, and the rest of the team behind *Redemption Alley* would like to thank everyone who has made production of the book possible.

Joseph Ardolino	L. Jay Bourgeois
Corbett Austin	Chris and Cynthia Buck
Howard and Elizabeth Barnett	James Burnett
Taylor Barnett	Mike Calbi (Lodi Lanes)
Lawrence Bechtel	Tracy A. Campbell
Lilly Bechtel	Bethany Carlson
Sari Bennett	Monica Chieco
Gardy Bloemers	Joseph Conigliaro

Teresa Cooper

Jeff Corwin

Jim "Crazy Horse" Crawford

Roni Del Rio

Nick Duke

Nicholas R. Duke Sr.

Jon Emm

Stuart England

Jay Flanagan

Carolyn Friedman

Bob Hadley

Andrea and Steve Holmberg

Lewis C. Johnson Jr.
  (aka Jr. Johnson)

Matthew J. Kessler, DVM

Paul Levesque

The Madara Family

Philip Maturo

Tim Michel

William Mullin

Len Nicholson

Viktoria Parvin

Chuck Pezzano

Debra Pick

Ann Purzycki

Sarah E. Ray

Ring Fever Productions

Francesco Ruffa

Susan and Kent Rychcik

Jamie Sacco

James Salisbury

Eric and Nancy Schmitz

Joseph Schwartz

Bob Sieski

Pat Spadafora

Bill Spigner

Storm Bowling Products

Mary Jane Strickland

Matthew Strickland

Ian Wren

Kimi Wren

INDEX

Underscored references indicate boxed text.

ABOUT THE AUTHORS

ROBERT "BOB PERRY" PURZYCKI was born in the gritty industrial town of Paterson, New Jersey, achieving fame in bowling and infamy for his mob ties before committing to a life of serving others.

STEFAN BECHTEL is the author of *Mr. Hornaday's War* and 10 other books that have sold more than two million copies and have been translated into a dozen languages.